THE INFILTRATORS

THE
INFILTRATORS

The European Business Invasion

of America

by

NICHOLAS FAITH

NEW YORK
E. P. DUTTON & CO., INC.
1972

First published in the U.S.A. 1972 by E. P. Dutton & Co., Inc.

Copyright © 1971 by Nicholas Faith
All rights reserved. Printed in the U.S.A.

FIRST EDITION

Published simultaneously in Canada by Clarke, Irwin & Company Limited, Toronto and Vancouver

Library of Congress Catalog Card Number: 72-173028

SBN 0-525-13305-4

TO

ROS

WHO BELIEVED I COULD WRITE IT

CONTENTS

ACKNOWLEDGMENTS

The biggest contribution to this book was made by the dozens of anonymous executives and officials whose words and documents provide its framework. But it would not have achieved reality without Peter Wilsher, the editor of the *Sunday Times* Business News, who believed, long before I did, that my discoveries about European companies in the United States were interesting enough to turn into book form. It was Frank Hermann, then the editorial director of Thomas Nelson, who bullied me into thinking through the implications of what I had seen. Norine Linnane in London, and Sheila Robinette in New York, kept managing to find the most obscure companies and articles for me, and Alison Taggart somehow contrived to translate my scrawl into coherent typescript.

FOREWORD

This is an engrossing and stimulating book. It should encourage others to follow suit—on both sides of the Atlantic.

It is a truism to say that trade, especially international trade, must be reciprocal. For the past twenty years I have been deeply involved with British efforts to redress the balance, in terms of Britain's trade with the USA. Just as American exports to the UK are still substantially larger than British exports to the USA so is direct investment by American companies in Europe substantially larger than European investment in the USA. But the growth of European investment in America is indeed encouraging. Perhaps if this trend continues we, the British, will be accused of trying to recapture our lost colonies by guile.

There has been much talk of late of a coming trade war, and a reversion to protectionism. In a recent speech Edward Heath, Britain's Prime Minister, said that America had used its energy and generosity as no other modern great power to protect its friends. But he foresaw changes:

> . . . the United States is acting drastically to protect its own balance of payments and its own economic and, later, defense poli-balance of payments and its own trading position against the erosions which they suffered. Everyone concerned with trade and finance knows that rough winds are beginning to blow across the world.

We all have to ride out this storm and refuse to allow it to drive us back into the safe harbour of protectionism. In harbour we will face fewer hazards, but deterioration is inevitable. That way lies a steady decline in world trade and in the fortunes of one and all.

During a speech to the International Club at Harvard Business School, some years ago, I focussed attention upon J. J. Servan-Schreiber's recently published *The American Challenge*. I suggested that the main lesson was not to spread alarm and despondency among European industrialists, but to encourage them to update their management methods towards the end that they could compete with the American invaders more effectively. What impressed me most about Servan-Schreiber's book was his conclusion that the mainspring of American progress was investment in individual education—investment in people, not gadgets.

Regardless of the fact that some of Servan-Schreiber's forecasts have proved to be faulty, this particular conclusion was almost certainly correct. To the extent that European businessmen have been able to establish themselves successfully in the United States market, the lesson, for Americans, is the same—see what you can learn from them and compete, as fiercely as ever.

It will be apparent that during my years in the USA I have learned the lesson that competition is good for us all. The more, the better.

Nicholas Faith makes no bones about US anti-trust laws. They cause some disquiet among European businessmen—if that is not an understatement. Sometimes we wonder whether those who implement these laws believe that adversity is good for our souls. A foreign businessman is ill-advised to make a move on these quicksands without the guiding hand of a lawyer. However, with all the confusion and all the inconsistencies, the aim of these laws is clear—to encourage competition and to protect the consumer. In principle I would rather wrestle with them than accept cartelism, or any form of ganging-up on the consumer.

Compared with European giants in oil, chemical and heavy engineering fields, we, Schweppes, are indeed small. Even compared with others in consumer goods our unit size is miniscule and, as a result, our earnings, to date, are small. My only claim to fame—perhaps notoriety would be a better word—is for having used unorthodox methods to lay the foundations of a profitable business with a big potential.

We are an offshoot of an old and, until recently, somewhat stuffy British company (founded in 1792) which recognised the limitations of the home market and began to develop markets overseas. Our success in this direction is indicated by the fact that when we embarked upon this course, just over twenty years ago, I doubt whether our overseas business contributed more than $2\frac{1}{2}$ per cent of our profits. That figure is now nearer 50 per cent. We are now established in most civilized countries around the world and in a few that are barely so.

We have learned things, here in America, that have stood us in good stead—at home, in Britain, and elsewhere in the world.

The chief lesson I have learned from the Americans is the overwhelming importance of marketing. Perhaps because it is peripheral to his main theme, the author barely touches upon this vital ingredient of success for European companies now well-established in the USA and American companies in Europe. I suspect that it was as important to them as it was to us.

Success in the USA depends largely on the degree to which we become marketing oriented. This applies to every company—domestic or foreign. America is the home of modern marketing.

Some two hundred years ago the British pioneered the Industrial Revolution, which was a revolution in the means of production. Over the past few decades Americans have pioneered in the marketing revolution.

Despite the fact that the rest of the world is rapidly catching up, I am still surprised to meet senior managers of important companies, American as well as European, who have not yet grasped what marketing is all about. They seem to think it comprises a series of gimmicks that can be grouped under the heading of advertising, selling and promotion. The essence of marketing is viewing products and services from the customer's point of view, seeing that the right goods or services reach the right customers, presented in the right way, at the right place, at the right time and at the right price. To Europeans I have continued to say, learn from the Americans. Take advantage of their generosity in sharing their know-how, then do it your own way—in our case, the British way.

Marketing research is the starting point. How else did the Japanese achieve their tremendous success with miniature radios and television? They spotted a gap in the market and filled it, before their competitors. They produced excellent products and preempted the market before domestic manufacturers, let alone other foreigners, could catch up. By and large, however, they used Americans to do their marketing.

I have made a nuisance of myself, saying these things to my countrymen, for the past two decades. In the process I have promulgated Whitehead's one and only axiom. It might also be of value to Americans so, with due modesty, I include it here:

> In tackling large, overseas markets substantial investment, over a period of years, is inevitable. The sum invested and the period of investment varies in inverse ratio to the skill with which marketing plans are laid and implemented.

Clearly direct investment, in plant and materials, must be considered separately. If those marketing plans are not well laid, however, a great deal of money will be wasted.

This concept was endorsed and vigorously supported by eminent Americans of the calibre of Marvin Bower, then managing director and now a director of McKinsey & Company, General James Gavin, chairman of Arthur D. Little, and Professor Edward Bursk of Harvard Business School, members of BEMAC (British Exports Marketing Advisory Committee) of which I was chairman.

To encourage others to invest in overseas markets may I add that here in the USA we, Schweppes, have proved this axiom. We invested substantially for four years. In the fifth year we broke into the black. By the end of the seventh year we had repaid all that our parent company had invested. Since then we have increased our profits at an average annual rate of growth of 40 per cent.

Although I am not in a position to gainsay the author, I doubt if Americans in Europe have made more, or worse, mistakes than Europeans in America. British, French and German companies have put more than an occasional foot wrong, here in the USA.

Values and attitudes differ widely in other countries and they are difficult to prejudge, even if that other country speaks approximately the same language. Failure to adjust to different manners and mores, failure to appreciate the extent and depth of local feelings and prejudices, are not uncommon. Personally, I doubt if any company, of any nationality, has moved abroad without making mistakes. The trick lies in correcting them rapidly and in learning from these mistakes—our own and others.

Many years ago, when the superiority of American marketing was first becoming apparent to me, I conceived a scheme by which American companies, which had demonstrated their expertise in this field, would take on British trainees who would, thereafter, return to their parent company. I found a number of takers but, for a variety of reasons, my plan died aborning. I refer to it now because, typically, Arthur (Dick) Watson, now US Ambassador to France, then in charge of IBM's overseas business, responded, "Yes, we will take some of your chaps—we think well of them—and put them through our regular training program, provided we are free to offer jobs to the best of them."

This direct, albeit self-interested, attitude made sense to me then and it does now. Typically IBM have been in the vanguard in employing native talent, even in the upper reaches of management. Herein lies the secret of adapting to different circumstances and surroundings. Herein lies part of the answer to the author's criticisms. By bringing along nationals of the country in which one is operating to the point that they, rather than the head office, are running the company, many of the pitfalls can be avoided. That is certainly our (Cadbury Schweppes Limited) policy, worldwide.

If American companies abroad are insensitive and unresponsive to local wishes and feelings, as the author infers, the solution may also lie in the choice of management—more particularly, the choice of a chief executive. It is certainly a mistake to send an "organization man" to develop an overseas company. He has an invaluable contribution to make on the home front but, off on his own, in charge of an offshoot, he is miscast.

Invited to address a European management conference in Montreux, earlier this year, on "What You Can Learn from the Americans", I put at the top of my list, dynamism, defined as "pertaining to energy or power in motion, action or change . . . vigorous, forceful, relating to or tending towards change." I elaborated on innovation and creativeness and cited examples. (A colleague in the audience, who runs our business in France, was asked by his Italian neighbour if I was in the pay of the Americans.) I also enlarged upon the functions and value of the entrepreneur.

If there is one lesson I have learned in building a British business in the USA, it is that overseas companies tend to prosper when they are put in charge of an entrepreneur.

I am flattered that Nicholas Faith includes me among his pioneers—the entrepreneurs, the mavericks—and I do not resent his suggestion that, coupled with other, more attractive attributes, the entrepreneur usually possesses a streak of native cunning. I would go further and say that he is usually self-oriented, if not selfish. But good or bad, this is the man who, in my opinion, should be chosen to run an overseas company.

What sort of man is the entrepreneur? Apart from the defects I have mentioned he is usually inclined to be a loner. He thrives best when he is left alone to run his own show. He shows up to advantage only when he is given his head. Supervision or detailed direction are irksome to him and, being a self-starter, he has no need of urging from others. He is an innovator and, more often than not, an unusually creative and vigorous being. He doesn't shirk responsibility and he demands full authority to go with it. He is a risk-taker and, being full of self-confidence, he is perfectly willing to stand or fall by the results of his endeavours.

I am tempted to comment on many more of the points made in this book, but I will limit myself to what I have said— on matters arising from my direct experience, upon which I feel deeply. Improved communication, Faith says, jets and the ability to dial a number almost anywhere in the world "ensures that control from the centre will become more, not less, rigid". Heaven forfend. Autonomy should be the keynote.

—Commander Edward Whitehead

European bookstores are bulging with books and pamphlets warning of the 'American invasion' or the 'American challenge'.... Yet, it is my impression that we are reaching a turning point. No longer will the tide run only one way. Today we are beginning to see a reverse flow of investment by foreign enterprise into the United States, and all the portents suggest that this is only the beginning of a process. European companies are more and more laying plans to expand their operations in America; in fact, within this past year we have seen several substantial American firms fall into European hands.

—George W. Ball, Senior Partner, Lehman Brothers, New York City, and former U.S. Under-Secretary of State, at a Conference on Foreign Direct Investment, October 1970

THE INFILTRATORS

CHAPTER I

INTRODUCTION

A great deal has been written about direct investment by American companies in Europe. The movement has been praised—as a spur to local management to adopt more modern methods, as a contribution to industrial investment, as a help to a country's balance of payments through the inflow of capital and the resultant reduction of imports and growth of exports. It has been attacked—as American imperialism, as a reduction of a country's control over its economy, as a fore-taste of a future in which the majority of the advanced-technology, high-growth industries in Europe would be under American control. The very methods used by the Americans, the structures which their companies have evolved to deal with their increasingly complicated empires, the motives which induced them to invest abroad, have all been copiously examined.

The movement in the opposite direction has been scarcely looked at except as an historical phenomenon. Direct European investment in the US has not been considered worth studying as a living force in the past few years. Yet even the most superficial examination discloses not just that it exists and thrives, but also that it is entirely different in character from the American challenge. Its roots are more widespread, its motivations and methods more varied and more sensitive to the requirements of the host country; in fact, it provides an exciting alternative to the somewhat rigorous and inflexible American bias as to the nature of direct investment. For where

the American presence abroad—however innocent its motives—
can easily look, indeed can become, colonising, imperialistic in
outlook, the Europeans in the US are explorers. They are, too,
explorers with a visible respect for what goes on around them.
Unlike the Americans abroad, they have come to learn—and
to teach their parent companies; they have not come to impose
alien patterns, alien products, alien notions of the way business
is carried on. So the relationship between the Europeans and
their American hosts, based on mutual respect, is by definition
healthier than the situation of American—and European—
companies in the rest of the world, based as it is on an implied
condescension towards the host. For, in the US, even the
biggest European companies behave like small ones. They do
not crash into the market; indeed until now "fear, disguised
as prudence", as one academic puts it, has prevented many of
them from going in at all. Instead they sidle in, relying on
specific specialised products, not the general momentum given
by their size. For they know they are exploring the biggest,
most powerful market in the world, and they are duly res-
pectful of the fact. But this knowledge of their own presumption
has not prevented increasing numbers of them from invading
the US during the past few years.

The investment figures in the table on page 14 show clearly
how the Europeans have been forcing the pace in recent years.
In the four years to 1970 they have, overall, increased the
value of their direct investments as fast as the Americans. In
any key sector—manufacturing—they have moved faster; in
another—petroleum—they have moved twice as fast. But despite the acceleration the Americans controlled $13·7 billion of
manufacturing assets, the Europeans only $4·1 billion—in a
larger market. So the impact of the Americans is inevitably
greater, and still growing. Despite American restrictions on
capital outflow, manufacturers contrived to send over three
quarters of a billion dollars to Europe in 1970; depreciation
and retained dividends gave them another $684 million of cash
flow a year for reinvestment. But the Europeans were moving
fast, and so far only a few hundred companies are heavily in-

volved in the US. There has been none of the imitative rush into the US by European companies anxious not to be left behind which has been such a feature of American corporate investment in Europe in recent years.

The European invasion is not just of statistical significance. It looks so completely different to the American challenge in Europe. To outsiders, the latter seems to consist largely of hordes of grey-flannelled organisation men imposing on a more or less willing European scene the same types of organisation, technique, products and industrial skills as they have employed in the US. Their impact has been concentrated on a few sectors. According to 1967 figures 85 per cent of the investment was in four industrial groups; vehicles, chemicals and electrical and mechanical engineering. The Europeans have invaded on a wider front, and the invasion has involved many very interesting personalities, some of them well known, like Adriano Olivetti and Commander Whitehead of Schweppes; others, equally successful but more out of the limelight, like Henry Lazell of Beecham and Pieter van den Berg of Philips. Their activities have been widespread and, in some instances, picturesque. And for them and other invaders, investing in the US was not—as it was for the Americans—just another business decision, but the adventure of their business lives. So the risks they ran, both personally and for their companies, were proportionately greater.

At the same time the assets the invaders brought with them were more varied, if less obvious, than those imported by the Americans into Europe. The Americans rely heavily, and not unreasonably, on the combined force of capital, corporate size, management depth and sophistication, and production techniques tried and proved in their own market, the largest and the one most responsive to new products in the world. Except in the field of electronics they have not, in fact, relied over-much on superior basic research.

The Europeans have fewer of all the obvious assets: they have less capital, a narrower financial base, and smaller financial markets to use when expanding their capital; they have no real managerial tradition. So they have had to rely on their wits and ingenuity—a state of affairs resulting in a variety of approach which makes their activities difficult to categorise. Many have brought specialised products or know-how, others have found a geographical or industrial gap in many spheres of operation—some as straightforward as newsprint or steel bars. Others have found a partner anxious to buy ready-made expertise, a state anxious to attract investment, a customer looking for a supplier reliably close at hand.

But however various their motives and means, all the invaders share the conviction that they are in the country to stay—for direct investment is the best possible token of permanence: it is never a short-term proposition, which is probably why the European effort did not slacken during the American economic slow-down of 1968-70. And, on the scale of which we were talking, such investment has an important symbolic element; it reflects the economic strength of the parent economy. So, it is no coincidence that the pace in the present invasion is being set by the Germans, whose invest-ment in the US rose more than seven times in the decade to 1970 to $675 million and nearly trebled between 1966 and 1970.

Yet the new invasion is not primarily or entirely a symbol of a newly-powerful Europe asserting itself in the US; nor is it merely a collection of individual success stories. It is, however, partly both of these things, and because the whole invasion is so fascinating and so little known, most of this book inevitably concerns individual corporate invaders, or attempts to isolate some attributes and experiences which are common to the Europeans.

These qualities add up to a European alternative of how direct investment should be undertaken in a developed economy. It differs from the American model, which is assumed to be the norm, in every way except its success. For a start—and here it is most unlike the American equivalent—there is the question of local ownership of some of the sub-sidiaries. Without such participation, large-scale direct investment is inevitably an imperialist phenomenon, making the guest country seem a mere outpost of empire. Where the Americans insist on 100 per cent ownership of their subsidiaries abroad, many of the Europeans (particularly the Dutch and the British) share the profits from their American operations with local investors by issuing a part of the equity in their local companies. This not only involves profit sharing, but ensures that profits are not drained away to a country with lower taxation. This local involvement applies also to managements. Whereas Americans start with their own men in virtually all key jobs, the Europeans minimise the number of men from headquarters from the very start.

And the heads of their US subsidiaries, unlike the Americans abroad, are rarely strangers to the country in which they are working. Often they are Americans. If not, they will have worked in the country (or Canada) for some years. Whereas Americans stand out, often arrogantly, against the social and economic framework within which they are supposed to be operating, the Europeans in the States have succeeded in blending with the landscape—and afford one reason why the Americans at home, who expect important individuals and concerns to behave in a suitably visible way, do not take the virtually invisible Europeans in their midst very seriously.

The European alternative is based on tact and consideration for the host country; an anxious attempt to think first of the customer and thus, by natural extrapolation, of the society to which he belongs, and a consequent adaptation of products and corporate methods and behaviour to suit local needs. This priority is completely different from the general attitude of the American company abroad, where the corporation's total welfare and profitability come before any consideration of specific national interests. Of course there are exceptions on both sides, but considerate Americans and arrogant Europeans are, alike, obvious exceptions.

The same pattern applies to the degree of freedom allowed by the parent company. Most of the examples of detailed interference from Europe are historical; by contrast only a few American corporations even make a pretence of allowing any real freedom to their subsidiaries—freedom of action which is taken for granted by Europeans in the US.

This contrast extends to the seriousness with which research, development and the marketing of new products by the subsidiary is taken by the parent. At one extreme we shall see how Shell's world-wide chemical activities were deliberately started in the US; how Philips in the US has a subsidiary making drugs and vaccines, uniquely in the group; and how Olivetti's engineers in Italy rely heavily on the requirements of its Olivetti-Underwood subsidiary in the US. In contrast the Stanford Research Institute found in 1963 that only 4 per cent of the research and development expenditure of the US corporations involved was incurred in Europe. The survey found also that it was rare for foreign-owned establishments to do the basic research and development for products to be sold internationally—let alone at home in the US market. Equally very few products are first introduced outside the US. (As a journalist I find this confirmed by the pride—and the consciousness of how different they are from the average—with which US companies in Britain who have been given world responsibility for a range of products, or have developed products which have then been adopted world-wide, announce the fact.)

Exactly the opposite applies to the Europeans in the US. It was automatically assumed by most of the groups I came across that their subsidiary could not be called truly successful until it had developed products of its own, or had been the first market where a product developed elsewhere had been launched. To many of them the US was a gigantic test market for new products. Clearly this contrast is helped by the size of the American market compared with any other. But it originates in the basic way a company thinks about its subsidiary's role within the group.

Corporate style clearly contains the very essence of the invasion. And the present and increasing success of an invasion conducted in such a style poses the implicit question on which this book is founded: if Europeans can behave like this why can't Americans? Why should European host countries put up any longer with the American order of priorities? Why cannot they insist that their guests be as responsive to local conditions as the Europeans are in the US? Why shouldn't Europeans insist that a proportion of the equity of all American companies in their midst be shared with local investors? These, and similar demands, have been dismissed in the past as not being conducive to the health of the companies concerned. Yet, it seems to me, on the evidence provided of European behaviour and profitability in this book, they cannot be so easily dismissed in the future.

The European presence in the US cannot be waved away as either narrow or of limited public interest. For the Europeans are ensconced in every nook and cranny of US life. Parke Bernet, New York's leading auction rooms and a subsidiary of Sotheby's of London, hold sales of such all-American objects as the old wooden statues of Indians which used to stand outside cigar-stores. Such all-American artists as Glen Campbell are heard on records sold by Capitol, a subsidiary of the British Electrical and Musical Industries group. A large proportion of the newspapers in the South are printed on paper bought from the US subsidiary of Bowater, the British group. The Girl Scouts go round US suburbia selling chocolate bars made by the US subsidiary of the Swiss Nestlé Company. Their parents come to collect them in their Volkswagen cars (having remembered to fill up with Shell petrol). When they feel tense they swallow Librium tranquillisers made by the American subsidiary of Hoffman-La Roche, another Swiss company. Alternatively they could pick themselves up with a nice cup of Lipton's tea, sold by a Unilever subsidiary. If in need of something stronger they can drink the best-selling Gordon's Gin or Vodka, distilled by a British-owned distillery in New Jersey, with a Schweppes' tonic. And before they retire to bed they are likely to brush their teeth with a toothpaste made by Beecham or by Lever's Pepsodent subsidiary.

Although Europeans—and the American public—seem

largely unaware of the European invaders, a few institutions and individuals have been taking active notice of them very recently. The top American banks (especially the Morgan Guaranty and the Chase Manhattan), some management consultants (especially Booz Allen), and some academics, are all starting to analyse the phenomenon.

But, unusually, officialdom was there first. The US Department of Commerce has had a special branch devoted to stimulating foreign direct investment since the early 1960's, in the interests of the balance of payments. It has even encouraged American journalists to write articles on the subject. For, according to the Department, 400 European firms are considering joining the 250 or so already established with direct manufacturing investments in the US, an impressive indication of the breadth of the new invasion. Three states have offices in Europe to attract such participation. Eighteen delegations from individual states were scheduled to go to Europe in 1970 to discuss future investment. On a more homely note, in Spartanburg, in the heart of South Carolina's textile belt, the local development director keeps a collection of the flags of European countries, so that he can hoist the appropriate one on the flagpole outside the Chamber of Commerce, when the relatives of one of the many German or Swiss or Austrian businessmen in town come visiting.

The impact of this activity is inevitably far less than its equivalent abroad if only because of the difference in scale between the economies of the US and individual European countries. In chemicals, the major industry where the Europeans have been most active in the US, they account for perhaps 5 per cent of the total capital invested in the industry. As Sir Peter Allen, then chairman of ICI, the biggest non-American chemical company, said of the US market: "It has grown every year at around $3 billion, the size of our total sales". And in more general terms, while there are five American-owned companies in the list of the biggest fifty in Britain, there is only one foreign-controlled concern (Shell Oil) in the top hundred in the US. There would be less than twenty in a complete list of the biggest five hundred. It is typical of the lack of information on the subject that a number of European-controlled companies (like Roche, and Brown & Williamson), which are candidates for the top five hundred in *Fortune*'s much-quoted annual list, are excluded because of the absence of reported figures*. Nor do the Europeans pose anything like the same threat in technologically advanced industries in the US as do the Americans in Europe, though a surprising number of the invaders can rely on some force of technical superiority.

In addition, the Europeans have tended to keep extremely quiet about their companies' parentage to avoid any nationalist reaction, while the Americans since the war have not minded being visible; so the impact of the Europeans tends to be over-discounted and that of the Americans exaggerated. But there is a much more fundamental psychological point involved, as I found when working on this study. The Americans long ago recovered from their xenophobia over foreign investment. So they are more relaxed about the foreign companies in their midst than are Europeans—a relaxation that often slips over into a sort of condescension and wonder at the quaint activities of the foreigners.

They are concerned about imports rather than direct investment. With the Europeans the situation is quite the reverse: with their lower wage rates, they do not now worry too much about the Americans' exports of goods but about the influence exercised over their lives by companies controlled from across the Atlantic.

When the American import problem exploded in August 1971 in the dollar crisis and the resultant import surcharge, the financial turmoil reflected an earlier shift of the economic and industrial power balance between the US and the rest of the non-Communist world. The crisis itself must in the long-

* So unimportant are these companies considered that *Fortune* does not even bother to explain their absence, even though, without them, and others like Ciba/Geigy and Nestlé, its list is inevitably misleading. Indeed, in its list for 1970, the magazine dropped Olivetti Inc. (formerly Olivetti-Underwood) merely because the parent had consolidated the US subsidiary.

term accelerate the European challenge: worries about new tariff barriers (which will long outlast the American import surcharge), the increased values of European currencies and the reserves of European countries will reinforce the technical and industrial strength of the companies involved. But this power—and the European challenge—pre-dated the 1971 crisis.

So my first task is to look for the roots of the recent invasion in terms of the figures—and of the collective European powers underlying them. I then go back in time, to tell the story of earlier arrivals to show that the European challenge and the European corporate style have deep roots in the US and to tell the story of some of the post-war pioneers of the present invasion. I discuss the techniques used in the invasion, to sort out real from imagined obstacles, and finally go on to show how Federal, state and local government departments encourage the invasion and how other official forces, led by the anti-trust division of the Justice Department, try to ensure that the invasion will not result in the same sort of control over vital national interests so regretted in Canada and in Europe as a result of the parallel but earlier invasion by American companies.

I have deliberately ignored the important Canadian investment in the United States for several reasons. First, as I discuss later, Canada emerges, in the thinking of many firms, as merely one region of a larger North America. Second, the Canadian-based firms with large interests in the US, like Massey Ferguson, Alcan or International Nickel, are more like regionally-based American firms than true outsiders. Third, there has been no recent upset in the balance between Canada and the US comparable to that between the Americans and Europeans. Canadian investment in the US is not much more than a third the value of the European, while the US had around $21 billion of assets in Canada and Europe alike at the end of 1969. And the Canadian firms in the US are relatively unprofitable and slow-growing—an awful warning to the Europeans that the mere presence abroad of a handful of well-known names is no guarantee of commercial dynamism, let alone economic independence. For, crucially, American domination of Canadian economic life is an accomplished fact, reversible only by a major political act of will on the part of the Canadians. The Europeans are not forced to contemplate the equivalent of the various extreme measures of Canadianisation-without-compensation now going the rounds.

Equally I have ignored the Japanese. They concern the future rather than the present situation. During the late 1960's, while the Europeans were gradually starting to replace an earlier flood of exports with direct corporate investment, the Japanese were at an earlier stage. They were still shying away from any investment in the US except to build up sales and service organisations and to receive supplies of new materials. Their reasons were obvious: the advantages they enjoyed—low wages and a protected home market taking the bulk of their production—would be thrown away by producing in the US. There was an additional, political, reason for staying out. The government authorities which control Japanese firms so closely would obviously not be anxious for major completely Japanese-owned subsidiaries to be built up in countries which would then demand similar rights in Japan.

Since the crises of August 1971, the situation has been transformed: a revalued yen, seemingly permanent hostility in the US towards Japanese goods, enormously strong Japanese monetary reserves. All are contributing factors in a new era which will assuredly see a flood of Japanese corporate investment in the US. Within three months of the import surcharge, Sony, the archetypal mass producer, had announced an investment of $1 million—and others were on their way. But not only is the Japanese invasion yet to come, it will also be a much simpler phenomenon than the European: the Japanese will be investing largely as the only way of leaping tariff barriers while the European surge started at the very time duties were tumbling as a result of the Kennedy Round. The Japanese, in fact, will be behaving in a much more orthodox way than the Europeans.

CHAPTER 2

THE FIGURES

THE growth of European investment in the US is a direct
answer to the famous thesis of Jean-Jacques Servan-Schreiber
in his book *The American Challenge*; he took the trends of the
1950's and 1960's, saw that American direct investment abroad
made the overseas activities of American companies into a
"third force" in world industrial life—and extrapolated from
what he saw. Realising (quite rightly) that the American advantage lay in organisation, in education, in the ability to
translate ideas into productive reality, he more or less despaired
of Europe's future in the absence of any coherent European
policy to improve the situation.

Now, a few years later, his conclusions look slightly ragged
at the edges and the book is likely to take its place among
similar volumes which treated a transient phenomenon as
permanent—books which tend to appear as a particular tide
is turning. In the 1930's, just as the flow of books and articles
proclaiming that "the bomber will always get through" was
reaching its height, the fast fighter plane and radar were being
developed in time to prove the thesis wrong in the Battle of
Britain. Since the war, the missile gap, so loudly proclaimed in
President Kennedy's 1960 election campaign, is another
military example of the same phenomenon. And, in the 1950's
two other gaps appeared, whose permanence was assumed in
most analyses of the time. One was the "energy gap", the
allegedly rapid run-down of the world's supply of fossil fuel.

This was quickly swamped by the development of atomic power and the repeated discovery of new oil reserves which more than kept pace with consumption. The other—a direct parallel to Servan-Schreiber's thesis—was the famous "dollar gap" based on the assumption that the Americans would be in permanent surplus in their economic dealings with the rest of the non-Communist world. Just as this was being minutely analysed by teams of economists the world over, it was, like the energy and missile gaps, quietly disappearing. A flood of European and Japanese exports to the US, and vast increases in the flow of capital from the US for both commercial and military purposes, saw to that. In the same way the American challenge, itself an undoubted fact, was being subverted just as Servan-Schreiber was producing an analysis purporting to show that no real response was possible under prevailing socio-economic circumstances. These circumstances were temporary; as soon as the special factors they included had run their course, there was nothing to prevent the restoration—through aggressive European investment—of an earlier balance.

The best way to understand Servan-Schreiber's attitude is to look at the figures in the table on page 14. These show clearly how very different were the first years of the 1960's, the ones on which Servan-Schreiber was largely basing his analysis, from the period before or afterwards. In the years from 1959 to 1966 the rate of European investment in the US slowed down. European-owned assets in the US rose in value by an average of under 5 per cent, against 8 per cent in the 1950's. And the flow of cash to these companies dried up completely—in fact for the three years 1963-65 the European companies actually withdrew investments from the US, at a time when the Americans were pouring between $1 and 1·8 billion a year into Europe. For while the Europeans were ignoring the US, the American challenge was reaching its maximum flow. The growth of US companies' assets in Europe had been rapid in the 1950's—an annual rate of 13 per cent from 1950 to 1959. But the figure for the base year was low—a mere $1·7 billion, a thirteenth of what it had become twenty years later. So it would have been

Europe v the United States

	Value of direct investments—in $ million					Growth in values annual rate per cent		
	1937*	1950	1959	1966	1970	1950–1959	1959–1966	1966–1970
Total Values:								
By US in Europe	1259	1733	5323	16209	24471	13.1	17.1	12.7
In US by Europeans	1337	2228	4452	6273	9515	8.0	4.9	12.9
By industry:								
Petroleum: By US	*NOT AVAILABLE*	426	1452	3977	5488	14.7	15.5	9.5
In US		349	972	1772‡	2768	12.0	10.9	18.9§
Manufacturing: By US		932	2947	8879‡	13703	13.6	13.0	13.6
In US		869	1501	2669‡	4061	6.2	7.3	17.4§
Finance & Insurance: By US		*NOT SEPARATED*				—	—	—
In US		870	1451	1758‡	1800	5.9	2.2	0.8§
Others: By US		374	924	3343	5207	10.8	20.1	13.6
In US		340	528	1701‡	888	5.0	6.9	-15.9§
By Country								
In UK	474	847	2477	5657	8015	12.6	7.4	10.4
By UK	833	1168	2167	2864	4110	7.1	4.0	10.9
In Common Market	498	637	2208	7584	11695	14.9	19.3	13.5
In France	146	217	640	1758	2588	12.8	15.7	11.8
By France	57	N/S	161	215	294	—	4.2	9.2
In Germany	217	204	796	3077	4579	16.1	21.2	12.2
By Germany	55	N/S	84	247	675	—	16.8	43.0
In Netherlands	19	84	245	859	1495	12.6	19.5	18.5
By Netherlands	179	334	892	1402	2121	11.5	6.7	12.8
In Switzerland	9	25	164	1210	1766	23.2	33.1	11.5
By Switzerland	74	348	716	949	1550	8.3	4.0	19.0
In other countries	384	356	1001	3648	6028	12.2	20.2	16.3
By other countries	139	377†	432	597	765	1.7	8.6	6.9

Source: US Survey of Current Business

* 1936 for figures of US investment.   ‡ 1967 figures, 1966 not available
† Includes French and German investment.   § Annual rate 1961–70

N/S Not separated.

logical for the rate of increase to decline. But it didn't; from 1959 to 1966 the annual growth rate was a staggering 17·1 per cent. The reason for both the European slow-down and the American speed-up was the same: the existence of the European Common Market.

The Treaty of Rome had been signed in 1958: immediately the American flow into the Common Market accelerated. Its very existence tempted abroad numbers of formerly reluctant American companies which saw the previously fragmented European market divided into at most two entities—and where some low-tariff items were concerned, even the distinction between the Common Market and the European Free Trade Area countries could be ignored. In addition, the EEC countries were growing faster than the US—which had been stagnant for much of the 1950's. For the first time American companies had a market of something near their own size into which to expand. And European firms had an unprecedentedly large market of their own which could profitably absorb all their resources, which might otherwise have been used for investment in the US.

The American drive was also speeded up by two comparisons their companies could make: of interest rates and profitability at home and abroad. In the first years of the 1960's American interest rates were far below those prevailing in Europe. Yet American investment in Europe during the 1950's had been very profitable: it had, in fact, been consistently and substantially more profitable for US companies to invest in Europe than at home. This profitability gap reached a peak in 1959 when American companies in Europe earned 18 per cent on average before tax on the net assets they employed—a figure one half above the percentage they would have earned on the same capital invested in the US. So the market was there; the capital available to the American companies was greater—and cheaper—than it would be for their European competitors; and their own companies in Europe were making money hand over fist. No wonder the rush was considerable.

The existence of the Common Market also changed the direction of the US attack. For the first five or six years of the decade American investment was no longer so concentrated on Britain as it had been. The British share fell by nearly 15 per cent from just under half to not much over a third of the total—a change of emphasis which damaged the entire growth rate of the British economy. For had the British been in the Common Market they would surely have benefited from some of the $9 billion which the Americans added to their assets in the Common Market during the 1960's, a figure nearly double the amount added to US assets in the UK. In 1959, the Americans had more invested in Britain than in the whole Common Market ($2·5 billion in the UK, $2·2 billion in the Common Market countries), by the end of 1970 they had $11·7 billion in the Six, and $8 billion in the UK. US investment flowed into every nook and cranny in Europe. Investment in France nearly quadrupled to $2·6 billion, in Germany it rose five times to over $4 billion in the decade, with most of the increase coming in the first seven years. Assets went up by over a billion dollars in Italy and Switzerland. * Whereas Sweden, Switzerland and Holland had bigger assets in the US than the other way round in 1960, by 1968 only the Dutch held the advantage by controlling more in the US than the Americans did in Holland.

The experience of the first half of the 1960's was not typical. Even between 1937 and 1950, when German investment was confiscated and one major British investment sold off, the Europeans increased their investment faster than the Americans, and European direct investment in the US rose above the value of the American participation in Europe; though the Europeans were greatly helped by their insurance company subsidiaries. In the 1950's the Americans naturally accelerated past the Europeans, but the period had a pattern of its own. Both flows were increasing—the Europeans more than doubled the value

* The Swiss figure is partly unreal, since much of it represents assets physically outside Switzerland but grouped for tax purposes in a Swiss subsidiary of the US parent.

of their investments during a decade dominated by the alleged
dollar gap and hence by an extreme reluctance on the part of
European central banks to allow direct investment in the US.
The Bank of England was especially strict. And this reluctance,
combined with greater Swiss and Dutch dynamism, meant that
the non-British investments in the US rose faster than the
British ones during the decade. Not that the British performed
badly: their assets nearly doubled, and, as Professor Dunning
pointed out in his survey of British investment in the US in
1961, "In the last ten years for every pound invested by US
firms in Great Britian—either in the form of reinvested earnings
or new capital—between 16s. and 18s. has been invested by
British firms in the US. If one leaves out the flow of capital
involved in the finance of takeover bids (in both directions) the
British record stands on a par with that of the US". This was
especially creditable because during the 1950's the UK remained the favourite target for US investment in Europe:
between 1950 and 1959 the Americans increased the value of
their investment in the UK by $1·6 billion, the same amount
as their investment in all the six countries which joined the
Common Market at the end of the decade.

Once the first impact of the Common Market on European
companies had been absorbed the pattern shifted again, though
the American flow into Europe was, by 1965-66, large, varied,
profitable, and geographically well spread enough to be capable
of self-sustaining growth. What happened from 1965 onwards
was a renaissance of European interest in direct investment in
the US.

In fact it was in 1966, the year before Servan-Schreiber's
book appeared, that the tide turned. In the first six years of the
1960's, the value of US direct investment in Europe went up
by 144 per cent; the corresponding investment by Europeans
in the US rose by only 33 per cent. In 1966, however, the
relative speeds of the two values shifted dramatically—and not
because US restrictions on investment abroad immediately
slowed down the American challenge; in fact the outflow of
capital from the US reached a peak of over $1·8 billion in 1966,

and the next year was still marginally above the 1965 level of $1·4 billion. Europeans, cynical about the seriousness with which the Americans take their balance of payments problem, can point to a continuous outflow of over $2 billion a year to US companies in Europe, even in 1970. But the Europeans' response was such that between 1967 and 1970 the value of European direct manufacturing investment in the US has risen at over 17 per cent a year—as fast a rate as that achieved by the American challenge at its height in the early 1960's, and well above the long-term rate of 13·14 per cent averaged by the Americans since the war. These figures were not just statistical legerdemain. The Europeans had under half the American rate of cash-flow provided by retained earnings: so they had to bring over capital, and they did. In the three years 1968, 1969 and 1970, the Europeans brought in over $1·5 billion—as much as the total imported between 1945 and 1967—and virtually the whole of this was used for investment in manufacturing and petroleum—not to service imports.

Even during the first half of the 1960's, a number of trends were working the Europeans' way. Two were negative: the American investment was slumping in profitability, and each dollar exported was buying less in asset terms. It was, in a sense, not surprising that American profitability in Europe declined —competition, much of it from other American companies, saw to that. Taking manufacturing investment alone, the American return slumped to below 10 per cent for the first time since the war during the German economic slow-down of 1967, and although it recovered substantially in the next couple of years, it will, surely, never again reach the dizzy heights enjoyed in the late 1950's.

The statistical position is complicated because there was an even more dramatic fall in the profitability of the American oil companies' huge investment in Europe. In the 1950's this had been not much less profitable than manufacturing. In the 1960's a combination of reduced product prices and the desire not to pay taxes led to actual losses, which reached a peak of $196 million in 1969. The total return on assets fell below 7 per cent at one point. Because part of the reduction in profit on oil was due to the companies' tax policy, it would be fairer to omit them from any comparison of real profit figures. But if the oil companies are included, the Europeans in the US were more profitable than the Americans abroad for some years in the mid-1960s, and the two groups have now been more or less equal over a number of years.

At the same time, the American dollar was less magnetic. In the period 1951-59, the Americans sent $1·7 billion to Europe—and their net worth rose by double that amount. From 1960-69 they sent an unbelievable $11·8 billion to Europe and their net worth rose under 40 per cent on top of their capital exports. Some of this fall in the value added by each dollar exported was caused by simple haste on the part of new investors, who probably tended to be less knowledgeable about other forms of finance, and had no cash flow to help multiply their efforts. Ironically, it was while thousands of companies were reducing their dependence on the US economy that the home country was enjoying the Kennedy boom. The companies involved had clearly not applied Le Chatelier's principle, well known to all students of chemical reaction. Broadly, this says that the further a process goes the more it inhibits itself. In this case the companies which were lured into Europe by the high profits they could see being enjoyed by the older inhabitants prevented any continuation of the bonanza, which had attracted them in the first place. The later arrivals spoilt the market for everyone.

While the American challenge was growing—but becoming less efficient by the criteria of either internal dynamism or of profitability—exactly the opposite was happening to the Europeans in the US. They expanded without the nourishment of new capital; they became more profitable. In the 1950's the Europeans, like the Americans, had contrived to extract $2 of net worth for every $1 they invested. In the 1960's they got $3—though the rate will go down now that they are expanding so fast, while the American ratio is once more improving. Both will probably settle at the 2-to-1 figure.

The Europeans' profitability was also improving. At the end of the 1950's the return on their manufacturing assets in the US had been 7 per cent or below—consistently under half the return enjoyed by the Americans abroad. This was not surprising. The British investments, at least, tended to be both inefficient and in the wrong industrial sectors. Professor Dunning's 1961 survey found that for the period 1958-60 the subsidiaries of British companies in the United States were less than two-thirds as profitable as the American norm. He also discovered "the greater part of British business capital is either concentrated in those industries whose profitabilty is around or below the national average such as textiles, mining and quarrying, metal manufacture, etc, or of such recent origin that optimum working conditions in the US subsidiary have not yet been achieved". Though even he found that only one in five of those companies which had not pulled out were disappointed by their investment, and that many of the more recent investments were of the right kind.

By the end of the 1960's the average return was probably up to 11 per cent—and the Europeans were making a handsome return on their investments in petroleum, against the loss being made by the US oil companies in Europe. This leap in profitability was partly due to the increased maturity of some of the inflow of the 1950's—which reduced the dependence on historic, low-profit investments. But it also reflects the growing confidence of European businessmen during the 1960's.

According to a 1962 survey by the US Department of Commerce, American-owned companies were a fifth more profitable than European-owned ones—largely because the Europeans felt that to compete they had to cut prices. Five years later the Europeans had caught up with the Americans. They had realised that they could compete on other factors apart from price—and, presumably, the rub-off from American managerial expertise came through in profits. To an increasing extent, local manufacture is replacing imported goods, on which the manufacturers already had a reasonable return: and they would not anyway be investing in the US unless they weren't going to improve on it.

During the 1960's, also, the Europeans were ploughing back a higher percentage of their earnings than the Americans. The Americans in Europe sent home around three-fifths—and are now under pressure to increase the percentage for balance of payments reasons. But even the British companies in the US —who were supposed to remit two-thirds of their earnings—in fact sent home only 45 per cent. And other Europeans sent back even less. So the Europeans, increasingly profitable, ploughing back their earnings, and making good use of such capital as they received from home, were well placed to launch forth. But the European presence after 1965 contained some major new elements as well as the dramatic increase in the investment figures.

The first, and biggest, novelty has been the extent of the German involvement. Until recently, ancestral fears of a third confiscation this century of German investments in the US had combined with fears of high wages and what the Germans call "your terrible American unions" to lead the Germans to invest less in the US than they would have done on a coldly calculated rate-of-return basis. In that sense the present German effort is making good an earlier lag—and the figures may understate the trend because for tax reasons some German companies invest in the US through their Swiss or Dutch subsidiaries, and consequently German-controlled investment counts as coming from Switzerland or Holland.

For even in 1966 (after German direct investment in the US had virtually tripled in seven years) the sales of their subsidiaries in the US were only a twentieth of their direct exports to the US. As Stephen Hymer and Robert Rowthorn have pointed out, the contrast with the UK, Switzerland and Holland, the three big traditional investors in the US, was complete; their subsidiaries' sales were twice as big as the parent countries' exports. Because of this lag, and because direct investments tend to be self-generating after a time (especially when, like the majority of German companies in the US, you do not expect any dividends at all from them), the present spurt is not at

all likely to be an isolated one. The number of companies involved, their pride and the momentum generated are all too great.

The Germans, the Dutch and the Swiss have been providing
the bulk of the new capital in the last few years. But apart from
the Swedes (whose assets are in fact lower than they were five
years ago) the invasion has been, in military terms, on a broad
front. For instance, the French (whose exports to the US were
eight times the sales of their US subsidiaries in 1966) have made
a come-back. The value of their investment had risen by just
under a fifth in the first five years of the decade. In 1966-69 it
rose by a half. Above all—and this forms the most striking
difference between the present spate of investment and any
other time in the past—the investors were not and are not just
a few exceptionally enterprising firms or individuals, but a
whole mass of them.

The impact of the European surge is complicated—and, more
importantly, minimised—by the fact that the American figures
for foreign investment are drawn up in balance of payments
terms, to show the net obligations to foreigners. In other words,
they show the net worth of companies, and lop off assets
balanced by long-term loans and other credit arrangements.
This arrangement minimises the size of the capital actually
controlled by foreigners—whereas when Europeans discuss
the American companies in their midst they think in terms of
markets, industries or companies controlled by the Americans,
and ignore the extent to which this state of affairs is based on
local borrowing. This can be considerable: in the case of many
new investments it is up to three-quarters of the total, and 100
per cent local financing is not unusual.

The way in which assets are measured matters enormously
when one is contrasting the Europeans and the Americans.
For the Europeans are more adept at making a little capital
go a long way: in continental Europe companies are anyway
used to relying on a small equity base and larger borrowings
than in Anglo-Saxon countries, and because of capital restrictions the British have successfully learnt the many and
various ways of financing overseas investment without much

outflow of capital. This careful husbandry of their own resources shows up, as we have just seen, in the figures for net
worth. It would, certainly, be even more dramatic if figures
were available for assets controlled as a multiple of net worth.
It is generally accepted, for instance, that every dollar in net
worth produces two in sales. And Dunning found in his study
of US investment in the UK in 1966 that the assets which the
Americans controlled were nearly double the figures for net
worth. The Europeans—poorer companies from countries
anxious in general to prevent an outflow of capital—tend to
start from a smaller equity base than the Americans. So the
multiplier for sales and assets is certainly greater in the US—
especially as the Europeans have found the capital market
there easier and bigger than the home one.* But the American
figures have other features which tend to underplay the
European presence.

They do not take into account real property assets; the
figures for capital flow do not include money borrowed in the
United States by American subsidiaries of foreign companies.
Nor do the figures show the sort of investment made by
Americans to help foreigners. So the figures eliminated an
obvious landmark like the then British-owned General Motors
building at the top of Fifth Avenue in New York. They ignore
the money borrowed by British Petroleum to finance its entry
into the United States (because it was the American-registered
BP Inc., wholly owned by the British parent, which did the
borrowing†); they do not even allow for the real assets on

* The American statisticians argue that borrowing creates an outside
obligation and therefore an outside participation (not to say partnership of a
sort) in the enterprise involved. Statistically they are correct; but they agree
that in terms of influence the controlling shareholder wields financial power
and influence to the extent of all assets employed in the firm regardless of
who finances them.

† Because the US statistics are concerned only with net obligations to
foreigners, what matters is whether the debt involved is in the books of the
parent company or not. If the local US subsidiary borrows the money then
the company, the asset and the debt incurred to buy the asset are all native,
and thus excluded from the figures. If the parent does the buying and the
borrowing, then both debt and asset appear in the figures.

which BP relied for its entry—the oil it discovered in Alaska. This oil does not count as an asset while it is still in the ground; so that BP's investment will not show in the figures for some years, until the loans involved start being paid off. The result is that the biggest single foreign commitment by any company anywhere in the world in 1969—the take-over by BP of Standard Oil (Ohio)—does not count, so far as the statistics are concerned. The figures also ignore the sort of challenge represented by the consequences of European exports to the US— a presence symbolised by the $350 million spent by Volkswagen dealers in the US to service the cars they are selling so successfully.

Volkswagen dealers may have a third of a billion dollars invested in premises and equipment, but through them they sell well over a billion dollars' worth of cars a year; and it is sales like those which represent the true measure of the European challenge. But there are other investments which are less effective in terms of economic power. These are the portfolios of shares held by individual foreigners, and by insurance companies owned by foreign interests (mostly British, with some Swiss). The balance between portfolio and direct investment is enormously important when one considers the assets likely to be controlled in the future by a given volume of foreign capital. Direct investments (with their much greater leverage through borrowed money and retained profits) account for a much higher proportion of American investment abroad than of foreign investment in the United States. So the American Challenge enjoys a multiplier effect in terms of economic and commercial influence abroad denied to foreigners in the US.

Even within the direct investment figures, the balance favours the Americans. They have so few investments in insurance abroad that their figures are lumped under "other investments". But in 1950 two-fifths of European direct investment in the US was in the form of insurance companies' assets. Most of these were in common stocks and bonds. These are portfolio assets, since they are held as reserve funds, and lack the multiplier effects of other forms of direct investment. But the proportion has been falling; by 1960 it was down to a third of the total; and by 1969 (partly because of the sharp slides in the stock market that year) it was well below a fifth. So Europeans have been getting better value than before, in terms of the assets to be controlled by a given amount of direct investment capital, as a higher proportion of an increasing amount of direct investment came to be in manufacturing and service assets. And, in the past couple of years, it is the manufacturing side which has been setting the pace, not the assets (warehouses, service centres, etc.) classed as "other" in the figures and used to support rather than replace exports.

But even if all the European direct investments were in influential sectors they would still be at a disadvantage in terms of economic power because the proportion of their investment in portfolios of shares and bonds is so much greater than it is for the Americans. Individual shareholders have little influence even on the companies they invest in, let alone on the business and economic life of the country involved. And since the war, the US stock market has exercised a fascination for European investors, which, until now, has been irresistible. In 1950 European direct investment in the US was $500 million (or a fifth) more than portfolio. By 1960 the portfolios had more than trebled and were half as big again as direct investment; and by 1968 the portfolios (including corporate bonds, most of which were probably convertibles) were $10½ billion, nearly nine times the figure of twenty years previously and double the amount of direct investment.*

So, whereas over half the American assets in Europe in 1969 were in the form of powerful direct investments, only 15 per cent of European assets in the US were in the same category. For private European investors have considerably helped the American challenge. First they have been plunging heavily—and mostly at the wrong time—in US stocks (helping the US

* The total of portfolio investment obviously includes a lot of money from non-European—including American—sources channelled through Swiss banks and therefore counted as European. But even allowing for this distortion the figures are extraordinary.

balance of payments and thus the American ability to invest abroad). Since the 1965 American controls on foreign investment, they have financed American companies by investing in the international dollar bonds issued in the US. Indeed, when Servan-Schreiber was writing, he assumed that European companies could not enjoy any real success in the Euro-dollar and Euro-bond markets.

He was wrong. In 1969-70 it was European companies which made the running in international markets. In 1968, according to the Morgan Guaranty Trust's figures, American companies borrowed over $2 billion in Euro-bonds, more than three times the total for all other companies. In 1969 and 1970, partly because of the continuing unhappy state of the New York Stock Market, they borrowed $1,780 million, $10½ million less than "other companies", most of which were European. These "other companies" have proved their drawing power without having even to issue proper accounts. An issue by Michelin, a model of non-disclosure, was so popular that its size was increased by a third from $40 million to $54 million; and Michelin will be using much of the proceeds to build a factory in Nova Scotia to supply the US market. ICI and the German chemical companies have also used the Euro-bond markets to provide capital for use in the US.

It is idle to pretend that European companies pose any overall threat to the ability of US companies to raise money abroad —though they can at least compete. What is more questionable is how far the US market will remain the Mecca for non-American investors it was in the 1960's. These investors have lost a great deal of money since 1968; and the institutions (like Investors Overseas Services and the many off-shore fund groups) which exploited their appetites so successfully have now either disappeared or have lost much of their appeal.

By now nine-tenths of the Americans' assets in Europe are in non-liquid form; they have, to put it brutally, spent the last few years borrowing short to invest long. This situation leaves them exposed in a number of ways. First would be a change in investment fashion. Any major shift by European investors out of dollar assets into anything else (gold, non-American shares or property or simply back into the bank deposits where until recently so much of the capital had been for so long) would leave the American position in Europe extremely exposed. Even more dangerously, the Americans could be hurt by any determined international effort to force them to live within their means. Some of the companies involved are now fully aware of their exposed position. Following the dollar crisis of August 1971 there is no doubt they were warned that they might be the victims of European revenge in a number of ways. The flow of funds from the US (virtually unaffected by earlier restrictions) would be cut back; or they could be forced to sell off a percentage of their shares to reduce the extreme illiquidity of US investments abroad.

But the signs of trouble had been there for some time. In June 1971 even so established a commentator as Lombard of the *Financial Times* could say that "the main cause of the US deficit is to be found, it cannot be too strongly emphasised, in the fact that the country is devoting far more to acquiring assets in other advanced countries than it can possibly afford —given its present export-imports performance". Such a statement reflects a very fundamental change in the balance of power between Europe and the US of which the growth of European investment in the US is only one example.

CHAPTER 3

THE NEW BALANCE OF POWER

> It may be a portent of things to come that the
> largest overseas investment commitment of 1969
> was made not by a US firm abroad, but by a
> British company investing in the United States.
> In one year this foreign corporation (British
> Petroleum) has acquired an equity interest in and
> will acquire eventual control over $1 billion of
> US assets.
>
> —James Leontiades, of the Wharton Business School,
> in *Columbia Journal of World Business*, July/August
> 1970

THE changes in the balance of power between Europe and
the US are visible in economic, political, technological,
managerial and industrial terms. The change in relative
general economic strength as expressed in the figures for balance
of payments, is well enough known but its full effects have not
yet been seen. Less apparent, but as real, has been the cumula-
tive effect in the last decade of the USA's problems—and the
progress made by the Europeans—on the willingness and ability
of the Europeans to invade the US.

Of all the factors, the Vietnam War was the most important.
For just as American overseas expansion was based on the havoc
wrought on Europe by two World Wars, so the Vietnam War
has not only revealed the limitations of American political
power, but has brought in its wake exchange controls on

foreign investment and a world-wide sense that the Americans were not necessarily unbeatable. To emphasise the change in relative economic strength, the German Government has been encouraging the direct export of capital by granting tax concessions to companies prepared to invest abroad, while President Nixon, who had hoped to remove the restrictions on American investment abroad, has been forced to ignore the subject and retain his predecessor's restrictive measures.

The strength of a number of European currencies against the dollar—itself a reflection of relative economic positions—naturally results in foreign direct investment. This completes an economic circle which began with strong exports. For instance the revaluation of the German Mark late in 1969 encouraged the Europeans to believe the dollar was no longer almighty; it also gave a double boost to German direct investment. The cost of home-produced goods rose, relative to those produced (possibly by the same concern) abroad; a revalued mark bought that much more in dollar assets—and with the alteration in the exchange rate finally made, there was no excuse for further delay.

In any case, if a currency is strong, investors like an asset valued in it, so they will pay a higher price for the shares of a company quoted in a strong currency than for that of its equivalent in a weaker one. This advantage (recently elevated to a total theory of foreign investment by Robert S. Aliber) has certainly played a role in the European challenge. The three strongest currencies in Europe recently have been the Swiss, the Dutch and the German—the same three countries which provided the bulk of the funds for new direct investment in the late 1960's. Aliber's theory cannot explain why the French and the British, with their classically weak post-war currencies, should have also been so active though he could say, with some plausibility, that any European currency is now strong compared with the dollar.

The combination of new found strength-through-joyful-balance of payments and the attitudes imparted by such strength is symbolised by the fact that the Germans are using

$150 million of the funds they provide to offset American defence expenditure in Germany as low-cost loans to smaller German companies who want to invest in the United States. As a result, the Americans are strengthening the German threat to their domestic industry in return for the money they spend defending the Germans.

By holding Germany's ally to such an unfavourable deal Franz Joseph Strauss (who negotiated the agreement when he was German Defence Minister) was, consciously or not, copying American behaviour towards the British in the first few years of the last war when the Americans obliged them to dispose of their portfolio of dollar securities on unfavourable terms and forced the untimely sale of American Viscose, Courtauld's American subsidiary, then one of Britain's biggest direct investments in the United States. These actions were taken to demonstrate to an isolationist American public that the British were in earnest in their prosecution of the war. Oddly enough the Americans behaved with much greater forbearance towards the Germans after the war. They discouraged American companies from buying German ones at what would have been real bargain prices. According to Professor Kindleburger, this was partly because many of the senior officials and generals involved came from the South and had an instinctive revulsion against anyone who came into a defeated country and, like the carpet-baggers after the American Civil War, took advantage of an impoverished and conquered people.

Vietnam is also involved in the dilution of another essential element in the American economic threat: the degree to which technically advanced industries, particularly electronics and aerospace, were supported by the government. Because of the enormous cost of the war—used in paying the troops and in simple, technically old-fashioned supplies like Coca-Cola, jet fuel, bullets and napalm—spending on advanced military projects has been savagely cut back, thus whittling away one of the major technological props of the American challenge.

Indeed, this support and the huge subsequent orders were

confined to a few industries, mainly electronics and aerospace. Away from these areas the gap always appeared narrower. In the words of K. Pavitt, an OECD expert on the technology gap, "when such [i.e. military and space] research is excluded and when corrections are made for differences in wage levels, the European Research & Development effort is about the same as that of the USA. Indeed industry in Switzerland and the Netherlands—and perhaps also in the UK and Germany—devotes a greater proportion of its resources to R & D than does US industry. And there is little evidence that European R & D is much less efficient. These four countries, together with Sweden, all have strong competitive positions in the world markets in high technology industries, and Switzerland's export pattern is even slightly more 'technology intensive' than that of the USA." This opinion is supported by Professor Dunning's finding that British companies investing abroad reckoned to get a slightly higher return in know-how from their investments in Germany than from those in the USA.

The American lead was and is in such glamorous and fast-moving industries that the narrowness of its base was concealed; as Pavitt says, military and space uses "played a very small role in pharmaceutical products and plastics". And it is no accident that the European challengers tend to have in common a technical specialisation in products, like drugs, plastics and fibres, where know-how plays an important competitive role. They are also products for which American government support—which, unlike that provided by European governments, is almost exclusively military in origin—was noticeably missing. The fact that these products are technology-based and fast-growing gives the European challenge the solidity possessed by the American invaders twenty years ago and rather lost in the mass invasion of the 1960's.

Even in the field of electronics we find a leading American stockbroker recommending clients to buy shares in the North American Philips group because of the great strength imparted by the enormous research efforts conducted by the parent company in Holland—giving as examples items as diverse as a rotary-headed electric shaver and a television camera tube. And, in its successful 1970 take-over bid for the Alloys Unlimited Company, the British Plessey group was a perfect example of the way in which the European challenge extends to the very base of American technology. For Alloys, with the motto "everything but the chip", is one of the largest makers in the US of all the micro-components (apart from the silicon chip itself) used in the solid-state devices which are at the heart of modern electronics. The American lead in these devices was supposedly unbeatable, based on the classic formula of an enormous and technically receptive home market and superb production engineering. Plessey's bid challenged this lead at its very foundations. Significantly, one of the reasons why Alloy's management was keen to merge was the access it would thereby gain to Plessey's research effort in Britain, which it considered low-cost and high-grade by US standards.

In one case, that of tyres, the technological advantage is so far in favour of the Europeans that Dunlop opened a large plant in the US in 1970 which will, initially make only ordinary cross-ply tyres. In Europe, by contrast, all the tyre producers (including the American-owned ones) are concentrating on the more advanced radial-ply tyres. And to invest in plant to make technologically obsolescent products is generally reckoned as the sort of insult offered by advanced countries to less fortunate ones—usually in the Third World outside Europe and the United States. It is easy, in fact, to exaggerate the technical sophistication required to succeed in the American market. After all, the whole American motor industry is now striving, unsuccessfully, to break the hold of a forty-year-old design, the VW Beetle, in the affections of a large percentage of the American motoring public. And certainly the American challenge in the motor industry owed nothing to American technical superiority; in fact the Americans, conscious of the importance of marketing, financial and managerial skills in the industry, go out of their way to brush aside the idea that advanced design of the product should play any part at all in the success of a motor company.

In one really convoluted case of technological back-lash European technology contributed greatly to the problems of an existing European investment in the US. The invention by the British Pilkington group of the "float" method of glass-making made all the existing ways of manufacturing plate glass technically obsolete. One of the last companies in the US to instal a new plant using older technology was, ironically, a subsidiary of the French St Gobain glass group. And because of the lack of profitability resulting from this ill-timed investment the company had to be sold off a few years later.

The invention of the float glass method, like many other innovations, carried with it the possibility of "technical multiplication". The classic example in the US of an important innovation waking up an entire industrial sector is the impact of the stainless steel razor blade introduced in the early 1960's by the small British Wilkinson Sword company. The new blade produced all the results desired by the textbooks: it stimulated other new products in response to the innovation: encouraged greater research efforts, and benefited the customers.

The same could be said of a number of more recent invaders. And many of these are going into partnership with Americans. Together, as I show in Chapter 7, the partners can increase competition in a sector in a way impossible for either partner separately.

In the past it has been fashionable to dismiss the potential impact of European technology by saying that there were few firms like Dunlop, Wilkinson, Plessey or Philips in Europe capable of the vital step of translating technological innovation into commercial success. In eight industrially advanced countries in OECD, after all, eight firms account for around half of all research and development (in the Netherlands the figure is five firms and 65 per cent). The Europeans were supposedly helpless, whatever they did. Either their industries were too fragmented to compete, or—when firms did merge—there were too few companies to provide an adequate response. All that has now changed. The Europeans are now getting the best of both worlds—from the solid corporate power of newly-merged European giants, and the adventurousness of smaller, but technically specialised, concerns. For the present European invasion has two separate strands, woven by big and small firms.

First, European companies in industries traditionally dominated by firms with world-wide manufacturing interests (tyres, oil, pharmaceuticals, plastics and chemicals) are completing their world-wide coverage; a classic case is ICI. A prime reason for the merger of Dunlop and Pirelli, two of the biggest non-American tyre companies, was to exploit the US market the better. And in industries like electrical engineering, big companies like the Swiss Brown Boveri group are being dragged in by their very success in direct exports to the US.

The European merger tide of the past few years has helped provide European companies with three of the major assets required for direct investment, all attributes previously largely confined to American companies. It has given them an adequate "corporate brain" of central staff services, and far bigger bases of capital and existing export businesses. All these are vital; for large companies are inevitably even more dominant abroad than they are at home. In 1962 seventy-six firms, mostly very big ones, accounted for 71 per cent of British manufacturing assets overseas. But these big companies also need the overseas investment. Only by such a presence abroad can they use their particular specialised assets to the fullest advantage. As Professor Dunning puts it: "It is not the production or technical or managerial know-how (or even the production of the goods that incorporate this know-how) but the extent to which this know-how is used which is the important determinant to economic development."

For what was so worrying about the European (especially the British) scene in the post-war years was the defensive attitude of many big companies, which never dreamt of challenging the Americans on their home ground, even though they were being challenged from across the Atlantic. Now all that has changed. Even the most diffident British companies are actively selling—if not yet investing—across the Atlantic.

The mergers in Western Europe—often triggered off by the impact of the Americans—have been accompanied by an obsessive interest in managerial education, corporate reorganisation, and the activities of management consultants. These efforts have often appeared faintly laughable, or even sinister, to Europeans. But they have helped to make European-owned industry more competitive, and they have been reinforced by the extremely valuable training ground provided by the American-owned companies in Europe. There is a constant drain from these concerns of able men fretting at the strict controls under which they have to operate and the knowledge that, in most American-owned companies, they cannot rise above the management of the subsidiary in their own country. And no European company now feels secure without its quota of men trained by Ford or Proctor & Gamble. These men, aware of the deficiencies as well as the strengths of their former employers, would naturally assume that their new employers can, and must, be present in the US.

Among smaller firms, however, a threshold of fear has been overcome. As Frank Sheaffer of the US Department of Commerce, the senior official trying to attract European investment into the US, puts it: "Non-Americans used to think that every firm in the States was the size of General Motors . . . they couldn't understand that 96 per cent of American manufacturing firms have less than 200 employees . . . or that every firm in the US is not a national firm." Because their idea of the size of American corporations was derived from the giants in their midst, they could not grasp that in reality American business is more fragmented, and has proportionately many smaller units than is usual in Western Europe. So, in fact, American conditions are more, not less, suitable for small businesses than European ones. And, as more and more European countries reach what Blake Frischia of the Chase Manhattan Bank has described as "the threshold of internationalism" in terms of size, and technical, managerial and financial competence, they will naturally want to be directly involved in the world's biggest market.

Indeed, the industrialists I have questioned seemed remarkably vague on the subject: given the size of the American market the obvious response to the question "Why are you in it?" is "Because it's there". As Jack Callard, the chairman of ICI, put it, "we have to go where it's big". But perhaps the best answer was given to me one Saturday lunchtime by a British electronics engineer who was in the middle of a sleepless weekend submitting a detailed specification for a valuable defence contract on behalf of Elliott-Automation's US associate: "Responsiveness," he said, "is the name of the game, and you can't be responsive from 4,000 miles away."

To translate this "responsiveness" into direct investment, however, is another matter. The process involves the possession of the necessary assets, and sufficient motives. Professor Dunning defined the first as a "package deal comprised of three ingredients: 1. Entrepreneurship, that elusive and ill-defined fourth factor of production; 2. Expertise, technological and managerial; 3. Money capital". Of these (fortunately for the still under-capitalised Europeans) he considered the third the least important. Since direct investment is perfectly possible without any international capital flow at all, but by using solely money borrowed in the host country, it is reasonable to agree, with Professor Kindleburger, that "direct investment belongs more to the theory of industrial organisation than to the theory of capital movement".

Direct investment must therefore, as he says, reflect an industrial superiority, a monopoly advantage possessed by the investing company big enough to offset the disadvantage of not being on home ground; so the foreigner's qualities must be exceptional—in other words, potentially profitable—enough to make up for the disadvantages he labours under against the local competition. The assets can, as we shall see, be many and various. So can the motives. When Professor Dunning looked at the (relatively) simple picture presented by British investment in the US ten years ago, he found that "there are few common features concerning the pattern of investment evolved"; he cites the obvious reasons, tariffs, transport costs, the break-up of licensing agreements, the need for a "window into US industry".

There are other, more bizarre reasons. Wilkinson Sword, for example, invested in its first plant in the US in the early 1960's, relatively soon after it had started importing razor blades, because, by finishing them in the US, it paid a smaller fee on the stainless steel coating patents held by Gillette than it would have if the blades had been produced in Britain. A decade later, in the first systematic study of European Corporate strategies in the US since Dunning, Lawrence G. Franko, found that successful investors "entered the US market to exploit a distinct, usually technological monopolistic competence."

The Europeans seem, mostly, to have specific reasons for investment. The Americans were more vague—and tend towards the personal and chancy: "The justification for many major actions," says Raymond Vernon in a recent book about US Corporations abroad, "could only be explained as a hedge against a murky future." This is echoed by Michael Brooke and H. Lee Remmers: they say "For all the talk about plans and strategies, the actual decision [to make a direct investment] often arose from some chance, almost freakish, event . . . amongst the most common were personal influences of one sort or another."

From their study of eighty corporations they came away convinced that the bulk of such direct investment is defensive: "The management," they say, "frequently appears to respond to this new challenge [of overseas investment] cautiously and pursues what have been called risk-minimising policies."

Professor Stephen Hymer and Robert Rowthorn have put forward the theory that even the American onrush into Europe was defensive, not offensive, in motivation. They claim that part of the notion of the American challenge came from myopia. "Europeans felt threatened because they saw US corporations gaining an increased share of the European market. They paid little attention to the fact that, in the world market taken as a whole, US corporations were themselves being threatened by the rapid growth of the Common Market and the Japanese economy and required a rapid expansion of foreign investment to maintain their relative standing."

Hymer and Rowthorn were thinking of growth rates compared internationally. It is more likely that the firms themselves were thinking of comparisons with other US companies in their own industry which already invested abroad. This comparison would naturally result in a good deal of imitative and defensive investment, following suppliers and customers as well as rivals abroad.

The European invaders—like the Americans in the 1950's—have no such defensive notions in mind. When the imitators follow, as they surely will, the present flow should, if the American precedent is anything to go by, speed up considerably. For the moment the impetus seems largely positive and provides a direct contrast to the norm established by Brooke and Remmers.

In this context even a reduction in the total investment figures can reflect increased—not reduced—aggression. Uniquely, the Swedish investment in the US has actually declined recently, from $239 million in 1967 to $208 million in 1970. This was mainly because of the sale for $57 million by the Swedish Electrolux company in 1968 of its 38·8 per cent holding in US Electrolux, one of the biggest single Swedish investments in the US. This apparent retreat concealed some aggressive behaviour. The parent company's former majority shareholding had been eroded because of successive rights issues. So the parent sold because the investment had become merely a portfolio one; without a majority it had no control, and could not generate a profit, or even a sales volume appropriate to the value of the investment—its proportion of US Electrolux's sales was not much more than the value of the shares. Yet when it reinvested $20 million of the money it reckoned to get $1 of sales for every 60c invested.

Electrolux managed to get out of a generalised business into a number of specialities like industrial cleaners and lawn mowers for professional use. It increased an existing investment in Flymo air-cushion lawn mowers, and bought the agents responsible for selling the fridges it produces for use in caravans. In other words it invested aggressively—yet the figures show an actual decline. Electrolux's new ventures and its attitudes were typical of the Europeans: how far they differ from the established norm amongst direct investors elsewhere can be seen by comparing European motives in the US with the general run—the respondents to Brooke and Remmers' questions.

These put tariffs and transport on top of the motive-list: "If there were no such things as tariff barriers or transport, we were repeatedly told, most companies would not be multinational." Both sound, defensive reasons: yet—except in a few special cases like dyestuffs—tariffs were barely mentioned to me as a reason, even where the American barriers were high enough to provide an excuse for investment. "Transport" was important—but the Europeans were talking about delays produced by the length of the freight pipeline, the intangible failure to satisfy customers, not—as Brooke and Remmers mean—the straight cost element. And an investment made in order to give better service reflects a more positive attitude than one purely made to avoid unnecessary costs.

There were other differences: I have already noted the absence of "me-tooism", of following customers or rivals abroad. And none of the Europeans were in the US to ensure adequate supplies of components or raw materials—both important considerations to Brooke and Remmers' companies. By contrast the few Japanese investments in the US are classically defensive attempts to guarantee supplies of raw materials—at the moment mostly lumber and fish. The next investments are likely to be in coal mines to safeguard supplies of vital coking coal for blast furnaces in Japan. And at least one of the rare Japanese manufacturing investments, a plant in Texas assembling Mitsubishi aircraft, was defensive and protective, a take over by the Japanese only after two local partners had proved highly unsatisfactory.

The single motive which the majority of the Europeans seem

to share but which is lacking, or muted, in most other direct investment is the desire to learn from their investment. The Europeans want their subsidiaries in the US to be, as Brooke and Remmers say, "a 'listening post' sensitive to local conditions and having access to research and other sources of knowledge in the country concerned". But they also hope that their American subsidiaries will grow into suppliers of new products and ideas for the rest of the group—and take early steps, by setting up research and development in the US, to ensure that they do.

In the past the simple "listening post" aspect of foreign investment was so important that a few large companies, like BP, Shell and ICI, had offices in the US, not to trade, but simply to learn. BP had such offices both in New York (for the commercial information) and in Washington (for the political scene). These were such key points that Sir Maurice Bridgeman and Sir Peter Allen, recently retired as chairmen of BP and ICI respectively, were among the high-flying executives who worked in these spyholes in the past. And Shell, despite its massive direct investment in the US, still maintains a separate listening post in New York.

Even when the investment is more than a token office, this learning role remains. In a sentence which might have been written with Unilever or Olivetti in mind, Brooke and Remmers say "companies argue that even an unprofitable national subsidiary can produce overall benefits to the firm". This argument has become unfashionable: European companies now expect profits as well as intangible benefits. But many of the case histories in this book show how valuable these benefits can be, whether they be tangible products or intangible managerial methods.

Another major motive, for companies big and small, is a simple impatience with intermediaries and middle men. Licensees are often the first to suffer from European impatience. Licences are withdrawn (or not granted for new products) or the licensee's company is simply bought up. Licencing a product (even when the licensing company has a share stake in the licensee) is especially inadequate where the licensing company is both aggressive and anxious to find out what is happening in the licensee's market. Licensees cannot be truly "responsive" to market requirements and are not doing research and development of the product to adapt it to the local market. Where licences are not involved, Europeans often buy up their local sales agents and then gradually expand their sales organisation to include more elaborate service facilities. A natural further step is to assemble machinery from components supplied locally, especially when these are standard equipment, or to manufacture parts which are especially bulky or do not require the sort of highly skilled workmanship on which so many European companies pride themselves. In these investments the Europeans are imitating the Americans, whose stake in foreign business grew as a later development of the industrial superiority first shown in their post-war export boom. They need cite no specific motive, for they are simply following the cycle laid down by Professor Raymond Vernon for products sold internationally: development at home leads to exports and then manufacture (and further development) abroad.

The Europeans' investments, in fact, followed export increases remarkably quickly—certainly more speedily than could be explained in purely defensive terms. For there are three major reasons why Europeans should in theory think of investing in the US at a later stage of their export development than Americans would in Europe. First is the wage gap between the US and Europe. This inevitably provides the Americans with a temptation to invest in Europe, and gives the Europeans a ready-made excuse not to rush into the US. Second, there is virtually no anti-trust legislation in the Common Market—and the US was a bigger market even than the EEC. So whereas US companies (especially in oil) could easily find themselves with management energies which could not be properly harnessed within the US because of limitations on expansion imposed by anti-trust legislation, and therefore needing an outlet abroad, European management could keep its energies fully employed at home. Whereas Europe was to

Americans a series of smallish markets (or one biggish one), the US loomed more formidable in European eyes. And American companies are more used to controlling subsidiaries 3,000 miles away than were the Europeans. Americans do it all the time; their country is over 3,000 miles wide. So they saw no more problem in exercising control over a subsidiary in London than over one in Los Angeles. Another intangible barrier the Europeans are leaping is the fact that the label "genuine imported" on many consumer goods carries much prestige in the US, a respect which leads to bigger mark-ups, and thus higher profits.

Yet the US is now a part of small companies' marketing strategy from the outset. One such, Eurotherm, a small British maker of solid-state temperature controls, has plans to assemble and then manufacture in the US even before it has sold any of its devices there: and this confidence is being expressed by a company less than seven years old, with total sales of only £1 million. At the other extreme is Volkswagen, whose sale of a billion dollars' worth of cars in the US involves virtually no direct investment apart from a few million dollars in corporate headquarters. The purchase, in 1970, of the company which makes air conditioning equipment for Volkswagen cars sold in the US was exceptional: the Volkswagen headquarters in Germany insists that this was a local initiative, financed by Volkswagen's American subsidiary.

Volkswagen is not alone in continuing to rely on low-wage, high-volume manufacture in its home country. But one particular industry, large electrical turbo-generators, shows how even the most reluctant European company is inevitably forced into spending considerable sums on facilities in the US once it has been reasonably successful in selling on the market (incidentally it also demonstrates the very different angles from which companies in an industry attack the same market).

The Europeans are currently attacking Westinghouse and General Electric, two of the world's largest companies. These two have found themselves short of manufacturing capacity and not necessarily technically superior to the Europeans, who have sold quite a number of generating sets in the US recently, even though their prices have to be at least 6 per cent cheaper than the lowest American-based bid (defined as being a set which is 50 per cent US-made); this stipulation is a protectionist measure applied by any US public or federal corporation. Now four European turbo-generator manufacturers are selling hard in the US. And of these only one, the British General Electric, is selling from a purely European base without any American partner. Two other companies are going in with American partners, both of them giant concerns, but both needing European technical expertise and production facilities. The German Kraftwerkunion, the merger of AEG and Siemens' interests in power generation, has a selling agreement with the American Allis-Chalmers company, which itself used to make generators until 1962. This agreement, and one between the British Reyrolle-Parsons group and North American Rockwell, are clear demonstrations of present trends. Until the agreement late in 1970, Parsons had been trying (unsuccessfully) to sell into the US from a base in Canada, where it could show American utility companies a successful factory assembling very large generating sets. NAR, for its part, was trying hard to increase its sales outside its troubled and cyclical aerospace business. From the beginning a certain amount of work on any sets will be done by NAR.

Parsons was not NAR's first proposed partner. It would have preferred to join with the Swiss Brown Boveri group. But Brown Boveri felt strong enough to go it alone. The world leader in large turbo-generators, Brown Boveri has been extraordinarily successful in selling them in the US and now has orders for about 15 million KW—equivalent to seven of the biggest power stations in England. It would probably have preferred to continue exporting direct to the US—despite the tariff barrier, and even though the US is the only large developed country where it is practicable to import these sets; in France and Germany Brown Boveri has for a long time had to have subsidiaries which construct the whole set, because of local unwillingness to buy such vital equipment from abroad. So it should have been resigned to the investment in the US. Yet it was reluctant. As the company says, "production of our designs in Europe results in optimum conditions regarding quality and economics" (even though some heavy casings are now made in Canada). But it was under considerable local pressure to invest. One of its best customers was a big power company from Virginia. So a delegation from Virginia, including the governor, Linwood Holton, went to Switzerland late in 1969 to spend three days with Brown Boveri's top management, selling the idea of investing in Virginia. The state obligingly re-zoned for industrial use the 400-acre site Brown Boveri wanted as well as 200 additional acres on a nearby farm. So, possibly reluctantly, Brown Boveri moved in—but on such a large scale that the investment is an earnest of a long stay. From the beginning it is installing the very biggest testing facilities, including 600-ton cranes, and enormous test beds for "overspeeding" and balancing of turbine shafts. Because of the size of the sets Brown Boveri is supplying to the US, these facilities will be bigger than anything Brown Boveri has anywhere else in the world. And because, as Brown Boveri says, "it is not anticipated that the facility and its personnel will be fully loaded by maintenance and service work . . . certain manufacturing and assembly operations will be performed" there. Only slowly will the company be drawn into an extension of its plant, depending "on the acceptance of our equipment on the United States market".

For all its apparent reluctance to leave its European base Brown Boveri is spending $10 million on its initial investment in Virginia. Brown Boveri's ability to go it alone in this field without US partners; the keenness of two giant US corporations to link with other European companies; the extraordinary efforts of the state of Virginia to attract Brown Boveri; the attempt by Parsons to use a Canadian base from which to sell into the US market: these are all facets of the new scene. It is a scene which combines European technical confidence with a slow acceptance by the Europeans of the need to invest directly in the US once past a certain sales point. The combination of an impressive commercial momentum by aggressive European companies, American pressure to have suppliers close at hand, and an anxiety to help on the part of the local American authorities is not confined to turbo-generators. The entrepreneurial spirit which creates the momentum required for direct investment is now found in more European companies than ever before, but it (and thus direct investment in the US) go back a long way.

CHAPTER 4

THE GIANTS

It's an axiom in the trade that all soap salesmen
are bastards. For what it's worth, Lever salesmen
are the nicest bastards in the business.
        —An American grocer quoted in *Fortune* magazine

Nice guys finish last
—Leo Durocher

THE European corporate style in the US is not a recent development. Indeed, Shell and Unilever, whose US subsidiaries (Shell Oil, Lever Bros, and Thomas J. Lipton) are the two biggest foreign direct investments in the US, were evolving the delicate mixture of qualities required, the loose but definite parental control, and the balance between bending to local susceptibilities and still looking for profits even before the First World War. And much of what they learnt is still applicable.

Of course, their very size makes them in some ways exceptional. Shell, in fact, still dominates the investment figures. The parent company's holding controls net assets of over $1·8 billion, accounting for 15 per cent of the whole foreign direct investment in the US and a fifth of the European total. Its 1969 sales of $3·5 billion made it the sixteenth biggest company in the United States. And, even though its sales are confined to the US, on its own it is the sixth biggest oil company in the world—bigger than others with a world-wide spread like

Phillips or Continental Oil. Nor is it a mere upstart. In 1929 it was the thirteenth biggest company in the country—and its relative slippage is due entirely to the spread abroad of other companies, not to its own slow growth. In fact, after US Steel and Ling Temco Vought it is the third biggest company in the US whose activities are entirely domestic. Yet Shell Oil does not account for the whole of the group's US activities. Asiatic, another Shell company with headquarters in New York, also handles the sale of a lot of Shell group products to US customers (including several hundred million dollars of jet fuel for the US Air Force). Shell is so big it is also capable of dominating the figures for capital flows. When the parent group took up its 69 per cent share in a rights issue by the subsidiary in 1968, the investment—of around $200 million—accounted for around half the total new investment by foreign companies that year.

For all its size, Shell's growth—and more especially the learning curve of its American experience—forms a true example of European methodology and motivation. It also had its fair share of luck from the very start. In 1912, a year after John D. Rockefeller's Standard Oil monopoly had been broken up by the American courts, the first cargo of Shell products landed. They came because "the Standard" was attacking in Shell's own backyard in the Far East, and this was Shell's reply—an aggressive response by one big company to an attack by another, a move typical of many in the oligo-polistic oil game. The products landed on the West Coast, because that was the nearest market to Shell's refineries in Sumatra. It arrived at the right time in the right place. Pro-duction of the Model T Ford had just begun to inaugurate the spread of the thirsty motor car which dragged up with it the US oil industry. And nowhere was growth faster than on the West Coast, where Shell's strength has always lain—it is still the biggest seller of oil products in Oregon and runs second to Standard of California in its home state. Shell's West Coast orientation was so strong that until 1950 its headquarters were in San Francisco. By accident Shell, like other later

48 THE INFILTRATORS

invaders, had found a gap in the market—in its case a geographical one.

Shell also had the advantage that the oil industry in the US is far more fragmented than it is elsewhere, for a number of reasons only one of which is connected to the sheer vastness of the country: the oil industry was the first major target effectively hit by the anti-trust authorities early in the century and has remained a favourite target ever since; the producing end is composed historically of a lot of small rich entrepreneurs with considerable political influence; and sales of oil products in the US are far more heavily concentrated on petrol (sold through thousands of scattered outlets) rather than on fuel oils (sold to relatively few buyers) than they are in the rest of the world. No one company has more than a tenth of the total US market for oil products, and it is exceptional, even in a giant company's home state, for it to control more than a quarter of the market for petrol. Even now only a few oil companies sell oil on a fully national basis.

In fact, for the first seventeen years of its history, Shell Oil—or rather its constituent companies—was almost completely concentrated in the Middle and Far West. During that period Shell grew fantastically fast, and its problems and advantages ran remarkably parallel to those of today's investment explorers. It could not pick and choose among its purchases, for instance. To get local production it had to buy oil fields which were not, to put it mildly, gushers. Sir Henry Deterding, the Dutch guiding light behind Shell's world-wide growth, was philosophical: "One has to start at the bottom in a new country and it is not always possible to get 20s. for £1." But Shell's men, at least in the Oklahoma fields, had an advantage denied to later investors. In a pioneer area, said one Shell man, "we were all foreigners. Everybody there was from ... New England, Oregon, Ohio, Pennsylvania—places which in those days of slow travel made them almost as far from home, and just as 'foreign' to Oklahoma ways, as men who came from across the ocean."

This advantage was not general. And in the 1920's Shell

faced a number of onslaughts as a foreign concern. As the owner of Roxana Oil Company in Oklahoma, Shell was attacked as "the foreign petroleum menace" in a paper friendly to Standard Oil. More seriously, in the early 1920's, Californian nationalism was invoked—"a kind of jealous feeling," according to Deterding—to prevent Shell's takeover of Union Oil of California. Shell had already taken over one rather ramshackle company, Union of Delaware, the creation of a group of Eastern financiers, whose major asset was a 25 per cent stake in Union of California. At the same time there was an attempt to launch a senatorial investigation of the group's expansion on the grounds that it was a sinister influence owned by the British government (other innuendoes pointed to Queen Wilhelmina of Holland as the proprietor). These rumours were spread by Albert Fall, President Harding's crooked Secretary of the Interior, who had his own oil scandals (the granting of the leases on the Teapot Dome oilfield) to conceal. They came to nothing. But Fall did succeed in persuading Arthur Brisbane, the leading columnist of the Hearst newspaper empire, of Shell's sinister nature. A local anti-Shell campaign, with the Hearst Press, which was powerful in California, behind it, frustrated the purchase of the remaining three-quarters of Union of California. So Shell found itself with a lot of minority shareholders in the combined Shell-Union group. Originally an incubus, Shell has found these shareholders their "greatest blessing", a phrase echoed by any Shellman I have met. The blessing expressed itself in the independence it—eventually—gave the management from undue interference from head office (Shell Oil has always enjoyed greater freedom than other Shell subsidiaries). And in the US, legal and financial requirements ensure that a quoted company with minority shareholders keeps up to scratch managerially if it wishes to avoid trouble. A quoted company can also raise money through fixed interest and through rights issues: it can (though Shell has not done so) use its paper to take over other concerns more easily than if it had to use cash. And, finally and crucially, the issue is a demonstration that the company really has "gone native" and dug its roots deep in a host country. In Shell's case it has meant that the parent has been scrupulously honest in its dealings with the subsidiary. Two sets of lawyers are employed, for instance, to ensure that the subsidiary does not pay too much for the research and other help it gets from the parent, which leans over backwards to avoid a possible charge (which could be serious under American law protecting minority shareholders) of imposing uneconomic burdens on the subsidiary. As a lawyer acting for the subsidiary once put it: "You sure have a doting parent." Such a relationship is completely different from that of a wholly-owned subsidiary whose profits can so easily be arranged for the convenience of the parent. This ability to juggle subsidiary profits—mainly by adjusting the price at which oil is transferred between subsidiaries in different countries—must have cost European governments hundreds of millions of dollars in the past few years in tax avoided by the wholly-owned subsidiaries of the major oil groups. Yet Shell seems happy enough with its US arrangements, so perhaps, whatever other oil groups may think, there are more important things in corporate life than tax avoidance.

In the 1920's Shell Oil itself could have done with more independence. In the early days of its existence, Deterding, ever-masterful even from 6,000 miles away, could not fully grasp the speed with which business moved in the US, the way everything was geared to the market place. Because of Deterding's attitude, for instance, Shell was unable to make as many acquisitions in the Oklahoma fields as it would have liked. The myth—and reality—of detailed direction from Europe lingered on. Even in the 1930's group approval was required for quite minor design changes in refineries. It was in the early 1930's too, that Monroe Spaght, then studying at Stanford University in California, and later to be the group's first American-born managing director, was offered a job with Shell. His professors were concerned about his future because they assumed that the company was dominated by the parent —and its Dutch element at that. "Don't stay long," they told him, "or if you pop up you'll be hit on the head by a wooden shoe." Ironically, Shell's determination to be a better citizen than native oil companies had led the company to give bigger graduate studentships than was usual, and Spaght had such a fellowship at the time of the job offer.

Yet, as Shell's subsidiaries expanded in the 1920's many of their advantages were due to the parent's backing. The first advantage was technical. Before the First World War the Europeans—which meant primarily Shell—were ahead of the Americans in many of the techniques used in exploring for, producing and refining oil. Shell was an early pioneer of scientific geophysics, and it was with the Amerada group, then owned by the millionaire British building contractor, Lord Cowdray, that Shell developed the use of radio waves for oil exploration. Another advantage was the way in which Shell, like many other European groups, took far more care of its employees than did American companies—a paternalism which still finds a ready response. It avoided lay-offs, it was among the first big American companies to have a provident fund. This care, at managerial level, paid off in the case of the teams which had worked, in the second decade of the century, at the Coalinga oil-field in California. Unlike other companies, Shell provided some civilised comforts for its people there. It acquired a good reputation, and excellent people who increased Shell's sales of petrol (then, as now, the key product in the US market) ten times over in California in the 1920's, pushing it up from fourth to second place in the market. Finally, the men head office sent to run the company were clearly highfliers (one of the first had been a nephew of Marcus Samuel, Shell's founder). In general, because an American subsidiary will inevitably be important to a group, companies almost always send promising people there.

Then came probably the worst trauma ever experienced by any European company in the US. After five years' thought, Shell moved into the Eastern American market in April 1929, only six months before the stock market crash of October that year. Nor was it a cautious venture but a multi-million dollar attempt to achieve in a few months the market percentage which had taken a decade or more to build up on the West Coast. To make matters worse, Shell also tried to spread into every American state, marketing "a mile wide and an inch deep", as Alec Fraser, the Scottish chief executive who picked up the pieces, put it. For Shell's crash, when the American slump came, was really violent. Because of the lateness of its expansion, more of its network was in an early, unprofitable stage than that of its major competitors, and its finances were overstretched. Unlike other companies it did not have the layer of financial fat provided by depreciation on old, but still profitable, assets. In all it lost a staggering $125 million in trying to build up its market in the mid-continent; and in 1932, at the depth of the slump, aggravated for the oil companies by the new oil discoveries in Texas, Shell lost $27 million, the worst result of any of the major oil groups, and a quarter of the industry's total losses.

So Shell had to reduce staff by a third in 1931, sell off a lot of oil leases and cut back on everything. Yet, in line with the hoariest of business truisms, adversity bred a much better company. Fraser banged together Shell's operations—previously scattered in Shell of California, Shell (Eastern) with Roxana in the middle—yet returned enough independence to separate areas, particularly California, to enable them to keep some initiative. He abandoned most of the thin, and for Shell disastrous, market between the Mississippi and the Rockies; yet retained Shell's insistence on aggressive marketing and quality. It was on April 8, 1933, only a few days after the newly-installed Franklin D. Roosevelt had announced a New Deal for the American people, that Shell announced its own New Deal for the American motorist.

This was not an empty gesture: it was boosting a better quality Super Shell petrol of an unprecedented 70 octane. But far more important than individual products, or even than Fraser's internal reorganisation, were the very considerable changes in the relationship between parent and subsidiary in the twenty years after 1930. Even in the 1930's Americans were steadily being promoted: all his working life, says Spaght, he found himself as the first American to do whatever job he was promoted to—right up to being group managing director. In the 1930's, too, Shell Oil was chosen as the group company to get into chemicals—one of the first oil companies to do so in a systematic way. And the reason was simple: the supply of excellent scientists available in California. Even by today's standards it was a bold move to allow a foreign subsidiary to lead an important, research-based piece of diversification; then it was a virtually unprecedented piece of "multi-nationalism". And it paid off: for instance all the development work on Shell's extremely profitable weed killers was done in the US.

But it was the war and its aftermath which really altered the relationship. During the war Shell Oil, like most other European investments, was inevitably almost completely cut off from parental control. Afterwards, equally inevitably, it became a key source of help in rebuilding the group in two ways. The first was financial. The group's shareholding in Shell Oil (then still called Shell Union) was used as collateral for a $250 million loan to develop vital new oil production in Venezuela. The second was managerial and technical. The balance of power had been so reversed that it was the Americans who had to come over in droves to teach the Europeans all the new developments in oil which had occurred during the war—including the epoch-making introduction of catalytic cracking in refineries. Yet at the same time the Americans within Shell Oil were urging their European superiors not to dissociate themselves from the parent—as they had done in the 1930's to avoid further nationalistic criticism—but to stand up and be counted as part of a world-wide group. In other words the relationship had grown up: as a corollary the parent's directors have been able to start making a more positive contribution within the last fifteen years—"a constructive sort of interference" is how Spaght puts it.

Not that Shell Oil's post-war history has been totally calm. It has, in fact, been cyclical, like that of its major competitors. In the 1950's the then managing director, though a former marketing man, concentrated on exploration, and the result was that Shell's share of the crucial petrol market went down by a tenth to 6 per cent, But in the 1960's everything came right. Thanks to the efforts of the 1950's, concentrated on the then new oil-fields off the shores of Louisiana and Texas, Shell Oil had enough crude oil. And Spaght, who took over as managing director of the company in 1960, reversed his predecessor's priorities. He took "the two people in marketing who were most disgruntled" with the existing state of affairs and let them loose. But he had learnt the lesson of 1930-32 well enough to ensure that their efforts were concentrated on Shell's existing markets, particularly those in urban areas—where the company could get the maximum sales out of any given sales outlet in an industry where such concentrated volume is priceless. By the end of the 1960's, it had increased its coverage of the country, giving "exposure" to 88 per cent of the population, 10 per cent more than ten years previously, even though Shell had 400 fewer stations and was still unrepresented in a dozen Rocky Mountain States. In addition Shell Oil led the American industry in treating the whole refining, transport and marketing process as one continuous profit centre at a time when many of its competitors were still thinking of the market as somewhere to dump the products of their oil-fields and refineries. No wonder Shell Oil's share of the petrol market jumped by over two-fifths to 8·8 per cent in a decade, putting it up four places to second in the sales table, while earnings per share nearly doubled.

Recently, the company has again had problems: over-ambitious expansion and a major refinery project that was two years late combined to deepen the general decline in profits felt by the domestic US oil industry in 1970 after a glorious decade. And the 1970's will see the arrival in quantity of oil from Alaska, where Shell has virtually no stake, at a time when other US sources of supply will be looking increasingly inadequate. For Shell is always happiest when sources of supply are predictable, and new leases are bid for on evidence good enough for proper financial calculations to be made. So it was with the off-shore Gulf of Mexico leases. But Alaska—like so many of the discoveries in the Middle East from which Shell was conspicuously absent—was not a matter of logical prediction, but geological hunch. It was characteristic that Shell gave up looking in Alberta just before a major oil strike was made there after the war.

Nevertheless, the story of Shell Oil is still one of the most successful in the whole history of overseas investment, reaching a logical climax when Spaght was brought back to London as a group managing director in 1965. This appointment marked a very late stage of multinationalism, of recognition that an overseas subsidiary, and consequently the executives who run it, could be the equal of the parent, a stage few, if any, other major companies in the world have reached.

Below the top level, there has been relatively little managerial interchange or mutual benefit—except technical. Americans, says Spaght, "don't travel so good"; and the large numbers who came to Europe after the war returned as soon as they could—Europe was not then, as it has since become, a peaceful haven for Americans worried by the strain of living in their own troubled cities. It was simply uncomfortable. It has also proved extremely difficult to fit American rates of pay into the rest of the group's pattern. And the other parts of the group have been too short of good men to spare them to work in the US. So, apart from the sphere of chemicals, and the invaluable post-war help, Shell Oil has been almost entirely an investment, providing a quarter of the total group profits, but not a basic managerial prop.

Precisely the opposite could be said of the second biggest European business in the US, Lever Brothers and Thomas J. Lipton, the two subsidiaries of the Unilever group. They have proved invaluable in every way except profitability. Not that they are small: their combined sales of $742 million in 1969 would have put them around 150th among US companies—not much smaller than such apparent giants as H. J. Heinz and Campbell Soups. Their assets of $363 million account for nearly 5 per cent of the total for European manufacturing investment. Lipton, mainly in the tea and packet soup business, is one of the most profitable and fast-growing companies in the extremely competitive American food business. Lever Brothers itself has a number of marketing successes to its credit.

Yet, to the outside world, Lever is known, and well known at that, only for its long and generally losing fight in the detergent market with Procter & Gamble. The twenty-five punishing years of this war have kept Lever's profit margins low. They are a mere fifth of P & G's world-wide average, and a third of the very comparable Colgate-Palmolive. Lever's well-chronicled conflict with P & G has tended to give the company a bad name —and because it is so much better known than the story of other European products, the mud has spread to European marketing as a whole. Because of Lever's lack of profitability it has been unable to float the company to the US public. Even the parent group's shares have performed too poorly in the Big Board of the New York Stock exchange to be usable as "paper" for takeover purposes.

The story is, on the surface, the opposite of Shell's. And yet, Lever Bros. has been of far more use to its parent than has Shell Oil by any criteria except strictly financial ones. In the words of Stefan H. Robock, a professor of International Business at the Columbia School of Business, Unilever's "effort is worth-while because the parent company learns the sophisticated advertising and marketing techniques that are practised here. Then it applies those techniques to its operations elsewhere round the world. The US investment thus fits into a world-wide strategy". Charles Wilson, in the standard history of Unilever, emphasises that the US subsidiary's principal use for the group has been the stimulus given to the group's technical and marketing skills. Unilever's ability to compete world-wide with giant American groups, not just P & G, but in foods as well, is crucially dependent on its possession of a sizeable US operation, not just for marketing skills, but for products and management training as well. This is not a new development. Fifty years ago the group's founder, Lord Leverhulme, was writing to his son: "We get enormous strength on the selling side in England by our knowledge of selling and advertising in overseas countries, especially in the US". This theory is very much the accepted wisdom among companies investing directly in the US. But it has not been thought through in most cases—it is just assumed; and in Lever's own detergent business the German Henkel business has repelled the assault of international groups in its home market without the help of a US subsidiary.

It is Wilson, in summing up Leverhulme's career, who provides the clue to Lever's mixed fortunes in the US, and indeed the key to almost every failure and success of European companies in the US. Leverhulme's failures, he says, "were all failures of imitative products. Lever's triumph was built on originality—Sunlight is the supreme example—and where he had nothing new to offer, in a market already overcrowded with competent and established competitors, not all his energy, optimism and advertising skill could command success. Where he led, he conquered; where he followed he fell".

In fact Lever's ventures in the US before the First World War were a classic lesson in the futility, not of me-tooism, but of trying to introduce purely foreign products into an alien market—a mistake more characteristic of American than of European companies. The ventures, like so many by the early makers of branded products—Singer, Nestlé, Coats—were part of an earlier wave of world expansion based on direct investment. For all its success elsewhere, Sunlight Soap was a failure in the US—the Americans preferred bigger "filled" tablets to the smaller, but more solid Sunlight. Lifebuoy's fate was worse, for many Americans hated its smell. In a similar refusal to depart from his successful English formula, Lever would not use the middle men—jobbers—used by his competitors like the already formidable P & G and Colgate. So Lever was virtually confined to the New England market where it sold directly to retailers. In 1913 Lever earned literally $733 on sales of $800,000. But that year everything changed with the arrival of Francis Countway, Lever's first American-born manager. And from then until P & G introduced Tide, the first synthetic detergent, in 1946, the story of Lever in the US

forms one of the marketing successes of the century. By 1920
sales had risen to $12·5 million by which time net profits were
$400,000. By the end of the decade sales had tripled, and profits
quadrupled. Even the Depression only slowed Lever down—
not for Countway the crisis problems that hit Shell. Between
1929 and 1934 sales rose by a third. By 1939 they were $91
million and net profits $7 million, and sales nearly doubled in
the wartime and post-war era before Countway died. Countway
was a great salesman. He concentrated on the hard selling of a
few products which he had chosen especially for the market.
And because there were only a few brands, production could be
properly mechanised. As Wilson says, "he gave up the attempt
to make Sunlight Soap a leading line in America and he
courted assiduously the wholesale merchants instead of selling
direct to the retailers"—using his direct sales in New England
as a large test market.

The first success was with Lux Flakes—which were especially
suitable for the new textiles (like rayon) then coming into use.
Lux Flakes, "fine soap which would not injure the most delicate
fabric", were a wow. So were Lux Soap and Rinso washing
powder. Countway went his own path, undisturbed by Lever
and his successor as chairman, Francis D'Arcy Cooper, even
though by 1923 Countway was spending $6 million on adver-
tising—almost as much as the rest of the group put together.
Countway invented the idea of Body Odour for his ads to show
how Lifebuoy soap would cure it, and suggested that the way
to avoid "undie odour" was to use Lux Flakes—it was a great
age for finding new slogans for existing products. With brilliant
timing he introduced Spry—a compound cooking fat—during
the Depression in 1936 when production of real lard had
slumped. In fact his only major failure was an abortive attempt
(before Lever had merged with the Dutch margarine monopoly
to form Unilever) to get into the margarine market in partnership with American Linseed. This was prevented by threats of
anti-trust action, leaving as a legacy a $1 million investment
in a refining company in the Philippines formed to provide
coconut oil for use in the margarine. But in general he was so

successful that Colgate paid him the ultimate compliment. Because of the success of Lux soap in their home market they launched Palmolive in Europe as their only possible retort.

Then in 1946 came Tide "the revolutionary washday miracle", the first successful washing product which was synthetic, not an animal or vegetable product. Soon, one housewife out of four was using it—and even though the Tide tide has come and gone outside the US, in the US it still flourishes. A quarter of a century later Lever has still not fully recovered from the impact. In fact the war of Countway and successors against P & G has several resemblances to Henry Ford and his successors against General Motors: man (Ford, Countway) beats corporate machine (GM, P & G); man fails to train up proper successors; machine completely dominates successors; successors avoid head-on collision with machine; successors never seem able to match machine's profitability.

Lever's problems were compounded by its foreign ownership. Unilever was afraid that too close a relationship would lead the anti-trust authorities to argue that the parent should submit to their jurisdiction. So the parent (known to Levermen as "the redcoats" or "the Englishmen") took less close interest than it would in any other subsidiary. "With normal subsidiaries," says one senior Lever executive, "we could have asked more questions, looked in more detail." But the failure immediately to produce an adequate answer to Tide had deeper roots than lack of managerial control. Countway didn't believe in synthetic detergents, he was used to relying on basic research done in Europe, and the war prevented such research A group then so dependent on fats and oils might never have done the work even in peace-time, but the war stopped the flow of any new product from Europe for twenty years and thus increased Lever's helplessness.

Countway retired in 1946, the year Tide appeared. His successor, Charles Luckman, presided over the most-publicised crack-up in the history of European investment in the US: four years during which Lever's sales slumped, one year by as much as $65 million. In 1949 the company lost $7 million (though even this figure was less than a third of Shell's losses in 1932). To add to the problems of fighting P & G, Luckman "nominated his own cabinet" and in the course of centralising a previously fragmented organisation, sacked many executives and lost many others. Luckman's basic problem was Surf, Lever's answer to Tide. When it was first launched, it did not work well: and when it was relaunched as a "no-rinse" product P & G was quick off the mark to claim that Tide, too, "washes clothes so miracle clean NO RINSING NEEDED". Surf lost $24 million. It was, like Ford's Edsel a few years later in the middle-price car market, an essential attempt by No. 2 to match No. 1 in its strongest area, the one where the basic profitability of the whole market was decided. Ford lost ten times as much money on the Edsel as Lever did on Surf: but Lever went one worse by repeating its error. Luckman had been fired, and three directors from Unilever's main board spent eight months in New York running the company before they appointed Jervis (Jerry) Babb as successor. Babb (remembered within the group as a promotions-mad executive who "gave away silk stockings with everything") launched Rinso Blue. P & G hit back with a remarkable display of marketing toughness and speed. In whatever test market Lever promoted Rinso Blue, P & G outspent it in advertising, giving away, and generally pushing, its two detergents Tide and Cheer ("It's New! It's Blue . . . only Cheer has the Blue-Magic whitener!").

Babb's successor, an old-time Lever man, William H. Burkhart, testified that after Rinso Blue had lost $7 million, "this led to the conclusion that we were facing apparently a hopeless task to get a real entry, a winner, into this field [and] we came to the conclusion that we would give up any further attempt to force our way into a winning position in the heavy-duty [detergent] field". So Burkhart, like Ford after the Edsel, avoided direct confrontation. In Lever's case this meant virtually running away for a time from the $900 million market in basic, heavy-duty detergents; in Ford's case it involved putting up only a feeble resistance to GM's Pontiac, Buick and Oldsmobile high-profit cars. Burkhart and his research director

Dr Llewellyn Parsons produced a number of winning products outside Tide's surging sway. Stripe, the first striped toothpaste (not one of Parsons's ideas), was a winner; so was Lux Soap offered in a variety of colours and a gold pack. Lifebuoy was re-perfumed; Lux Liquid was a wow as a dishwashing detergent; Wisk, a liquid clothes washer, Dove Soap, three-quarters synthetic detergent, one quarter coldcream ("Dove creams, creams, creams, your skin while you wash") and Imperial, a luxury margarine, all made money.

But the unavoidable struggle against Tide took its toll. *Fortune* magazine summed it up:

> Before the war, the two companies had been fairly evenly matched in the laundry-soap business. But between 1940 and 1956, P & G's estimated share of the market rose from 34 per cent to nearly 57 per cent while Lever's share fell from 30 per cent to 17 per cent. This shift naturally had a profound effect on the earnings of the big soap companies. From 1951 through 1956 ... the sale of Tide and its other laundry soaps and detergents yielded [P & G] profits totalling about quarter of a billion dollars before taxes. In the same period Lever and Colgate were both losing money in the laundry products field ... in the early 1950's Lever barely broke even, and the $3 million that it earned in 1956, on sales of $282 million, was only about a third of what Lever had earned in a good prewar year.

To add to Lever's troubles, P & G's profits were enough to give it real aggressive power against Unilever in the rest of the world, while Colgate could use its non-US earnings to boost its ailing operations at home. *Fortune*'s figures (and Burkhart's confession quoted on page 60) both came from a hearing which set an official seal on Lever's impotence. Lever had bought the rights to "all", a "low-sudsing" detergent suitable for front-loading automatic washing machines, from Monsanto Chemicals, a company unused to the hot pace of consumer marketing (its chairman found the $12 million marketing bill for "all" "rather horrifying"). The anti-trust people objected that this would reduce competition. In order to prove the opposite, Lever had to show its own need for "all" to keep competition going.

As Lever's lawyer summed it up, "the purpose of this testimony, Your Honour, is to show that not only did we not lessen any competition, but with all of our own talents and skills and funds we have been scarcely able to keep our head above the water".

In the 1950's Lever's troubles had been too drastic for it to fulfil its historic stimulating role within the group. In the 1960's things were different. The US subsidiary has fought back in the detergent market; in the face of P & G and a newly-revived Colgate-Palmolive it has improved its share of the market with a number of derivative products like "all" in liquid form and as a powder for use with cold water. But the figures remained unimpressive—sales were $413 million, net profit $10·2 million in 1962, only $491 million and $5·2 million six years later—though the 1969 profits were depressed by the considerable cost of launching the "Drive" enzyme detergent. But Lever Brothers, and more especially Thomas Lipton (bought as an investment in 1946 but now a highly successful subsidiary), have worked very closely with the group all over the world. Lipton itself has broken away from its former basic sales of tea to expand into a number of other packaged foods; it is the market leader in "dry" soups and salad dressings. Ironically, the non-US rights to Lipton's greatest strength, its teas, iced and flavoured, do not belong to Unilever so cannot be exported. But the group contributed Vesta prepared meals, and ideas on the techniques of dehydration which helped Lipton to sell its "dry" soups. Lever imported the "soft" Imperial margarine ready-made from Europe—and its success helped it to become the second biggest margarine producer in the US. But such successes show up the limitations on the mutual help that can be expected between subsidiaries— and thus on the support provided by Lever's US operation to the group world-wide. In 1970, after several lean years in the US toiletry market, Lever scored a great success with Close-up toothpaste; this was a new product because it used silicon as the abrasive which actually cleaned the teeth. From a promotional point of view it could be pushed as a mouthwash-cum-toothpaste; it looked different from the usual toothpaste (it was a red, transparent jelly); and it had a distinctive taste, including cinnamon and wintergreen. It quickly captured over a tenth of the market—most of it pure gain from Lever's point of view, and a clear boost to morale.

Yet other Lever companies were slow to take it on. Only in Germany and the US is there a market for mouthwash, so that particular advantage was of no use in the rest of the world. Outside the US the Lever companies had reasonable shares of the toothpaste market—so a success by Close-up would inevitably not be pure gain. And in the US nothing seems much use against Tide. The use of enzymes in detergents developed in Holland enabled Lever to pioneer national US sales of a detergent containing them, not just a product in which to pre-soak clothes before washing (the first use of enzymes in Europe.) Characteristically the only powder to be unaffected by the enzyme onslaught was Tide—which is where Lever's post-war history started. And the group's senior men freely admit that only when Tide retreats will Lever Bros stand a chance—though judging by experience in England even then P & G will be much the more profitable company. The time to find out could come soon: the present drive against detergents as a source of pollution could easily lead to fragmentation of the detergent market in the US similar to that in Europe.

Until the day of fragmentation—and maybe after—Lever's experience remains a hard and salutary lesson. It needed to be in the US to compete effectively with the Americans in the rest of the world; but because its products were for the most mass of all mass markets, it has been operating on too big a scale to be able to use the basic European weapon—specialisation. And in Procter & Gamble it has faced one of the world's greatest organisations-in-depth in its principal market. Yet Lever's success when away from P & G's hypnotic influence—in foods and in toothpaste—shows how far bad luck, rather than mediocre management, has led to the stigma which still surrounds Lever's US operations.

To contrast Lever with Brown & Williamson, the US subsidiary of British-American Tobacco, is to write a short morality play: Lever exemplifying the gay life based on advertising and marketing skills, succeeded by a quarter of a century of unprofitable purgatory; Brown & Williamson, the tortoise against the hare. B & W was quiescent and uncompetitive before the war when the cigarette was a me-too product, sold by advertising as repetitive as anything Lever dreamed up. Then came post-war success, based on two specialised products, Kool, the pioneer mentholated filter cigarette, and Viceroy, one of the earliest ordinary filter-tips. The contrast now seems complete: Lever, virtually static in a dynamic industry, B & W dynamic in a static one. No wonder B & W's profits are probably over twice those of Lipton and Lever together, even though sales (just under $500 million) are only two-thirds as much.

British-American Tobacco itself was the artificial product of the great tobacco war of the first years of the century, between Imperial Tobacco (Players, Wills) and an early American challenger, J. B. Duke's American Tobacco. BAT was simply a jointly owned company in which both sides put the companies they owned outside their own countries. A 1911 anti-trust suit removed the American shareholding, and allowed BAT to enter the American market. But it hesitated and it was only in 1927 that it took over B & W. B & W brought with it only one brand of cigarette (and that disappeared pretty quickly) but two brands of snuff (Tube Rose and Granny) and no less than thirteen brands of plug, chewing tobacco, including Bloodhound ("A dog-gone good chew"). The company itself was as bucolic as its products, run until after the war by men BAT now describe as "tobacco farmers". But they understood that for a small company it was useless competing head-on against the giants for the mass market where the cigarette was "just an ordinary white tube". So B & W brought out its two filters—well before their time—as well as Raleigh, the first coupon cigarette, and Wings, a ten-cent brand born of the depression.

In 1948 B & W still had only 3 per cent of the cigarette market. Then came the first of the lung cancer scares which have given B & W its chance. The first great success was Viceroy, boosted by a 1950 article in *Reader's Digest*. BAT admits the "name was against it. everything was against it—except the product", and by 1955 B & W's market share had more than trebled to 10 per cent. Not only did it have successful products. It sold hard to supermarkets at a time when this was not usual in the industry. Then the Americans counterattacked, but B & W had a second success with Kool in the 1960's. This put its market share up to 17 per cent—and B & W and Philip Morris are rated as the two most aggressive members of the industry. Ironically when American Brands (formerly American Tobacco) invaded Britain in the late 1960's by taking over Gallaher and, later, a large chain of opticians, it looked as though it was fleeing from the clobbering B & W was giving it in its own market.

B & W's success rests on specialisation: but like Volkswagen, it is operating in so big a market (and one where the particular specialities are becoming more widespread) that it can grow to what seems a considerable size by European standards. "Can" does not mean "will". But BAT's peculiar skill, in a business which consists exclusively of far-flung subsidiaries, lies in choosing the right people: "we believe," they say, "a large element of our control is by selecting people and training them to think as we would think in their circumstances." BAT then gives its men "quite adequate authority", even though group headquarters has a very clear and detailed breakdown of the key figures, profits and market shares, related to B & W's budget forecasts. But its care in the choice of top executives has meant that since 1949 only two men—William Cutchins and Edwin Finch—have run B & W. And, since the then chairman, Sir Duncan Oppenheim, allowed B & W to expand after the war the venture has been a model one.

It has also contributed in the intangible ways Lever has

found so valuable: not in executive man-power—problems of payment have, as usual, prevented many direct transfers of people. But BAT says that "things tend to start in the US—most of the group's thinking is done here, or in Germany or in the US". And B & W contributes, apparently, more to group management training than it gets. All this, and over a third of group profits as well. And B & W does not seem panicked about tobacco's health problems; or the fact that, as an unquoted company, B & W has been unable to diversify. It could point to the very mixed success enjoyed by other tobacco companies—including BAT itself—and feel, not unreasonably, that B & W's cautious ventures into specialised sea-food represent a better start than many other splashier ventures. Yet B & W has reached the end of the specialist road—even though in 1970 it launched Loredo, an up-to-date kit for rolling your own filter cigarettes, to provide a cigarette for one cent each, a clear attempt to carve out another specialised market.

But Kool has a third of the menthol market, and BAT sees clearly that saturation is near. So it will probably have to diversify. It is a tribute to B & W's success that further specialist successes would not be big enough to provide any growth. This is a turning point likely to be reached by any really good specialist European invader. To diversify, B & W will have to go public, and is clearly waiting for the right moment. And this leaves an enormous question mark over B & W: if its judgment about diversification, or about coming to market, is wrong, it could drift with an industry which, at best, will be static in the next few years. And, looking round, it can see what this has involved for European-owned companies which have ossified in unexciting markets. As Stephen Hymer puts it: "Companies do not die like ordinary trees. They are like California Redwoods."

CHAPTER 5

THE VETERANS

SHELL, Lever and Brown & Williamson are only three of a whole host of companies in the US whose European ownership dates back to before the last war. The country is, in fact, littered with the monuments to earlier eras when the balance of power between Europe and the US did not seem so hopelessly one-sided as it did for the twenty years after the last war. In sewing thread and knitting wool, in insurance, drugs and dye-stuffs the companies hark back to an earlier imperialism, of British wool and cotton textiles, and finance and engineering, and to German and Swiss dominance in the commercial applications of chemistry. In fact, had it not been for stern protection, the two World Wars, and the double confiscation of German companies, there might have been few major US-owned dyestuffs or pharmaceutical concerns—a possibility the Americans are not keen to remember. As it is, the earlier invasion lives on in the names, if not in the ownership, of the companies involved. At least two major American pharmaceutical companies, Merck and Schering, were founded as offshoots of German parents towards the end of the last century. Sterling Drug still sells aspirin called Bayer after its German inventor; and in dyestuffs, GAF (General Aniline and Film), the now American-owned former IG Farben subsidiary, is turning its back on its foreign origins. It refers to its IG Farben days as "the period of our history that we'd just as soon forget".

Of the "redwoods" still owned by Europeans the British-owned insurance companies are always cited as the most rotten. They were not helped by operating in a tightly regulated, highly political industry, with low margins and poor management. The parent groups, too, were not over-bright. But for twenty years after the war the subsidiaries were shielded from the wrath of their British superiors because the investments, many of them equity stocks, which the US subsidiaries held as reserve funds were considered such major assets that the generally depressing trend of their actual underwriting experience could be overlooked. It is only recently that a crossover point has come in view with the increases in underwriting losses gradually making up ground on the income and capital gains from the investments. Because these companies are still so important—with assets of over a billion dollars at the end of 1969, still nearly a third of the British total—their lack of profitability (and their reputation for poor management) has adversely affected the whole managerial and financial reputation of British investment.

As the riots in American cities have shown time and again, the badly managed British companies were insuring an undue proportion of the most riot-prone, the most blighted urban property. To make matters worse they failed to understand, as *The Economist* pointed out in a 1967 survey, that a significant minority of American brokers and agents could be found whose "ethical conduct is inconspicuous or absent". In the area of motor insurance not one of the British companies was able to follow the best of the Americans into direct writing (avoiding agents) and swift follow-up of accidents—which saves enormous sums in claims egged on by profit-sharing lawyers. In management (to quote *The Economist* again), "much could be said about the reputation that the British companies have managed to acquire for themselves—justifiably or not—of paying their American employees salaries that are low by normal American insurance company standards". But even in this depressed area the new European competitiveness is stirring—and there is a clear indication that the companies are in a mood to grasp a profitable underwriting position very soon or else follow the many British companies who have sold out. This change is, in fact, part of a belated, general, overhaul of the British insurance industry. The Royal, by far the biggest, with 2 per cent of the market (representing $500 million in premiums), is now adopting the standard remedies: a better-paid management, represented on the main board; withdrawing from unprofitable activities; more automation to cut costs; reorganising its activities to serve different classes of customer rather than different markets—for instance separating commercial and personal customers. And the Royal, which can justifiably say that there was a whole "industry malaise" and that "in a market of this sort you can't behave differently from everybody else", is not alone in seeing that the part of the industry not dealing with motor insurance will soon be rid of uneconomic competition. For in March 1971 Commercial Union, another large British group, spent $66 million buying control of Employers Group Associates, an American insurance group in which it had previously had only a 35 per cent interest.

This was a contrast with the 1960's, when the industry's bad record, and the poor reputation of the British-owned groups, had led to a steady withdrawal from the market. And six weeks before CU's bid, a British group with interests in reinsurance, Triumph Investment Trust, bought a specialised concern based on Hartford, Connecticut, for $15 million, the first such purchase for some time.

It will take a long time for the British insurance companies to rid themselves of their deservedly poor image. And because they were operating in such an unexciting industry, they gained none of the managerial feedback which should be part of direct investment. The same can be said of a whole raft of British investments in manufacturing industry which seem to have pursued an independent life of their own in the past twenty years in a useful but undynamic way. In some cases parental control was so loose that it is doubtful if they truly fell within the definition of "direct investment" used by the Bank of England for purposes of exchange control: "direct investments," it says, "are those in which the investor actively participates in the management and operation of an overseas enterprise." Firms like Coats Paton, English Sewing Cotton (now English Calico) and Baker Perkins have often done well in the US, but their activities in the rest of the world do not seem to have gained anything except profits from their investment. Nor have these companies tried to turn their American subsidiaries into a springboard for expansion in the US.

Until late in 1970 the same could have been said of the R. T. French subsidiary of the British Reckitt & Colman firm. French is so American that its ready-mixed mustards are exported to grace the dining tables of American embassies abroad. In addition it has been more successful than the parent. Now, the parent has reorganised its activities into product groups, and Cedric Rowntree of French's has been put in charge of the world-wide food group—of whose $165 million turnover French's contributed a quarter.

This piece of managerial feedback is, as Gwen Nuttall put it in the *Sunday Times* Business News, "as though General Foods had given the British head of the UK company control of Maxwell House in the United States and put him in charge of developing new products in all the markets". "As though": a brave and sensible move by a British group which would be unthinkable for an American one. Executives from overseas subsidiaries are virtually never allowed to come in to reorganise the home market for their American parent companies—the only possible exception being at Heinz. More typically, when one particularly powerful Briton, Robert Appleby, tried to sort out the domestic problems of Black & Decker, he was soon put off by local opposition.

The British have in general performed notably worse than the Swiss or the Dutch companies since the war. Both these countries' groups share a delicate touch in dealing with foreign subsidiaries—with their tiny home market they need them, but can usually blend harmoniously and politely with the commercial landscape abroad because they know the home government has no gunboats to back up their country's commercial imperialists. Hence their attitudes abroad are ideal when dealing with the American market. So it is no coincidence that four Swiss companies, Nestlé, CIBA, Geigy, Hoffman-La Roche, and one Dutch, AKU, have been able to keep abreast or even ahead of native managerial talent in growth industries both before and since the war.

Nestlé's enormous American interests—with sales in 1969 estimated by *Forbes* magazine as $720 million—are partly a legacy from the days before the First World War when brands of food, Nestlé's Milk and Chocolate, Lipton's Tea and Colman's Mustard, were manufactured throughout the world and the first multinational global battles started. Its technical leadership in instant coffee—which has given it second place in the American market, of which it has over 16 per cent—and its inherited strength in chocolate—where it has 10 per cent of the market—have helped. So of course has its style of management which is deliberately multinational. The (very real) control from Swiss headquarters is exercised extremely discreetly, and each company adopts the nationality of the country in which it operates.

The group's touch has been less sure with the companies, like Crosse & Blackwell and Findus, it has taken over. Nestlé's management is very home-grown with a strong family atmosphere among directors of subsidiaries who tend to understand each other better than they do executives of other companies. And Nestlé is not used to the sort of ruthlessly effective purges which American groups inflict on ailing companies (like Rootes in England) they take over.

This background is particularly intriguing now. For during the 1960's Nestlé was gradually building up its shareholding in Libby, Macneill & Libby, the famous, but only marginally profitable, canner of fruit and meat. At the time, Nestlé assured the anti-trust division of the Department of Justice that it had no intention of taking control. It has now been forced to do precisely that by Libby's declining fortunes (in 1969 it lost money)—and the take-over was allowed by the anti-trust division under the "ailing company" clause which permits otherwise unacceptable take-overs if the victim might succumb without help. Because Libby was in such a bad state Nestlé has removed the whole Libby top management in a move unique for Nestlé—and for the Europeans as a whole.

Libby is not the only historic meat packer to be in trouble. Armour (now owned by Greyhound Corporation) sold off three of its specialised chemicals and adhesives companies late in 1970 to Akzona Inc. (until 1970 known as American Enka), the little-known but highly successful US subsidiary of the Dutch fibre producer AKU—now merged with the salt and pharmaceutical group KZO to form Holland's third billion dollar group, AKZO. It is symbolic of the country's internationalism that all three have sizeable US interests; all, unlike the Swiss companies, with some American shareholders.

Until recently, KZO had only one wholly owned US investment, in drugs (mainly birth pills) through the Organon subsidiary. But it did have close links with International Salt, a leading American producer of salt. AKU, however, had been producing rayon in the US for over forty years through the 56 per cent-owned American Enka, with headquarters at Enka, in South Carolina, until last year the only company town in the US called after a foreign-controlled concern. In fact the name was given to the post office, and then to the village which grew up after the plant was founded. By producing there, AKU was one of the pioneers of artificial or synthetic fibres in the South. Since 1945 American Enka has been very successful in an industry where European technology is at least the equal of American. AKU differed from other European fibre producers after the war in that it had an American subsidiary already in existence, whereas most of the other European fibre producers (except Courtaulds) had to begin with joint ventures with US companies. And AKU's success makes one wonder how dominant Courtaulds would be today on the US fibre scene if it had not been obliged to start again from scratch after the war. American Enka steered clear of the high-capital manufacture of raw materials and stayed close to the market place, selling nylon and rayon to the carpet industry, and specialities like

Enkasheer (a nylon hosiery yarn for panti-hose) and Crepeset (a fine denier crimped yarn for the nightie and lingerie business).

This specialisation, based on excellent research by the parent company, has made it a favourite of US financial analysts and (after thirty-five years of continuous dividends) gave it pre-tax profits in 1969 of $45 million on sales of $257 million and a good stock market reputation.

Then in 1969 its merger partner KZO made a friendly cash offer for just over half the shares in its former technical partner, International Salt. The two were complementary: International mines salt from rocky deposits, KZO gets its salt through evaporation. The bid was held up by the anti-trust authorities. They were convinced that KZO had giant salt pans in the West Indies and so could have entered the US market without waiting for an American partner. Thus KZO's bid for International would have removed a potential competitor into the US salt market. In fact, the story proved to be baseless (it is International which is getting into the evaporated salt panning game in the Dutch Antilles) and the bid was allowed. KZO was clearly making an aggressive move, not just buying up a complementary business. Shortly after the merger it announced plans to broaden International's range of products by investing in the chlorine-based chemicals which the parent company makes in Europe.

The merged AKZO has now amalgamated its US interests in a quoted company, thus marking a departure from the group's present policy in Europe of acquiring full control of its interests: a clear case (and one very different from American corporate habits) of adapting the group's corporate style—and the reality of its ownership—to local conditions.

AKZO's willingness to share the profits with the local investor (and with key executives through stock options), the avoidance of over-heavy capital commitments which would involve a loss of control, while still being able to raise money on the local capital market, form one element of its success. The ability to rely on the parent company's research (the only three Dutchmen in senior positions at Enka were all in technical jobs) and to choose specialities for a market from the varied results of such researches form another. The luck of having such a vehicle after the war when European competitors notably did not is a third strand. A fourth is the new aggressiveness shown recently—and the fact that this is accelerated rather than slowed down by mergers at home. Some, or all, of these elements crop up in all the success stories of more recent investors.

Even before the merger which formed Akzona, American Enka, with sales of $257 million, was firmly esconced in the top 500 companies in the country. But there are two Swiss groups which are even bigger (though neither are in *Fortune*'s annual list because of lack of information). They are Hoffman-La Roche and the recently combined CIBA and Geigy. The last two—and Sandoz, another Swiss chemicals group—were forced to invest directly by the heavy protection afforded to domestic producers of benzinoid dye stuffs by the American Selling Price system of protection after the First World War (the American industry only grew with the war and it was feared that the infant would be swamped when the Germans, historic leaders in the field, returned after its end). The ASP system (which meant that imports have to sell at the same price as the American's own products) has led to tariffs which are still as high as 100 per cent in some cases and forced the Germans and the Swiss to manufacture in the US.

The German interests were confiscated in 1942, but the Swiss have remained with a curious concern, the Toms River company. This produces dyes in quite separate vats on the same site, for three companies, CIBA (which has 58 per cent of the company), Sandoz and Geigy. The Europeans are still strong in dyestuffs (CIBA and Geigy between them had 18 per cent of the market), hence the fact that all three major German chemical companies (BASF, Bayer and Hoechst), ICI, and even Philips Lamp are in the dye business in a big way. Some of the Swiss companies are so well entrenched and so American in outlook that the lobby trying to end the ASP system has difficulty in getting their whole-hearted support for a measure which might hurt their important American investments more than it would help the European parent. For dyestuffs remain an exceptional area for European investment, one where the rationale is largely an attempt to overcome a tariff barrier.

But the Swiss companies have not only been defensive. They have attacked aggressively in ethical drugs (those prescribed by doctors), herbicides (weedkillers) and the specialised Optical Brightening Agents used to make detergents and textiles appear whiter than white. The success enjoyed by the American subsidiaries of CIBA and Geigy (and their link through Toms River) created an anti-trust problem which delayed the merger of the Swiss parent companies—who took a lot of persuading that they were in any danger of having one of their two US companies forcibly chopped off if they persisted in their merger plans without dealing first with the US anti-trust authorities, who considered them too strong individually to be allowed to merge.

Eventually, a settlement was hammered out, in July 1970, allowing the parent groups to merge, a remarkable event for a number of reasons. First was the way in which two giant Swiss companies had to await the pleasure of an American government agency before merging (an issue dealt with more fully in Chapter 13); second was the relative harshness of the conditions extracted by anti-trust; third was the meekness with which these groups accepted the sentence. The settlement also gave an unprecedented amount of information about CIBA and Geigy's US business. Geigy sold $280 million, 45 per cent of its world sales, CIBA half as much—but still over a quarter of its total.

Their biggest success was Geigy's quarter share of the $500 million herbicide market, mainly through its strong position in the maize and beet protection business. Geigy also had half the $60 million market for Optical Brightening Agents and the two companies between them 30 per cent of the OBAs used in textiles. Together, they sold $53 million worth of dyestuffs; and in ethical drugs the two groups specialised in the oral diuretics used to control the flow of urine and to lower blood pressure.

Specialisation all the way: as CIBA says proudly, "most of our products you can't buy from anyone else".

The anti-trust decision has forced the merged group to form a new company. Through this it has to sell off to an Eligible Purchaser (i.e. one without a substantial interest in the products concerned) some of the products made by the weaker partner in each field. So CIBA has to hive off its dyestuffs and accept conditions which include undertakings not to hire back any of the executives involved for three years, and to supply the new company with products from Toms River. CIBA also sacrifices its $6·2 million sales of herbicides and Geigy loses a number of drugs, anti-depressants as well as diuretics.

The Eligible Purchasers will then be competing, with the weaker half of a product range, against CIBA-Geigy, whose salesmen will be offering both halves; not a state of affairs which seems likely, on the face of it, to lead to the anti-trust dream—a vigorous new competitor to challenge CIBA and Geigy; though Revlon, which bought the drug interests in summer 1971, could live up to anti-trust's hopes.

But the groups themselves have been able to adjust well enough to local conditions. They have to live with one of the most pernickety of all US government agencies, the Food and Drugs Administration. Most important, they seem to have worked out a *modus vivendi* between subsidiary and parent with a few Swiss on the subsidiary board, and a few others in key technical positions within the subsidiary, but with ample opportunity for Americans to get ahead—and with pay slightly above the going industry level to compensate for the absence of stock options.

The Swiss maintain enough of a research effort for all their US subsidiaries to pass a classic test as to whether a group is sincere in its protestations of decentralised control: that some important new products have been introduced by the subsidiary ahead of the parent—though, of all the European-owned drug companies, the one with the most outstanding record of research is probably the British-owned Burroughs Wellcome corporation.

Its research director, Dr George Hutchings, and his team, have spent a quarter of a century investigating the use of chemicals to suppress the growth of diseased cells—researches which have led to uses as various as the remission of leukaemia, the suppression of undesirable effects during organ transplants and a cure for malaria. Other European-owned companies also seem more prepared to work on long-term programmes than are American ones, even at home, let alone in their foreign subsidiaries. This is why the Europeans say they find it comparatively easy to get good researchers to work for them. Burroughs Wellcome's scientific successes are matched by the commercial bonanza enjoyed by the biggest Swiss chemical subsidiary in the US— the Roche subsidiary of Hoffman la Roche.

Roche began selling in the US sixty-five years ago; before the war it hired a "super-salesman" Elmer Bobst, who, like Francis Countway at Lever, was highly successful. (Bobst was hired on the advice of a graphologist: the evidence, his letter of application, was in fact written by his wife.) Then, just before the last war, "the invasion of Switzerland became a definite possibility", as the company says. So the chairman moved to the US bringing with him some of his key scientists, a decision which gave the group's top men an exposure to local conditions unequalled among European companies. During the war Roche's US subsidiaries became the principal manufacturer of drugs within the world-wide group. But it lost Bobst, who wanted a share stake in the US company: the close-knit Basle families which then controlled Roche (and still do) wouldn't part with absolute control. He left, and built up the US drug firm, Warner-Lambert. Roche survived: and its laboratories at Nutley, in New Jersey, produced, after the war, the pioneer tranquilisers Librium and Valium, reckoned "the most profitable products ever produced by the pharmaceutical industry", and successively the best-selling drugs throughout the 1960's. (Roche was helped because both drugs were introduced before 1962, when much stricter rules for the testing of new drugs were imposed.) The result is that

Roche is the second or third largest manufacturer of ethical drugs in the US: its sales are near the half-billion dollar mark —40 per cent of the group's world-wide total.

But Roche is not just a two-drug company: its post-war success was founded on its dominance of the market for Vitamin A; and it is pioneering large-scale work on medical electronics. Roche also pioneered the idea of the "product team", a group, including a doctor, formed to develop a new drug without arousing inter-departmental jealousies; it also caters to its customers' every whim; farmers who prefer to mix their own chicken feed are even provided with their computer programmes. The relationship between Roche and its Swiss-based parent company is odd enough for the American-born president of the subsidiary, Dr. "Barney" Mattia, to express himself with far greater freedom than is normal for someone who is technically only in charge of a subsidiary of a foreign company. For, early in 1969, just after the industry had been convicted of price fixing, Mattia came out solidly against the industry's trade association and a self-justificatory advertising campaign it was running, in an interview with *Life* magazine: "We should not be investing in such a programme, but should be investing in research in drug metabolism to learn how to better control side effects." He went on to say: "I can't honestly say the drug prices are cheap. I think they're reasonable only for those who can afford to pay the price," a line of thought which induces Hoffman to give away, through doctors, 37 million pills to needy patients each year. This sort of independence is rare enough in the clubby pharmaceutical game. For the head of a foreign-owned company to behave like that was doubly unusual and it is a tribute to the way in which the Swiss companies fit into the landscape that he and his company could simply be labelled as nothing worse than that traditional American nuisance, a maverick.

CHAPTER 6

THE PIONEERS

Most of the major European direct investors in the US during the twenty years after the war could, like Dr Mattia, be described as mavericks. But Adriano Olivetti, Sir Eric Bowater, Henry Lazell of Beecham, Commander Whitehead of Schweppes, were mavericks in their own country before they went abroad. To be a maverick implies that you have a lot of self-confidence. And it needed a great deal of that quality for any new European company to enter the American market, especially by itself without a US partner, at a time when even the biggest European companies were, as one senior man put it, "scared just a little bit silly about marketing here."

Even now we find that entrepreneurial companies, one-man bands, are prepared to plunge into the US market as direct investors much earlier in their company's growth than more formal organisations. It is no accident that Willy Korf, the only European now making steel in the US, is one of the smallest, yet most independent, steel makers in Europe. For entrepreneurs characteristically believe more fervently than organisations that what they have to offer is unique. A good example is Peter Wilson of Sotheby's. In the six years after he took over Parke Bernet, the leading New York auction rooms, its turnover multiplied twenty times; yet the take-over was accomplished on a managerial as well as a financial shoestring. For Wilson had few trained people to spare to reinvigorate a business where know-how and experience are the only assets.

These early comers were enormously important to European self-confidence: they proved that a European company could conquer the US market. No wonder, therefore, that some of their names, uniquely among the invaders, are well known—but as explorers, adventurers, with deeds of daring to their credit, rather than as successful organisation men. More important from a business point of view, they helped to change the image—and the reality—of the European presence in the US. They were visibly, glamorously, in high-growth areas, whereas until their arrival Europeans were associated, somewhat unfairly, with stodgier activities. But, they were also convinced, like any good direct investor, that they had something unique to offer. Given their inadequate resources, given, too, the assumption at that time that the US was untouchably superior in all matters industrial and managerial, they also needed nerve in a big way.

The model for these early post-war adventurers was not a one-man band, nor even an organisation usually thought of as a piratical enterprise, but the solid Dutch Philips Gloeilampenfabriken. Yet North American Philips, 66 per cent owned by the parent's shareholders, has grown to be the biggest single European-controlled manufacturing company in the US (though the Lever subsidiaries together form a bigger company).

The story of NAP, like that of many of the other post-war pioneers, harks back to the simpler world of the Victorian self-made businessmen conquering the world through his own God-given intellectual strength and probity (the native cunning usually combined with the uprightness is omitted by the hagiographers). The story of NAP started in 1938 when a young Dutch lawyer working for Philips in Holland came across a wheeze devised over 4,000 years earlier by an Assyrian merchant. He put the business interests he owned outside his own country into the Assyrian equivalent of a holding company (doubtless registered in some Assyrian Liechtenstein) so that his property should not fall into the hands of the Egyptians who were about to take over Assyria. The lawyer mentally substituted Holland for Assyria, and Hitler's Germans for Egyptians. In due course, two Philips trusts were formed with local directors, one to group Philips' holdings in the British Empire including Canada, and the other for the Western Hemisphere, including, for some reason, Portugal. These trusts were to come into operation if an enemy invaded Holland and to remain in existence for the duration of any occupation and while "dangerous conditions" persisted. Whereas the other Philips companies have gradually returned to the direct ownership of the group's central operating company, the US Philips Trust has remained apart.* Even now the shares in NAP are held, not by the central holding company but in a trust; the individual shareholders have a non-voting beneficial interest in the Trust—they have, incidentally, received only one dividend from the Trust, and so separate was it kept that this was distributed separately from the group's own dividend. All that Philips had in the US to put into the trusts was a small factory making medical X-ray material with profits in 1938 of $1,000. During the war, Philips had subcontracted with US manufacturers to make war material but in 1945 found itself with virtually no tangible assets. It then lost most of the little it possessed through an untimely venture into projection television, and the outlook seemed grim.

Yet twenty years later NAP has total assets of nearly $420 million and net worth clear of debt of over $200 million. And until a couple of years ago, when the Philips headquarters induced the Trust to take a capital injection of a further $50 million, it had only received $5 million from home during its whole life.

So Pieter van den Berg, who is still NAP's chairman, looked round for companies with money and products with whom to go into partnership. All he could offer was Philips' name as good men and true and, crucially, access to the Philips' world-wide research and development effort—since the Trust had automatic rights to all the group's patents and products. The first company he persuaded was a maker of timing devices and within twenty years Mr van den Berg had been so persuasive

* It is so separate that it cannot, technically, be referred to as a "subsidiary" of N.V. Philips, which, for its part, is not the "parent" company.

that Philips owned 30 per cent of a sizeable well-spread manufacturing group, mostly in the electrical component business and called Consolidated Electronics Industries. In 1968 this merged with the Trust's wholly owned subsidiary, North American Philips, which was mainly a selling and assembly operation. In addition, the pharmaceutical interests, grouped in a company with the charming name of Pepi and 66 per cent owned by NAP, were hived off as a separately quoted business.

NAP's story is summed up in a report from the American brokers Donaldson, Lufkin and Jenrette at the time. After saying that the merger made industrial sense since it involved amalgamating a mainly component group with one more involved in the retail market, they go on: "NAP's access to the products and highly regarded innovative capacity of N. V. Philips makes this merger more than a simple vertical integration. NAP can selectively import products from N. V. Philips' entire line (these imports account for perhaps a fifth of NAP's business). If the product sells poorly, NAP merely phases out its investment risk in manufacturing facilities. On the other hand, if an imported product sells well and is judged to have a strong future, NAP can begin manufacturing in the US if it makes economic sense."

This process works both ways: the outstandingly successful Norelco rotary electric shaver was one import, and a gramophone motor now used throughout the world by the parent company one export. Pepi, of course, is on its own, as the only major pharmaceutical company within the Philips orbit. It has gained approval for the world's first effective vaccine for German measles (rubella) and was a pioneer in techniques as diverse as one-shot packages for hospital drugs—and growing vaccines in kidneys, which apparently provide purer soil than the eggs usually used.

But Philips' boldest recent decision in the US was to take a cassette developed by the parent and let any manufacturer in the US make it under licence, while the Lear Corporation, which had developed a superior product, kept its product to itself. So, as Philips had forecast, their cassette swept the market, thanks to the promotional efforts of a number of manufacturers who took up the licence, while Lear's faded.

Despite isolated acts of this sort some observers felt that Philips' management lacked impetus once the empire had been put together. But recently, just before and since the merger, NAP has shown greater dynamism. This change has come with a new chief executive, Pieter C. Vink. NAP say they were lucky to get him from Philips' Australian subsidiary, outsiders that this appointment (combined with the $50 million new capital from the parent) may have marked a shift towards normality in the cloudy relationship between NAP, the Trust and the parent company. For, even now, it is the Trust's directors, all American citizens (though a couple, including Mr van den Berg, were born in Holland), who control the company through a governing committee which meets once a month to decide policy. In theory, and, so NAP will tell you, in practice, all relationships between the parent and NAP are at a technical level.

Explanations for the continuing independence still enjoyed under the original trust deed come at three levels. The most obvious explanation, that it is for tax purposes, is unlikely: the Dutch tax authorities treat NAP as though it was an ordinary subsidiary. The second, offered by NAP, is that the structure is needed to retain its relationship with the US Department of Defence. Less than a tenth of NAP's business is in defence material, yet the company's classification as being suitable for high security work is greatly prized. This is not so much for the size of contract involved as for the hold it gives on its best scientists who, so NAP tell you, will not work for a company that does not have access to really advanced work, especially in electronics, knowledge of which is confined to secure companies. But this does not make sense. If all Philips wanted was defence orders, it only requires an all-American board of directors (if necessary setting up a special subsidiary for the purpose) and the assurance that over 50 per cent of any product was manufactured in the US. It would not have to retain the elaborate arrangement of the Trust and the policy by which the head office at Eindhoven is kept at bay.

But there is a third possibility; that NAP was personified in Mr Van den Berg, that he was left alone because he was so powerful a person and so successful, that now he has retired from day-to-day management and been replaced by someone accustomed to the usual Philips group control, the days of the Trust are numbered, in years perhaps, but numbered all the same.

In 1969, in fact, for the first time, and without any explanation or fanfare, the accounts of NAP were effectively consolidated into those of the parent. The impact was enough to transform Philips from the sixth biggest company outside the US into the third biggest.

The relationship between an (in theory) totally permissive parent and a totally independent offspring makes the Philips story probably unique in the history of direct investment. But NAP was also lucky in the range and variety of products which the parent could offer and in the fact that they were mostly small household appliances—where taste the world over is much the same. Other pioneers in consumer goods did not have the same parental back-up or the same transferability of product. The result is that they are mostly at an earlier stage of their US development than NAP. So Beecham and Schweppes, two of the British pioneers in the consumer field, are together much smaller than NAP. Yet they are following the same path and are likely to grow even faster—even though Vink of NAP has declared that his aim is for sales nearly to double to $1 billion by 1974.

It is not obvious to the outsider that Beecham's Brylcreem or Schweppes' Tonic Water were the sort of unique selling propositions on which fortunes could be made, and major businesses founded, in the American market, but they were; and their stories, whose outlines are well enough known, tell us how sheer nerve can carry the day despite mistakes.

The very success story of Schweppes, based on the Englishness-in-depth of Commander Whitehead, has been a snare and a delusion for other British companies who gained the misleading impression that being terribly British was not only desirable but was enough even in non-consumer industries to compensate for other deficiencies. This has led to such marketing atrocities (recalled even by competitors with deep blushes) as an attempt to sell advanced electronic equipment for a new aircraft by a salesman with a bowler hat and an umbrella arriving at the potential client's in a Rolls-Royce carrying a Union Jack. They, like other Schwimitations, lacked Whitehead's marketing brain—as well as his style and flair.

Whitehead's Englishness has now blended completely with the US landscape (in front of which he is frequently photographed, immaculate in riding kit near an equally well-groomed horse). He is a director of a major cigar company and tells students at the Harvard Business School, in the best poacher-turned-gamekeeper tradition, "Do as I say, not as we did." In fact what Whitehead, then world export director for Schweppes, did in the early 1950's was to go for the wrong market with the wrong distributors—a combination of mistakes which has been fatal to many a marketing effort. Bottlers, who are also distributors, are vital in the tonic business which basically consists of importing the quinine and then bottling it with local water, making extremely sure that this is pure. Schweppes went first of all into the New York market in conjunction with Pepsicola. At that time, for a couple of years, the whole of Schweppes' initial operation was based on a partnership with Pepsi. But Pepsi had access to a different, much wider market than Schweppes was seeking and the two companies' objectives were too diverse to be reconciled. So the partnership was soon dissolved—though individual Pepsi bottlers retain the Schweppes franchise.

New York was simply too big a test market. And it was a matter of the luck of the brave that made Schweppes' Tonic a success. The famous ads, concentrated in the *New Yorker* magazine, and devised by that other flamboyant British émigré, David Ogilvy, caught on so well (helped by a well-timed strike which hit the rival Canada Dry) that tonic became a national drink within four years. Whitehead has no illusions about the secret of the success: "We built a successful business on the few, despite the charisma people didn't really like the stuff." But he had three safe marketing props. First was the fact that Schweppes' Tonic really is a better product than its competitors. Second, he knew that in aiming for his particular market—which wanted the cachet given by any imported product from a drink actually fabricated in the US—he could emphasise his Englishness hard and get away with it; when he recorded some advertisements for radio stations in California many of his listeners "had never heard an English voice before" and he became a celebrity overnight there. Third, once Schweppes had started to choose its own bottlers, it made sure that they would take seriously what might otherwise have been a marginal product for them by insisting that they share the local advertising fifty-fifty; and because it was selling a superior product (at a premium of a fifth over the competition's price) Schweppes could offer them profitability to compensate for relative lack of volume. But for nearly ten years Whitehead had only one line to offer—a fact often cited by other companies as a reason why they cannot get into the US market by themselves.

This inability to mount a wholly controlled operation based on only one product has proved true even for Wilkinson's, whose stainless steel razor blades, the biggest single technical advance for sixty years in the field, became a legend within a few months of their introduction in the early 1960's. In late 1970 Wilkinson made a wholesaling arrangement for its blades in the US with the giant Colgate-Palmolive Group. But Wilkinson was strong enough to retain control of its US marketing operation; Colgate, glad to take advantage of Wilkinson's reputation, merely undertook the physical distribution of the blades. Even among American companies it is generally accepted that one product cannot support a sales operation in a competitive consumer area. Lever Bros acquired the rights to "all" detergent because even a company as big as Monsanto was unable to make money out of one successful product.

But Whitehead succeeded without much support from home. The operation was mounted on a remittance from Britain of under $10 million, all repaid within five years. And Sir

Frederick Hooper, Schweppes' chairman, was by no means fully in sympathy with the flamboyance and riskiness of Whitehead's adventure. Indeed, it was Schweppes' uncertain start in the US combined with the fact that Whitehead, who previously had been at the Treasury telling British industry that they ought to export more, really felt involved in the US operation, that led him to abandon the total export job in favour of concentration on the US.

Schweppes' mistakes continued when in 1963 Whitehead agreed, reluctantly and under much pressure, to start selling Bitter Lemon in the US. He was worried about everything to do with the stuff. "It was less profitable, all those damn lemons—very expensive," he mutters even now; anyone else would certainly have obeyed the marketing rules and dropped it when the drink failed in two test markets. But he would not admit failure and staked his whole show-businessman-type reputation on the result, going so far as to fly in helicopters between suburban supermarkets. It worked. Bitter Lemon (made from Californian lemons) was a national drink within a couple of years—at a suitably premium price.

Schweppes then faced a problem which confronts any successful specialist: it had no other products which it could launch in the same way and refused to rest on its laurels—even though sales of tonic are still growing around 10 per cent a year. The public would not buy its soda or its ginger ale at a premium price—and wanted its ginger ale à l'Américain, sweeter than the English taste. Whitehead—accepting that he could not sell the Americans on a third drink whose taste they did not really like—realised that he had grown too big to rely on specialities. Backed by a carefully chosen American marketing team he is now competing head-on with soda and ginger ale at normal prices—while marketing a range of ready mixed cocktail mixers (a bloody mary ex-vodka, a sour without the whisky) as premium products. So Schweppes is now growing up: and it has a delicate couple of years ahead during which it is to merge with Cadbury's business in the US to match the 1969 merger of the two parent companies. Since Cadbury, like Schweppes, is

largely selling to supermarkets (through imported large chocolate bars and chocolate biscuits rather than locally bottled
drinks) the problems should not be too severe to prevent the
likely flotation of the combined operation in a few years. Then,
specialist US food manufacturers could be induced into joining
the group.

*   *   *

Beechams started slightly later than Schweppes, and at a far
less sophisticated level; its sales in 1970 were $84 million, three
times those of Schweppes, and its subsidiary has gone through a
much wider gamut of experiences with commercial (and
government) problems than the relatively uncomplicated
Schweppes business. To start with, Beecham had a more
difficult, yet potentially more rewarding job than Schweppes.
It was competing head-on with a number of large and tough
US corporations in toiletries, one of the most hard-fought-over
battlegrounds in the whole US consumer market. But because
the battle was on so large a scale, sales volume followed
marketing success to a much greater extent than with Schweppes' more specialised products.

Henry Lazell, who has retired as managing director of the
whole group but remains chairman of the US operation, will
still quote to the visitor the triumphant ditty with which his
Brylcreem hair tonic conquered the country:

> Brylcreem a little dab will do you,
> Brylcreem you look so debonair,
> Brylcreem the girls will all pursue you
> They love to put their fingers through your hair.

Beecham went into the US for two reasons. One was simply a
matter of principle for any company engaged in a world-wide
battle with American companies in proprietary drugs and
toilet preparations. As Lazell puts it: "If we can't stand up to
these so-and-so's on their home ground then we can't stand up
to them anywhere in the world." The other reason was that
Beecham's sales in Canada were being badly hit as thousands

of Canadians living near the US border were attracted by ads for rival products on the US television channels they could receive. So, with $2 million from its Canadian operations, Beecham went in, aiming fairly and squarely at the youth market. Lazell then tried to repeat the success with Silvikrin Shampoo, but it proved to be the wrong type of product for the US market. In the early 1960's, however, he found another winner, Macleans Toothpaste. This brand was aimed not at the market afraid of bad breath or tooth decay but at young girls anxious to ensure that the fangs they were putting (figuratively) into their young men were white and gleaming.

Lazell was clever and lucky in concentrating his ads for both products during the late-night movies on television, then largely ignored by most American advertisers because the audience was smaller than in peak hours—though it was the right young audience for Beecham. But Beecham, like Schweppes, has had to change direction sharply after two specialised successes. And Lazell had to face furious counter-attacks from US manufacturers who lost money for years trying to beat off Brylcreem. Score, a greaseless dressing launched by a US rival, was an immediate success but Beecham counter-attacked with ads (which were eventually judged unacceptable as "knocking copy") showing how greaseless dressings allegedly made boys' hair stand on end. And Macleans has slowly lost ground against new toothpastes.

But in 1968 Beecham issued some of its shares to the American public (raising over $11 million) to build a US plant for a major new product developed by the parent, its semi-synthetic penicillin, Penbritin. Previously, Beecham had sold a non-exclusive licence for it to Bristol Myers—and to compete, with only one product in the pharmaceutical business was a major act of self-confidence. But the confidence was justified; and Penbritin's success allows Beecham time for the toiletry research lab it established in 1966 in the US to come up with products suitable for the local market.

But, as if to show that the US is a land of peril for even the bravest, Beecham then faced some new problems. OA, a non-licensed competitor, is importing Penbritin from Italy, and the anti-trust division of the Justice Department is using Penbritin as one of its test cases to change the present system of new drug marketing in the US. Another new drug was held up by another government agency, the Food and Drug Administration, for over a year. Yet another government agency, the Securities and Exchange Commission, stymied Beecham's attempt to expand through exploiting the quotation of its US subsidiary. To foil the efforts of financiers anxious to use their own shares to buy up companies with sizeable, but unadvertised assets, the SEC now insists that any element of "goodwill" in a purchase has to be written off over a maximum of thirty years. This is crippling for Beecham which was looking for companies in toiletries and drugs where the goodwill represents (quite legitimately) the majority of the assets of a company; and because Beecham Inc. is not a large group, the write-offs would have ruined the profit record. At the same time Beecham had proved, through a couple of issues in the notoriously finicky Euro-dollar market, that it was one of the very few British companies with any real appeal to the international investment community. So the US quotation became less vital as a means of raising capital while its attractions to help with take-overs was being diminished.

The logic of this dual change was expressed in early 1971. Beecham then bought up the minority shares in Beecham Inc.; it also paid $54 million in cash for S. E. Massengill, a reputable family-controlled drugs company from Tennessee, which had a national sales force in the drug business, as well as a number of specialised toiletry products, like douches and deodorants. Beecham had to pay a high price for Massengill since cash sales bring tax problems not found in sales for quoted shares, but it faced other potential purchasers, none of whom, however, moved as quickly as Beecham.

After the take-over Beecham now, finally, has a proper balance in the US. Its existing national sales force in toiletries can push Massengill's products; in drugs it no longer has to rely on jobbers to sell its one product. It has Massengill's sales force to sell, not only its own products and Penbritin, but also other Beecham products (particularly drugs for animals to hospitals and vets).

But problems are not only government-created; they can arise from the very success of an enterprise. For instance, Bowater Inc., the US subsidiary of the British Bowater Paper Corporation, would appear to be yet another inspirational success story, of a great man, a founder, (in this case, the late Sir Eric Bowater), whose skill and daring and foresight established a great commercial empire from humble beginnings. Indeed he did, and taught a lesson in how to use American partners to one's best advantage into the bargain. Not only that, he established the company as such an accepted part of the industry that the Bowater party is now a social highlight of the American Newspaper Publishers' Annual Convention in New York. But his successors face a severe problem as to how to deal with the inheritance. They have to find an equal daring to prevent Bowater in the US from stagnating, as other British investments have done.

Because paper (especially newsprint, Bowater's speciality, of which it supplies one-sixth of the US market) is made on so vast a scale, the story of Bowater in the US is essentially that of two plants. One is at Calhoun in Tennessee in the middle of the fundamentalist Holy Roller country, which seems at first sight to be devoted entirely to the production of hot gospellers and walking horses. The impression is reinforced by the fact that the Calhoun mill is, unusually, free from smells, and dirty water. Bowater is notably absent from lists of paper companies accused of polluting the countryside.

The Calhoun plant was only the second major one in the South. One had been put up just after the Second World War using Southern pines for pulp, with money partly provided by newspaper owners. The Calhoun mill itself was built at the request of a number of Southern newspaper owners who guaranteed to buy its production for fourteen years, and went to Bowater because they thought so highly of its production engineering skills. With these contracts in hand Sir Eric could go out and borrow most of the money he needed. Ever since it was opened, the mill has been a fabulous success but, in the last few years, because Bowater has been committed to a high dividend policy it has been "bled every year", as one senior man puts it. The next development, a pulp mill, nearly went sour on the company, and was only really saved by a subsequent coated paper plant which now supplies *McCalls* magazine. Yet although both these plants were profitable, they did not generate enough capital to pay for a new one. So for Bowater's next project it had to find a new partner. It could no longer rely on long-term contracts, but Bowater's know-how and the bargaining skill of Vic Sutton, the Canadian who was then the director in charge of Bowater's North American operations, ensured a very favourable deal with Sam Newhouse, who owns more newspapers than anyone else in the US—a man who gave his wife *Vogue* magazine as a birthday present. For just over $5 million Bowater got 51 per cent of a $60 million newsprint plant at Catawba in South Carolina, the biggest in the world, with the banks falling over themselves to lend $50 million to any company backed by Sam Newhouse.

Now Bowater can show an empire valued at $150 million as a result of an investment of less than $20 million. It is rounding out its North American operations by investing in a big way in British Columbia. For Bowater combines Canada and the US in its thinking. This is natural in a product as sensitive to transport costs as newsprint. Bowater's pre-war plant in Newfoundland supplies the North-East of the US, and its other two cover much of the South and South-Western United States. From British Columbia it could supply California. But this Canadian development merely delays the day when Bowater will have to decide whether to expand in the US, and, if so, by going public in order to diversify or by staying with its existing range of products. In 1969, Bowater ducked the opportunity to buy a pulp mill in Louisiana when British Inveresk Paper was forced to sell up. At the time the outlook for pulp prices and profits looked unpromising. But since then the situation both in pulp and paper has started to look up. For the biggest US paper company,

International Paper, is being transformed from a production-oriented group into a leaner, more profit-conscious group under the guidance of a former chairman of the giant American Telephone and Telegraph group.

The change in International should give Bowater and other US-based paper companies the opportunity to edge prices upwards, as they allow the American market to follow the European levels in that direction. An increase in profits would give Bowater an excellent opportunity to go public and thus diversify, like other paper companies, into such natural areas as wood and building products. But this change depends on a decision to go against Bowater's previous practice and retain the bulk of profits in the US. Yet Bowater has not fully restored a dividend cut years ago and is worried when British financial analysts automatically ask when it will be put back to its former level, especially as, like most other paper companies, it had to reduce its dividend still further in early 1971.

In these circumstances an American company would simply not restore the dividend and retain the money, knowing that US financial analysts and investors go by the record of a company's earnings, not its dividends. The continuing lack of sophistication in some British financial circles would present an easy way for Bowater to excuse itself from further forward movement in the US. But this would be an admission that the US market, infinitely bigger than the British, was not going to be allowed to dictate the pace of Bowater's general progress. Given the record profits from the US subsidiary, however, Bowater may be able to get the best of both worlds by raising more money locally to build the additional newsprint capacity it will need in a few years' time.

In the last decade, one European company (apart from Hoffman-La Roche) has been faced with this problem of an American company which threatened to lead on and in many ways dominate the group, and has let it do so. The group involved is Olivetti, one of the very few Italian companies with direct investments in the US. The story of the impetuous takeover of the ailing Underwood Typewriter Corporation eleven years ago, with the first fatal investment made in eight days, the eventual complete take-over and the investment of $100 million —by far the largest single direct investment by a European company in the US in the twenty years after the war—is part of business history and deserves to be. Underwood was losing money at a dreadful rate ($40 million in 1959/60); sales were only $95 million from 12,000 workers (by 1969 sales were up to $163 million, the number of employees down to 6,200). But most of the companies available for purchase by Europeans are inevitably going to be run-down, as Libby was, and as was Wyandotte chemicals, bought by the German BASF group in 1969. If the company is not visibly in decline, there is likely to be trouble from the anti-trust authorities (who can allow otherwise objectionable take-overs if the company involved counts as a "failing" one); there is likely to be a native counter-bidder— not to mention objections from the existing management.

But now Olivetti-Underwood has become to the parent what Lever in the US is to Unilever world-wide—in itself not an outstanding investment, but providing the rest of the group with techniques and disciplines which are quite invaluable to its commercial survival. Even now, Olivetti-Underwood, though in a growth industry, has been comparatively low-growth and low-profit since Olivetti's initial dynamism wore off. What makes the story of the feedback from the US so extraordinary is that for the first few years after the take-over it was Olivetti which was engaged in a massive managerial reorganisation of Underwood. Squads of Italians were flown over, given crash courses in English and set to work on Underwood's bemused salesmen. For while Olivetti expected to find that Underwood's manufacturing facilities were in a bad way and its product line outdated, it was shocked by the demoralised state of the sales force which it had counted on as a major asset.

In addition, Olivetti discovered that the Italian habit of paying salesmen purely on a salary basis so as to make them more service-oriented could not be applied in the US. But it discovered a great deal more—and was sensible enough to learn, particularly in the field of production planning and financial control. In the latter field the present managing director of Olivetti-Underwood, Gian-Luigi Gabetti, has organised standard financial measurements and reports in most of Olivetti's world-wide subsidiaries based on a US model. And it is the men from the US who naturally play a major part in planning the production and design of new models at home in Ivrea—even though very few of these men are now Italian. To satisfy the American market, for instance, Olivetti has produced its first calculator without a print-out device; and its Programma 101 microcomputer was introduced in the US a year before it was marketed elsewhere.

Olivetti has also carried out the single most difficult operation required by a foreign company: it shut an old factory which was a major source of employment in the town where it was located. Under these circumstances, tension is inevitable, yet, thanks to elaborate consultation machinery (and thanks also to the fact that the board of Olivetti-Underwood was almost entirely American), the move—from Hartford, Connecticut to a small Pennsylvania town—was smooth. Even the timing—during a boom year in 1968—was right.

Yet the Italians have often admitted that, had they known the depth and extent of their final involvement in Underwood, they would probably not have made the original investment. But, since then, they have been highly convincing in rationalising the situation. "The experience of Olivetti-Underwood is a source of strength for us and conditions our response in many ways. It keeps us modern and aggressive," Roberto Olivetti told *Fortune* Magazine in 1967, and he went on to say how provincial and sheltered life seemed from Ivrea compared with the hard real world in which Olivetti-Underwood exists.

Even so, whatever its final investment result, the case of Olivetti and Underwood remains unique. As one Olivetti man put it, it was "perhaps the first time that a European company has come to the US and has taken over what was then described as an ailing American corporation, has tried to reshape it in accordance with its basic philosophy and ideas and has rebuilt it as an active force in this market". For the final result, as the

Italians clearly see, was not just an Italian-owned office machinery company. The take-over led to a genuine rejuvenation of the parent/teacher company through an infusion of ideas from the new environment in which the teachers had to do their instruction. And few teachers—certainly not American companies in Europe—can claim to be so open-minded.

In one way, however, Olivetti's problems with Underwood were easier than those encountered by the French Pechiney aluminium company in its dealing with Howmet, now its subsidiary. For the Underwood people at least realised they were down and out when taken over by the foreigners. But Howmet was in better shape, and knew it. Indeed, the major reason for the investment, apart from the fact that both companies were in the aluminium industry, was that, as Pechiney admitted, Howmet had "dynamic management". Pechiney's problem, since it took its first interest in Howmet in 1962, has been to harness this dynamism without losing control. The process has seen the departure of two chief executives, and it was only in 1970 that the clerical staff took the reality of control by the French seriously enough to start, apparently of their own volition, to learn French.

At the same time Pechiney, like Philips and AKZO, has merged a wholly-owned subsidiary (in this case Pechiney Inc.) with another group which it controlled but did not own entirely. And, just as Philips's two companies were complementary, so were Pechiney's. Its wholly-owned subsidiary sold aluminium; Howmet fabricated it. But whereas Philips's 30 per cent-owned Consolidated Electronics was a judicious mixture of businesses developed under Philips's own guidance over twenty years (with older managers, former owners of subsidiaries, tactfully retired when necessary), Pechiney had not had the same control over Howmet.

Howmet had been developed since the war. It has shrewdly specialised in two growing uses for aluminium, for sheet and for use in buildings. It also bought a number of businesses which shaped other metals, like titanium, for the exacting requirements of the airframe and aero-engine businesses. Getting a grip on this company was a problem: one president, Bill Weaver, who had been largely responsible, both in production and in sales, for Howmet's growth, left amicably enough. But he complained to a number of investment institutions that Pechiney was interfering in Howmet's affairs. A second president, John Burke, remained on the board after he resigned as president in 1969. He tried to diversify the company (as was fashionable at the time); this involved buying more companies, often by issuing more stock; and Pechiney knew that the more frequent and bigger the take-overs, the more its control over Howmet would be diluted. Burke's departure came about largely because of the troubles of a company he had bought in 1967 for $11 million. This made landing gear for aircraft and was caught, like so many others in the same industry, in the considerable squeeze suffered by the whole aero industry in 1969-70. So Burke went, to be replaced by André Jacomet, a brilliant French lawyer who had organised many of Pechiney's overseas operations. He makes an incongruous figure; dumpy, dishevelled, a yellow Gauloise dangling from his lips, talking in French in a beautiful office overlooking the trees and water of Greenwich Sound in Connecticut, an office bequeathed by his predecessor.

Pechiney's problems in the Howmet corporate jungle contrast with the great success of its direct investments in the US. These involved American partners, who, like the Southern newspaper owners in Bowater's case, were happy to help a foreign firm to establish itself because its production expertise gave them some control over their own sources of supply. Pechiney, like Bowater, had been selling its products into the United States for a very long time; and Pechiney had the additional, and unusual, advantage that its financial adviser, André Meyer of Lazard Frères, was himself of French origin, but had become possibly the single most respected investment banker in New York.

Pechiney's first joint venture was called Intalco. The partners were American Metal Climax, which took half the shares and provided the finance; Howmet (which by 1964 had a substantial Pechiney shareholding, and which took a quarter share to provide itself with a supply of its major raw material); and

Pechiney, which also took a quarter, provided the know-how and sold its share of the production through its existing US sales company.

The consortium looked long and hard for the cheapest supply of the major raw material it required, electric power; because of the low price it obtained on the West Coast and through Pechiney's production expertise the plant was one of the world's most efficient and has been highly profitable since the day it opened in 1966, a mere two years after the agreement to go ahead. It was so successful that in 1969 Pechiney and Howmet went ahead with another plant, in Maryland, called Eastalco, without the help of Amax.

Even after Eastalco came into full operation in 1970, Howmet/Pechiney, now the US's fourth biggest aluminium company, still only produces half its own requirements of metal—against an industry average of three-quarters. And Pechiney has had other problems. Its first scheme for merging Pechiney Inc. and Howmet was approved by lawyers and shareholders but turned down by the revenue authorities late in 1969. A revised scheme went through a few months later: but Pechiney took the most elaborate precautions to ensure success. It asked for and got permission from the owners of a majority of the Howmet shares it did not own. It arranged for a $10 million loan from another Pechiney subsidiary—with a further line of credit available if necessary. It spun off 80 per cent of Howmedica, the Howmet division operating in the highly-rated medical field, whose value was greater as an independent company than as part of the lower-rated Howmet. In the end, to satisfy the taxmen, Howmet had to merge into Pechiney Inc., which then changed its name back to Howmet. But because Howmet had merged into Pechiney Inc., instead of the other way round, Pechiney had to reveal to the New York Stock Exchange a great deal of information about its activities; in the end, though, it found this useful and, unusually for a French company, adopted the idea of a consolidated balance sheet for the group as a whole (Rhône-Poulenc, another French company with large US interests, does the same).

Even after the merger Pechiney has to live with the continuing problems of the US aerospace industry. It also has to reconcile the very different interests of its own shareholders, who want two thirds of the profits distributed as income, and those of the continuing American minority in Howmet, who are more concerned with measuring the earnings per share; and Pechiney's problem is the more immediate because its interests in the US are now greater than those it has in France itself.

The problems on which M. Jacomet broods as he looks out on the as yet unpolluted Connecticut landscape—and indeed the barriers encountered by many of the pioneers—must appear remote to most European businessmen. The confidence given to the pioneers by the prestige or size of the parent groups, the very fact that these were mostly household names, removes them from the ordinary run of business life.

But there was at least one pioneer company, lacking these assets, whose American experience, like that of AKU among the veterans, contains most of the key elements required for a successful invader. This is Foseco, a group little known outside its own industry, which makes specialised lining materials for foundries and steel works. Foseco's chairman, Eric Weiss, had moved his company from Germany to England in the 1930's and had, in fact, been selling into the US from 1933 onwards through an agent, Sam Frankel. Soon after the war Frankel gave up his rights over the Canadian market—and soon Foseco was selling more material in Canada than in the whole US. So, in the early 1950's Frankel was bought out—mainly for the rights he held, rather than any physical assets he possessed. For he was operating from cramped facilities in Brooklyn, hundreds of miles east of the major steel works in western Pennsylvania, Ohio and Illinois.

The take-over symbolised Weiss's determination to establish a world-wide base for his products. But Foseco was then a small concern, and Fred Eastwood, the man who took over, had not been trained specially for the job—indeed he had been due to take over Foseco's Australian operation when Frankel's licence was bought. By simply going out and selling hard, Eastwood doubled the previous rate of sales—$250,000 a year—within a few months of his arrival in early 1954. Eastwood found, to his surprise, but like many other newcomers in different fields since then, that his competition did not generally come from large companies. The few that were in the field treated lining and coating products as "just one of their lines", and the divisions involved were rather neglected offshoots. Most of the competition, in fact, consisted of small, localised companies. And all the Americans underrated Foseco, refusing offers of cross-licensing, and assuming that Foseco could never make it.

They were wrong: Eastwood flourished and, as the business grew, he moved west to be nearer his customers, first to Columbus and then, in 1958, to his ideal location in Cleveland, the heart of the foundry industry. It was also near the airport, the Ohio turnpike road, and a trade publishing house which could provide Foseco with useful statistics. He had two separate markets to aim at: foundries, small customers who appreciated the technical skills which Foseco's salesmen could bring with them, and the steelmakers themselves, large buyers who tended to be interested more in price. So Eastwood aimed, as he says, to "service the hell out of these foundries". And he succeeded. Foseco Inc. barely lost money even in its first year of operation. And, although no dividends were paid for a time, royalties were, and growth was fast enough for Foseco to be self-financing.

In the late 1950's, as part of Weiss's general policy of integrating overseas companies into the countries where they operated, Eastwood (who had had a heart attack) was replaced by an American professional manager, and a minority stake in Foseco Inc. was sold to an investment group headed by Jock Whitney.

In the next decade, Foseco Inc. came of age. The local competition sat up, took notice and fought back, especially by cutting prices with the steelmakers. A number of large American companies, like Ashland Oil and Combustion Engineering, either expanded their own operations or bought into the field. In the early 1960's, too, the parent group was floated on the London stock market and the Whitney interests exchanged their shares in Foseco Inc. for those in the parent company. By the end of the 1960's Eastwood was back in charge. The American manager had built, if anything, too elaborate an organisation; although sales had expanded to over $15 million—a quarter of the group total—profits had not risen in line.

So Eastwood had to slim the organisation; but there was no fuss, because he, like other European managers, assumes that executives are not sacked on the spot, after the American fashion, but given weeks and months to look around for new jobs. He also found a new speciality material, produced originally by Sandviken in Sweden but developed in the US by Eastwood himself, which enabled Foseco to break an American rival's monopoly in the crucibles used in one particular process where American practice differs completely from European.

Foseco is now wholly integrated into the American scene: it is self-sufficient in materials and is building new plants near customers outside Ohio. It has emerged as the price leader over much of its range of products; and there are no problems because of nationality. It was 1954 when Eastwood swore that "the first steel mill or foundry that refuses me an order because of my nationality, I'll take out naturalisation papers—and I'm still British". Nor has he problems with the parent: "They told us to go to the US and make money and we won't bother you . . . we refer to them more than they do to us". Foseco Inc., which has had less than a dozen non-American executives in all its years of operations, has more applications from executives in Foseco's other overseas companies to come and work in the US than it can take. Yet Foseco Inc. is helpful to the rest of the group in finding new products which can be exploited globally—for instance, a nodular iron now being produced in Germany.

Of course, Foseco has difficulties: a two-month teamsters' (lorry drivers') strike; the General Motors' strike; local problems. But in the end Foseco's story is a triumphant vindication of two of Eastwood's points: "service is worth dough" and "the safe thing about the company is that the products worked". What has changed in the last few years is that vastly more European companies have gained confidence in their products working well enough to compete in the US, and have found that direct investment, with or without partners, is the best way to get the maximum profit out of their competence.

CHAPTER 7

PARTNERSHIPS AND SPECIALITIES

FOSECO's whole product range consisted of speciality products. But most other companies, when marketing or investing in the US, look for the gaps in the competition's offerings. As Lazell of Beecham puts it: "Anything new or unique you can promote . . . aim at a segment of the market." In adopting this attitude the Europeans are, as usual, behaving completely differently from the Americans in Europe whose approach has tended to be broader, selling a wide range of products not necessarily adapted to the local market. So, it is not surprising that the pace in the invasion is now being set by the European chemical companies. For these, unlike many large companies, have a wide range of products, not necessarily produced in large quantities, to offer in a host of fields—plastics, fibres, dyestuffs, resins—and can choose the fastest-growing, least capital-intensive markets to aim for. Alternatively, the European company can combine its own product range with that of an American company it takes over, in order to provide a more complete package. Plessey achieved this aim by taking over Alloys Unlimited. More recently, the British Bestobell group, by taking over General Connectors Corporation, a small specialist business in California, enabled the combined company to supply all the ducting required to carry air round aeroplanes (which are, apparently, "full of air rushing around at high temperatures"). GCC makes the titanium bellows required at the top end (600° C!) and Bestobell the silicon-impregnated rubber used at lower temperatures. Crucially, and a reason for many take-overs, GCC was well known to its customers, and provided the European company with a ready-made entrée and sales force.

In one recent and unexpected case (who would have thought the Germans could lead the female fashion field against the Americans?) Schulte & Dieckhoff, a leading German manufacturer of panti-hose, was able to raise $7 million (out of a total of $9 million it required), to set up a number of factories in Puerto Rico, from Chadbrown Inc. an American stocking manufacturer. In return for the $7 million, Chadbrown acquired shares and the right to buy half the factories' products—due to be 600,000 pairs a day within two years of the first investment in 1969. In this way S & D can protect itself against the growing threat of action against textile imports—as well as complete its coverage of the US supermarkets where it sells its panti-hose.

Specialisation does not just express itself in products. Bowater and Pechiney were worth-while partners for Americans because of their production know-how, not for the products they had to offer. Burda Druck, a German printing machinery company, followed Bowater's deal with Sam Newhouse in helping another publisher to get his independence from his suppliers. Burda and Meredith, an Iowa publisher, have formed a joint company to build a rotary gravure plant in Lynchburg, Virginia, to print some of Meredith's publications, including their bestseller, *Better Homes and Gardens*. This constructive use of partnerships— to enable both sides to get into new businesses—has a decidedly aggressive air about it. And it is the American company which needs the European expertise, and so is sending new employees to Germany to train for up to eighteen months. This is, as Meredith says, "a unique opportunity for a man to live and learn from the experts".

Druck is characteristic of one trend: the way as Frank Sheaffer of the Department of Commerce puts it, "a growing number of smaller firms, which in the past were interested in licensing US companies to make their products, are now beginning to talk about setting up joint ventures with a US partner".

Other firms are disentangling the question of which products are more suitable for manufacture rather than for licensing. In 1970 the German Demag company invested directly for the first time in the US by building a factory to make hoists and overhead cranes. These are relatively standardised: in its other products—heavy, one-off steel mills and the like, enormous lines of machinery costing millions of dollars—Demag still finds it more profitable to sell the necessary technical drawings rather than invest in the US in an industry which is capital-intensive, highly cyclical and competitive.

Not that all the partnerships can be called aggressive. But then the motive for investment can vary widely, even in the same industry. The German Krohne AG, makers of flow and liquid measuring devices, formed a joint company with the American Porter Industries because of tariff barriers; yet, in the same industry the British George Kent group went in, alone, and built a factory in Puerto Rico to make water meters, since Kent had seen a regional market gap for them in the South.

In exploiting such a gap, Kent had spotted one of the keys to the success of the recent invaders, the "disintegration" of American business, as one executive called it; "a series of regional markets with few economic power centres", as another put it. Willy Korf, the German who is the only foreign steel maker in the US, started with a small mill, costing $10 million, a "community plant", in Georgetown, South Carolina, making bars for reinforcing concrete from local scrap metal—the first mill for some way around. This was so successful that he has expanded it to serve an area rather than a town. To do so, he has joined with an American partner—Midland Ross Industries—which is putting up a pelletising plant to process imported iron ore for Korf to use.

Korf, with his regional, pioneering, plant, in an industry—steel—traditionally dominated by the biggest of the big battalions, is an extreme case.

But the expertise, and the specialisation, need not have very much to do with the products or their manufacture. Dunlop has had a great success recently with its golf balls in the US. It had a good—but not unique—product to offer; so the company gave its balls a special appeal by selling them only through golf club professionals. The pros loved Dunlop and sold hard, secure—as they were not with American manufacturers' products—from price-cutting competition elsewhere. And because the American market for sporting goods—around $500 million a year—is so huge, Dunlop has not needed to take an enormous slice of the market to achieve a turnover of around $20 million.

On a larger scale, Dunlop, in its tyre business, shows the great advantage enjoyed by the invaders: because they do not have a market position to protect they can choose the type of business to go for, and because the market is so large, a small specialised share can be extremely large. After the war, avid for growth, uncertain of its marketing ability, Dunlop, like other European companies, found itself supplying the fast-growing but, by definition, cut-price, low-margin, own-brand market for sale through supermarkets, discount stores and mail-order catalogues.

After a severe and humiliating crisis in the early 1960's— when the company had to admit publicly to the unions that it could not afford to pay the same wages as other tyre makers— Dunlop found its feet. It sold, under its own name, to large petrol stations, and protected the brand's value by using another name, Remington, where smaller outlets and price-cutting were concerned. And Dunlop—unlike the larger, native, tyre-makers—is able to concentrate on the more profitable replacement market, a form of negative specialisation. It could afford to turn down the chance to provide "original equipment" tyres—those fitted to new cars on the assembly lines—for the sub-compact Ford Pinto because the contract would not have been profitable enough. Dunlop is too big to be able to avoid OE business in its other markets, if it wishes to get a worth-while turnover (and American tyre companies in Europe have to be in OE for the same reason); but it can pick and choose in the US—so that its profit margins there are now higher than in much of the rest of the world.

Dunlop's 4 per cent of the US tyre market brings in an eighth of its world profits; similarly the French Air Liquide has the same proportion of the US industrial gas market, and gets 15 per cent of its profits from there.

Profitable expertise in a capitalist society does not only consist of production, marketing or technological know-how, it can simply be financial. European stockbrokers and merchant banks are belatedly copying the Americans and opening offices across the Atlantic. Some of these offices—like those of a couple of British stockbrokers on the West Coast or of German banks in Boston—were started in order to service European investment portfolios by being closer to the companies themselves. In one case in 1971 the aggressive Belgian Banque Lambert actually took control of Witter, a New York brokerage house, the better to control its US investments. But they soon spread—British names like Cazenove are to be found on the underwriting lists of purely local share issues in California— and sometimes a conflict is inevitable.

In New York the British merchant banks with offices there run a complete gamut in overcoming what one journalist has called the "crusty clubbiness of Wall Street" in the lucrative and prestigious business of underwriting and managing new issues. At one extreme, there is a US subsidiary which does no underwriting at all, in order not to damage the bank's valuable contacts with US banks in Europe. At the other is Robert Fleming whose founder masterminded the massive Scottish portfolio investment in the US a century ago. Fleming is a cautious outfit but its New York office, founded in 1968 under Laurence Banks, an uncompromisingly sharp young man, has challenged Wall Street head-on (Fleming had less to lose in Europe). He no longer relies on the power of the parent's $1 billion US investments, but bids for a piece of the action like the most carefree of freebooters. In between come Hill Samuel (tied to London), and Kleinwort Benson (working within the system successfully), to get a slice of business.

Financial acumen can, of course, be applied in simply controlling US businesses, without necessarily understanding the business involved—hence the success of the US subsidiary of Charles Clore's Sears Holdings. When he formed Sears Inc., by purchasing Consolidated Laundries, the largest contract laundry business in New York in the mid-1960's, what he had to offer was his skill and judgment in picking the right companies to buy. Since then Consolidated has expanded steadily from its New York base. Sears failed to buy the family tobacco firm of Dunhill after prolonged negotiations; but succeeded with the Highlander knitwear group which Sears Holdings had come to know as a customer of its Bentley Engineering subsidiary which makes knitting machinery.

Sears Inc. has suffered because the Clore name, unknown in the US, failed to give his company the same glamorous market rating as he formerly enjoyed in Britain. Without such a bonus, his particular expertise does not have its fullest scope. But at least Clore's financial know-how—and that of his right-hand man Leonard Sainer—have given him a successful business. And, unlike many earlier British investors, he does not ignore the investment—either he or Sainer attends every monthly board meeting.

The same could not be said of one of his earlier ventures, his purchase in 1960 for $14¾ million of a large office building, 40 Wall Street, which he sold five years later for what it had cost him (though he made a capital profit because, by 1965, there was a 25 per cent premium on dollars repatriated to Britain). Clore had bought the Wall Street building at an inflated price from that most visionary and improvident of property developers, William Zeckendorf senior, during a rash of British property development in North America. This fashion has been superbly described by Oliver Marriott in his book *The Property Boom*; it exemplifies almost everything that can go wrong with an invasion which relied on a special skill which was more apparent than real in a business where the conditions on different sides of the Atlantic were almost completely different. The British, used to a home market hungry for offices, and to easy money from pension funds and insurance companies, did not bother to adjust for American conditions, where the developer was an object of suspicion to most sources of long-term capital. So the British were unprepared for conditions which included finding tenants for a building long before they could raise the money for it. Nor were they accustomed to tenants, who, aware of the strength of their position, used it to get a share in the equity of the building or to force the developer to take their existing offices, together with the risks and problems of re-letting them (a process known as "take-back").

Nevertheless the peculiar qualities of one developer, the late Jack Cotton, enabled him to make a handsome profit out of the infamous Pan-Am building which blocks the view down New York's Park Avenue. He had the right partner, Erwin Wolfson, a well-respected builder-developer who understood, as soon as he met Cotton in 1959, how well suited he was for the US; "Jack might have been a warm-hearted American Jew." What Cotton contributed to the building, according to Marriott, "were two British ingredients in development: hunch, and an ability to persuade banks to lend money"—before, not after, a tenant had been found. In addition Cotton had to export $5·7 million—the biggest single capital movement since the war from Britain to the US. But the gamble on building a $96 million office block without a tenant paid off when Pan American Airways decided to lease a quarter of the building before it was finished.

But even Cotton's scheme hit snags: "take-backs" increased costs by an unbudgeted $3 million; and Cotton assumed he would get a dividend from the building within a few years—ignoring the American habit of depreciating a new building quickly over the early years of its life for tax purposes. Yet the Pan-Am building was basically such a vindication of Cotton's hunch that he started dreaming, with no result, of a $200 million development over railway land in Chicago even before he had finished the Pan-Am building.

Cotton had hunch and he had a reasonable partner. One disastrous British venture, the partnership between Kenneth Keith's Hill Samuel merchant bank and its associated property and insurance companies and William Zeckendorf had neither.

In the early 1960's Zeckendorf was, as usual, in financial difficulties. Against the advice of the New York financial community Keith was confident he and his group could harness their American partner's superb creative talents and yet confine him financially and stop his compulsive wheeling and dealing. They could not; and the error cost them over $20 million, as the property market sagged, and Zeckendorf kept on buying, rather than selling, as he had promised. But then, as another British property developer, Max Rayne, told Marriott, Zeckendorf had phenomenal powers of persuasion. "When I was really worried about the joint company with Zeckendorf, I sent over two quite unusually tough negotiators to try and contain him and see that he spent no more money. Two days later they phoned from New York: 'Mr Zeckendorf has some other very interesting projects over here. Would you like to put up some more money?'"

In fact Rayne did very well out of Zeckendorf, acquiring the Savoy Plaza Hotel on Fifth Avenue near Central Park (which became his General Motors building) partly because Zeckendorf was unable to pay the interest on a loan. But the object lesson in how to use partners in American property development is given by Jack Rubens, a man who had managed to resist Zeckendorf's blandishments—even refusing an invitation to lunch with him and the Mayor of New York.

Rubens' pet scheme, started in the mid-1960's after the Hill Samuel group had retired hurt, had been proposed to him in London by four young Americans, an agent, lawyer and architect among them. It was for a large office block in Boston, where there had been no development for half a century. When Rubens went to investigate he found the city's largest bank prepared to lend money to Rubens' Central and District Properties to build anywhere except Boston, which they described as a "dead" city. Reasoning that a city of over a million inhabitants which was also a major financial centre could not really be dead, Rubens went ahead. Before construction was complete, he had found another major bank as tenant, Boston was in the midst of a development boom, Rubens put up another block—and his partners became rich men.

Rubens had stumbled on the secret of any successful invasion, an unappreciated gap in the market. He had also been able to contribute an asset rare among the invaders, a financial solidity not found in the equivalent local companies. For property is such a speculative affair in the US that Rubens had to take a list of his more prominent institutional shareholders with him, to convince Boston's financial world that his was no fly-by-night concern. Rubens' success is being followed through on a bigger scale by the heirs of the Hill Samuel-Zeckendorf empire, the Star Property group's Tri-Zec subsidiary in Canada. Tri-Zec is now expanding rapidly in both Canada and the US helped by a partnership with the extremely rich Cummings family. The Cummings want to be active in an international property group; there are none in North America so they are lining up with Star, and have merged their property company with Tri-Zec. They also sold to Tri-Zec one of the largest office blocks in Detroit, a city, like Boston, largely ignored by developers, late in 1970 for over $14 million—yet the Star group contributed under $1 million in cash.

Property developers have few assets: money, credit, flair, an eye for the market. They cannot be expected to play an important role in the new invasion, though even here the British are eyeing the currently depressed New York property market for possible bargains; and when, in spring 1971, Max Rayne sold his share of the General Motors building he retained his profits in the US for possible future use. At the other extreme—similar only in that European groups are as large as, or larger than, their American equivalents—come the big chemical companies. Six of these have turnovers of $2 billion or more. All are bigger than any American chemical groups except Du Pont and Union Carbide. To these six—three German, BASF, Bayer and Hoechst, one French, Rhône-Poulenc, one Italian, Monte-catini-Edison, and one British, Imperial Chemical Industries—can be added two billion-dollar fibres groups, the Dutch AKZO, and the British Courtaulds.

I have already discussed in Chapter 5 how AKZO's American interests have expanded so successfully on a basis of superior technology in specialised products and avoidance of over-heavy capital commitment in raw materials. Six out of the other seven are now expanding so fast in the US that they form the spearhead of the present invasion; only the Italian group, in the throes of a complete internal overhaul, is stagnant. Because they are so big it is surprising that the six have been relatively so inactive until recently, especially as chemicals, plastics, fibres, are all industries where the Europeans—particularly the Germans—have traditionally been technically very strong. All the companies have numbers of specialised products eminently suitable for exploitation in a huge sophisticated market. This has remained more fragmented than in Europe because its growth has been relatively recent, occurring when the anti-trust authorities were more active than when other large industries, steel, oil, motors, were being organised. The American fibre producers cannot, for instance, integrate forward into textiles in the way Courtaulds especially has done in Europe. So conditions ought to be ideal for the Europeans.

Yet, even after several years' expansion, 1970 sales by these companies' US subsidiaries probably accounted for no more than $1 billion, or 2 per cent of the chemical industry's total sales of over $50 billion. Even the addition of the $500 million of chemical sales by Shell Oil, sales of polystyrene and other chemicals by the Belgian-controlled American Petrofina*, and the results of joint ventures, brings the total to under 5 per cent of the market. This stake shows not only the present modesty of the European invasion, but also its growth potential. For historical circumstances have delayed the invasion: the delay will ensure that it is the more formidable and permanent now that it has arrived.

One of the five major investors, ICI, was kept out of the US by its global cartel arrangements with Du Pont until these were finally broken by an anti-trust action in 1952. Rhône-Poulenc had sold its US company between the wars to a group which had itself been swallowed by Du Pont. The three Germans were the successors to IG Farben, whose General Aniline subsidiary

* See Chapter 10.

was confiscated when Germany declared war on the US in December 1941. Courtaulds' subsidiary, American Viscose, had been forcibly sold off during 1941 at a ludicrously low price in order to convince Congress that Britain really did have its back to the wall.

So none of the companies—except the Dutch AKU—had any base from which to build after the war. And none felt in a position to do very much: ICI, for instance, licensed American companies to make polyethylene, a plastic which was one of its major research triumphs. The first to arrive was Rhône-Poulenc, with a two and a half room sales office in 1948. Then Courtaulds returned with a modest rayon plant in 1951—the first direct investment. Two years later the French bought back their former subsidiary from Du Pont which had decided to get out of aromatic chemicals. For the next decade the story is of small-scale individual ventures, and a number of larger partnerships. Hoechst, for instance, started with a small purchasing office in 1953. In line with the IG Farben tradition that there should be no emphasis on a foreign name (and because German names were then still suspect), this was given the ambitious name of the Inter-Continental Chemical Company. Hoechst then took over a one-man shop run by an ex-IG Farben man, one Harry Grimmel, an inventive genius whom Hoechst describes as "the Leonardo da Vinci of dyestuffs". The Europeans tended to start with sales offices and then to advance through the acquisition of small sales companies; their direct investments were mostly in dyestuffs where the American Selling Price system of duties gave an overwhelming advantage to local producers. There were other acquisitions, mostly small companies with which the Europeans already had links: BASF bought a company making polystyrene under licence; Rhône-Poulenc acquired a pesticide and herbicide company with which it had become associated; and Hoechst bought Azoplate, a company which presensitised offset plates for use in printing, in order to learn the technology, and a family-owned pharmaceutical company, whose chairman happened to be the grandson of one of Hoechst's founders. In fact the chemical companies' plans during the early and mid-1960's foreshadowed those of many other companies a few years later.

Courtaulds and Rhône-Poulenc became very large producers of apparently old-fashioned products: Rhône-Poulenc's Rhodia Inc. accounted for a third of all American production of cellulose acetate (cellophane), and Courtaulds became the second biggest manufacturer (after its former subsidiary!) of viscose staple for rayon. In Courtaulds' case this was not so much a matter of a fatal reliance on an ageing product; rather it has been a cashing-in on a situation where the Americans, assuming that rayon was a declining product, have largely ignored the market, which has remained sturdy and profitable, helped by an increasing demand for rayon used in tyre cord.

But none of these added up to very much: even including a sizeable chunk of imports, not one of the companies had sales of as much as $50 million by the mid-1960's. The main thrust was through partnerships with major American chemical companies mostly to make synthetic fibres, where the Europeans were especially strong. ICI started Fiber Industries as an equal partnership with Celanese; the ICI share subsequently slipped to 37½ per cent when ICI took over British Nylon Spinners, which had a minority stake in Fiber Industries, and accidentally lost BNS's share. BASF went in fifty-fifty with Dow Chemical in Dow-Badische; Hoechst with Hercules Powder in Hystron— rather later than the others; Bayer with Monsanto in Mobay; and Rhône-Poulenc with Phillips, one of the earliest American oil companies to invest heavily in chemicals, in Fibers International. This last was a pioneering venture into, quite literally, new territory since the plant involved was put into Puerto Rico to reduce taxes and be near customers.

Although all these agreements reflected European hesitation and a sense of inadequacy even in areas of technical strength, the American partners made widely dissimilar contributions, and the fate of the five has been different. Three are still going strong: Fiber Industries (in which, as ICI says, "we swapped our technology—mainly in polyester fibres, like Terylene—for their marketing"); Fibers International; and Dow-Badische, founded in 1958 and probably the biggest ($200 million invested with all profits reinvested). But Monsanto was forced to sell its half-stake in Mobay in 1962, seven years after the partnership was formed, by the anti-trust people who ruled that Bayer could have entered the US market in Mobay's major product, poly-urethane foam, by itself. So, by American standards, Bayer had been inhibiting competition by joining with Monsanto, an actual rival as well as a potential polyurethane producer. Bayer made a considerable fuss at the time. But cynics within the industry claim that other potential American partners had told Bayer of the inevitability of anti-trust action if it formed a joint company, that Monsanto also knew of the possibility, but that they both preferred to turn a blind eye. Their strength was such that Mobay had half the market for its products, and of course the final result of anti-trust beastliness was that the Europeans emerged with a much bigger stake in the US than before its intervention.

The acquisition of Monsanto's share of Mobay put Bayer temporarily in the lead as far as the Europeans were concerned —for all the joint ventures were on a different scale from the solo efforts and all have sales of over $100 million. But the other Europeans were ready to go ahead on their own. ICI's European investments (which had, characteristically, pre-occupied its managerial talents and employed its capital for the first half of the decade) were by then on a largely self-financing basis and ICI was grouping its scattered US subsidi-aries into one amalgam so as to give a basis for expansion. BASF did the same in 1968. Already in 1965 Hoechst had made its American subsidiary a trading as well as a holding company. In 1969 Hoechst bought out its partner in Hystron—Hercules had never been actively involved in the management, and its main contribution had been the production of the DMT base material for the Hystron fibre; Hystron itself had always been run by Germans. In 1970 Hoechst bought out another American partner, Stauffer Chemicals, with which it had had a joint venture in PVC for packaging for seven years. In this case, too, and notably unlike the other companies' partnerships, it was the

European company which had taken charge of marketing from the beginning; Stauffer, like Hercules in Hystron, provided only the raw material (in this case polyvinyl chloride), and the finance. So Hoechst was in a stronger position to take over the whole venture than the other Europeans—especially as its two partners were noticeably smaller and less aggressive than the groups to which the other Europeans had become attached. It is because of this foresight and marketing skill that Hoechst's effort in the US looks the most promising of all the European groups.

Rhône-Poulenc has been less active than the others—it has had to suffer a great deal of internal reorganisation following a series of mergers in 1969-70—but it too made a $10 million investment in aromatics (and Vitamin A) on a new site in Texas. But this was overshadowed by the efforts of ICI and, especially, BASF during 1969, the year the European involvement in US chemicals really took off. ICI was already investing in a number of schemes, including a $20 million plant in New Jersey ("behind the Statue of Liberty)" to make fluon—the coating which gives non-stick pans their particular quality. It then announced the spending of $50 million on a plant to make Melinex polyester film, used, for instance, as the base for magnetic tapes. That same autumn BASF, which had already built up a $15 million investment in magnetic tape, as well as in orthodox chemicals, completed the take-over, begun earlier that year, of an old-established firm, Wyandotte Chemicals, with sales of $150 million, for $95 million in cash. This was the biggest single investment by a European since Olivetti had taken over Underwood ten years before. But whereas the earlier take-over had been greeted with a mass of publicity, BASF's bid received little or no attention. Perhaps the idea of a European company taking over an American one was no longer new ("man bites dog *again*" is not an arresting headline); but it was also swamped by news of British Petroleum's doings in the US. Wyandotte, an old family firm based on a town of the same name in Michigan, was in a poor way when BASF bought it—otherwise, as BASF admits, it would never have had the opportunity of doing so.

The flow of money in 1967-69 was large enough to give a permanent boost to European chemical interests. But these years also probably represented the limit to the size of individual investment of which these companies (apart from ICI) were capable—this limit was emphasised in 1970 by the general shortage of investment funds among the German companies; by their failure to announce any major new developments that year; by Courtaulds' announcement that it would postpone its Courtelle plant, a decision born, like many that year, of a combination of tight money and a sluggish US economy; and by the withdrawal by BASF, allegedly because of local opposition, of its plans to spend $200 million on a petro-chemical plant in South Carolina. This retreat, one of the few cases where the European invasion caused enough controversy to rate headlines in the American press, is examined in detail in Chapter 11.

There are other, intangible barriers to any immediate further inroads. ICI, for instance, was anxious to expand in the US in the pharmaceutical and plant protection products in which it is very strong. It has to wait for the Food and Drugs Administration, and for field and clinical trials, before introducing new products. Many older ones are now sold by American companies through agreements made when ICI was less aggressive in the market, so it will be nearly 1975 before the present sales plans in these fields can be carried out properly.

But ICI speeded up its progress—and virtually caught up with its German rivals—with its take-over, in April 1971, of Atlas Chemical for $155 million in cash, funded by loans raised in the international capital market. The bid was ironical. For Atlas was hived-off from Du Pont in 1912, and both companies still have their headquarters in Wilmington, Delaware; with the take-over, ICI supplanted Du Pont as the world's biggest chemical group, and its US headquarters will now be in the same town as Du Pont.

But there was more to the bid than irony and size. There had to be, for ICI paid a stiff price—23 times earnings—for a company with a static profits record. ICI acquired a sales force—and an FDA-approved laboratory—in a number of the fields on which its hopes were pinned, notably in ethical drugs. With the acquisition ICI reached its 1975 minimum total US sales figure of $200 million four years ahead of schedule; but even this figure is under 5 per cent of its present total turnover, a ridiculously low percentage for so large a market, and only two-thirds of its sales in Canada. After the Atlas take-over it is probable that further major developments will have to wait: none of the companies can, at the moment, afford to import enough capital to make a major splash; their present investments need a year or two to generate cash flow for further expansion; none of them has a quoted subsidiary to use in order to allow take-overs for shares or a capital base for the issue of loan stock or new shares. The only exception is AKZO's subsidiary, Akzona, which has a twenty-year start on the others, and is still forcing the pace.

Because their American activities are still so small compared with their total sales, the proportion of the market they hold so very much smaller than it is anywhere else in the world, their technical position in many fields so strong, because these companies are, by now, strongly entrenched in fast-growing products and the American competitition is so much less overwhelming in size and technical competence than in other industries; for all these reasons, any pause, such as occurred in 1970, in the announcement of new ventures, take-overs, or major new investments, is bound to be only temporary. And already in 1967-69 the Europeans felt strong enough to go it alone: none of their ventures involved local partners. For it is, as Courtaulds says, "always possible to get the money for a good project in the US"; and, there are powerful local forces anxious to encourage the Europeans' investment, especially in the mid-South where these companies are concentrated.

CHAPTER 8

WHERE THEY GO

IT was natural for the chemical companies to put their fibre
plants in the South, for that is where their customers, the textile
companies, are now mainly situated. But proximity to customers
does not fully explain the fact that the majority of new European
investment in the US is concentrated in a handful of States
running between Virginia and Georgia and back into the
Appalachian Mountains.

This concentration of foreign investment in an area which
does not have a long history of industrial development and
which is comparatively short of job opportunities is not confined
to the United States. In Europe American and other foreign
investors have been more ready than native companies to move
to such relatively underdeveloped areas. Because foreign companies have no existing factories to think about and no pre-
conceived notions as to where they ought to be located, they are
therefore freer than their native competitors to move where the
inducements are greatest, the labour most readily available. In
one case at least, that of the American electronic companies
who have been building factories in Eastern Scotland since the
war, the invasion has helped the whole area to move away from
older established industries and towards newer, science-based
ones. Recently, a whole host of smaller companies has been set
up by enterprising former employees of the bigger groups. But
this concentration, dependent on one industry, makes the new
prosperity vulnerable to recessions—there were, in fact, a

number of substantial lay-offs in these factories in early 1971 because of world over-capacity in many electronic products.

The twin results of foreign investment, a new boost, and a new vulnerability, took twenty years to show in Scotland. The technical spin-off is likely to be accelerated in North Carolina, probably the most sophisticated of states in its dealing with foreigners. Under the aegis of an experienced former Governor, Luther Hodges, the state has designated large areas in the thirty-mile-sided triangle formed by three of the state's universities (two of them, Duke and Chapel Hill, among the best in the South), as the Research Triangle Park. This has already attracted a number of Federal research institutions, some connected with the growing pollution business, as well as science-based companies which have set up their research headquarters there. In late 1970 Burroughs Wellcome Inc., the single biggest subsidiary of the British pharmaceutical group, and itself a sizeable operation with a $60 million turnover, moved its headquarters and research centre into the middle of the triangle and its production facilities to Greenville in the same state. Only North Carolina could provide the particular combination required by Burroughs Wellcome of an adequate labour supply on a new site (it was formerly housed in a rather cramped site near New York) and the sophisticated researchers and research facilities and contact with federal laboratories available in the Research Triangle Park.

As yet there is no sign that the European industries in the mid-South have become so dominant that the area's prosperity depends on them. But their increasing number in these mid-Southern states will in the future give them a degree of political leverage which is normally lacking in international groups. For multinational corporations have no votes; in times of trouble—and unless their own government intervenes—they can rely only on the political muscle of their employees or their local friends. And all of these are likely to prove fair-weather allies.

The South is not alone among American regions in having relatively high unemployment and low job skills (the most vulnerable is the island of Puerto Rico whose brochure trying to attract new companies says, pathetically, that of Puerto Rico's 800,000 workers "almost 12 per cent are available for immediate hiring"). The South may be peculiarly receptive to Europeans because, since the American Civil War, it has largely been an economic colony of the North so that it tends to welcome alternative industrial masters—especially from Europe, since another Southern tradition is an anti-isolationist and pro-European stance in international affairs. For the Europeans looking at the rich market of the North-Eastern coastal belt south from Boston to Washington through New York and Philadelphia, the states south of Washington form one of the two natural areas in which to invest. They are frightened of the cost of building and wage and tax rates in the great cities, yet they want to be close enough to them not to be penalised by inordinate transport costs. For the same reasons European companies often have their headquarters, not in New York, but in the suburban areas around the city. In moving out of Manhattan the Europeans were setting a trend which has now been followed by many large American corporations which had delayed partly because they already had an existing headquarters building in New York. As ICI explained, "we didn't have the same mausoleum in New York as our competitors" (and as ICI itself has in London). So in Stamford, a dormitory town in Connecticut, we find ICI's new headquarters in a rather uninspired block in the centre of town, and Schweppes in a notably inspired one on the outskirts. As we have seen, Pechiney is in nearby Greenwich, Nestlé in White Plains to the north of New York and a number of chemical companies, including Hoechst and CIBA, are in the more salubrious parts of New Jersey.

These suburban areas are not suitable for many labour-intensive manufacturing industries—though there are quite a few pharmaceutical groups scattered round New York. So for their factories these groups go south or north in a double outflanking movement. The strongest thrust is in the South but there are also many companies which are attacking the North-Eastern markets through factories in Canada. In quite a number of products there is free trade between the two countries, so that

EUROPE'S
THREE-STATE
BEACHHEAD

KEY

SPARTANBURG Major centres with important
European presence

GREENVILLE   Major centres with small
European presence

Catawba   Smaller towns with important
European presence

Georgetown   Smaller towns with small
European presence

0   20   100
miles

Europeans can use Canada as a regional base from which to assault the whole North American market. Michelin is building a large factory in Nova Scotia to supply the American truck market with the steel-corded radial ply tyres for use in trucks, buses and heavy earth-moving equipment in which the company has a world lead. Because of the free trade in cars, Nissan, Volvo and Peugeot, the only three foreign motor companies to have assembly plants in North America, have all pitched themselves in Canada's maritime provinces.

Similarly, because of free trade in agricultural products, ICI has a fertiliser factory in Ontario which serves a "two-country market", including Michigan and Indiana as well as Ontario. In cases like fertiliser and newsprint, both high-volume low-cost items where transport costs are important, companies often treat the North American market as a series of regions running north-south and not as two specific countries. As we have already seen, Bowater supplies newsprint from Newfoundland to the North-East United States and will supply California from British Columbia. This view of the market can lead to a drift southwards. Before Demag opened its crane factory in Cleveland, Ohio, it was supplying the American market by exports from Canada. It already had warehouses in America to service sales and it was the most natural thing in the world to add a factory.

As with factories, so with people. A number of British companies, including Bowater and ICI, which had important investments in Canada before they invaded the US, now have their US subsidiaries run partly by Canadians who are used to the North American market and form ideal interpreters between Europeans and the Americans. This use of Canada as a base, especially for exporting to the US, is likely to be a permanent feature of the industrial scene. So some of the capital invested by Europeans there ought to count towards the total of European money investing in the American market.

The logical alternative to Canada is a Southern state as near as possible to the North (which is why Virginia and North Carolina, the closest, have been so successful in their efforts).

Not that the newcomers are always logical. One German electronics manufacturer was trying to sell his products for space uses and went for advice to the Department of Commerce in Washington—which has a special office devoted to encouraging foreign direct investment in the US. His first instinct was to put his factory as near as possible to the launching pads at Cape Kennedy in Florida. Because, he reasoned, his products were going to be used in the rockets fired from Cape Kennedy, the orders would naturally be forthcoming there. The Department of Commerce gently dissuaded him from this idea; they analysed the location of the headquarters of the companies to which he was selling as a guide to where he should put his plant, and found that he should go anywhere near a line drawn from New York to Chicago. The German is now selling successfully to the Americans; his factory is on the outskirts of Philadelphia, miles away from the logical area. But his brother-in-law lived there.

The Southern states in fact face considerable competition in their search for investors. For every state has its own development organisation designed to attract new industrial investors and there is a natural inclination for most of the states east of the Mississippi to look towards Europe as well as to native companies; even the New England states, which usually look to Canada for new jobs, sent a mission to Europe to find new investors in early 1971. Europe seems altogether too far away to be a source of capital for states between the Mississippi and the Rockies. And to West Coast states the potential foreign investor tends to mean the Japanese who seem far less attractive than Europeans. The state of Washington did a study in 1970 on whether it should make an effort to attract foreign investment. The study group, which included local bankers, businessmen and academics, concentrated on the Japanese—who had recently bought three large grain elevators in the state. The study group was confronted, as they put it, by the combined weight of Japanese business and industry, what they called "Japan Incorporated", and by the very considerable protection afforded by the Japanese themselves against foreign investment. So they worried about the possibility of the wrong type of investment, and were far more cautious in their attitude than anybody on the East Coast, where most of the states seemed to try and outbid each other in order to attract the foreigners— but then they are concentrating on Europe and not on Japan.

This spirit of competitive welcome is a vital one for any company. A *Fortune* survey showed that the attitude of the host community was the single most vital factor in the location of new plants. It is particularly important for a European company making its first investment in the US, and needing help and relatively impartial advice and the psychological assurance that it has a friend in this large strange land. On the other side of the coin, many states impose bans on foreign-owned institutions which may prove embarrassing to future Federal governments. A number forbid foreign participation in the insurance and alcoholic drinks businesses. More importantly—and this is presumably a relic from the days when the Americans were afraid of domination by European financiers—all states except New York, California, and Massachusetts now forbid foreign-owned bank branches. American banks are now active—and relatively unrestricted—in Europe. And this one-sided state of affairs could in the future prove embarrassing with the Europeans who always find it difficult to believe that the Federal government's powers over the individual states are relatively limited.

As with restrictions, so with positive efforts, the base is the individual state and not the Federal Government. The pioneer, way back in the late 1950's, was in fact Luther Hodges, then Governor of North Carolina. In 1959 he sent the first industrial mission to Europe to try and attract investment. And it was only when he moved to Washington as Secretary of Commerce in President Kennedy's cabinet that his Department started the "Invest in the USA" programme as one answer to the then-emerging American balance of payments problem.

Even now the Department of Commerce only acts as a ringmaster to try to co-ordinate the states' individual efforts. Although there is a special attaché at the American Embassy in

Paris helping such investment, three states have offices in Brussels arguing in favour of their particular patch; in 1970 eighteen states were due to send missions to Europe to attract such investment. At least one of these missions came to Europe completely independently of the Federal government which has to fight hard to make sure that the others do not degenerate into junkets for local politicians. Recently, in fact, there has been some tightening upon these missions, and wives are no longer allowed on them.

These missions inevitably overlap in their appeals. For there are likely to be only a limited number of possible investors in any country, especially as the states all tend to be looking for the same sort of companies, fast-growing ones in machinery and electrical engineering. Yet the missions claim some impressive success ratios. These are expressed in terms of "hot" or short-range prospects and longer-range hopefuls. Up to a fifth of the calls made by one mission (which may be anything from fifty to two hundred) are counted as hot. There is obviously a high drop-out rate and an element of double counting because of companies which express great interest to two or more states. Yet the numbers are startling when contrasted with the total of less than 300 European companies which had invested in manufacturing facilities in the US by 1969; and the longer-term effects of the states' crusading efforts must be to make the US market much closer and more attainable a target than it had previously seemed to thousands of companies all over Europe. For all the missions emphasise that they do not expect imme-diate results and are treating their efforts as part of a continuing campaign.

These missions are now going further afield. The one which North Carolina sent over late in 1970, the fifth in a decade, swept through six countries: West Germany, England, Switzer-land, France, Holland and—it was the first mission to venture there—Austria as well. North Carolina, which ten years ago was looking for any company it could get, now feels it can be choosy, and is happy with smaller companies since it finds that the most intractable problems of unemployment lie in smaller communities where even a factory of 200 people would be welcome. This idea of spreading your welcome as wide as possible is echoed by another experienced specialist, Dick Tukey of Spartanburg in South Carolina, who says he would prefer "fifty companies, each providing a hundred jobs, rather than one providing five thousand".

But not all the effort is made by Southern states. Two of the three states with offices in Brussels, New York and Illinois, are not Southern at all (Virginia is the only Southern state represented). Two of these offices grew out of an earlier concern with promoting exports. But Virginia, which only started in 1968, began with the double job of encouraging exports from Virginia and direct investment into the state. Other states are less keen on such offices; North Carolina considers them a waste of money and does not even have one in Washington. The problems of such expenditure were highlighted in late 1970 when a new governor, anxious to save money, closed the office which Ohio had previously maintained in Brussels.

All the states have a bewildering variety of local inducements to offer. They will all carry out feasibility studies for the potential investor (or ask a local university to do so). Most will give all the information required by a company thinking of moving to a particular area. The complexity is such that Ohio's development department advertises a "one-stop service" to supply information on, among other things: financing, taxes, transportation, markets, labour supply, production material, sites and buildings, community plans and living conditions, education, utilities, water and sanitary facilities, topography, soil and climate, laws and regulations, and research and development. And any new investor needs a local guide to the maze of financial help alone obtainable through relief from Federal, state and local taxes (all of them assessed separately), the special depreciation allowances available and loans and grants from a bewildering variety of sources. The Federal government provides up to 65 per cent of the capital required in development areas through Economic Development Administration loans, and further help from the Small Business Administration and Small Business Investment Companies, as well as the Economic Opportunity Act for the long-term unemployed.

Then there is the labyrinth of local finance. A typical, but by no means lavish, state is Illinois*. Besides advertising itself, for unfathomable reasons, as the Tall State, and, for obvious ones, as "the market center of the nation", Illinois lists sources of credit and funds and guarantees as varied as the state's development authority, industrial buildings revenue bonds, local industrial development corporations, banks and insurance companies. It omitted the railways and the promoters of industrial parks and estates, always ready with friendly neighbourhood finance.

The biggest financial inducements to invest are available in Puerto Rico with exemption from Federal and local taxes, flexible depreciation and a powerful local economic development organisation. This help is so appetising that several of the twenty-five foreign firms investing on the island are owned by the normally reluctant Japanese, who think of it as more as an underdeveloped country than as part of the US. Their investments include a 1,200-room $50 million hotel, a plywood factory and a relatively historic plant, owned by Matsushita, and started in 1965 to build Panasonic radios. Puerto Rico also contains one of the most astonishing success stories among recent investments, Schulte and Dieckhoff, which, attracted by the labour costing a fifth less than on the mainland, was employing 5,000 Puerto Ricans making panti-hose in eight factories within eighteen months of starting up.

Panti-hose and transistor radios are products which do not involve heavy transport costs. Companies fabricating bulky machinery or goods consumed in large quantities, like Demag with its cranes and Foseco with its lining materials, have to be near their markets, an advantage to states like New York, Illinois and Ohio in the heartland of the American industrial scene. To offset their reputation for labour shortages and costs,

* Its constitution forbids the tax concessions to new industry, popular elsewhere, because established concerns would then be forced indirectly to subsidise newcomers who could well be competitors.

these states can provide other inducements besides their convenience for the market. New York makes the case that it is a state full of old industries and therefore needs a continuous flow of new ones. This is a point not generally exploited by European regions like the West Riding of Yorkshire which are not depressed by the normal criteria of income or unemployment but nevertheless require a shot in the arm from new industry. The decentralised American political system provides a boost to such "grey areas" more easily than is possible in centralised European countries where the national development effort is naturally concentrated on the worst areas.

When the New York State development people were told by a local bank that Dexion, a British company which makes slotted angle racks for storage purposes, and which already had a warehouse and sales office in New York, was looking for somewhere to build a factory for its products, they were able to guide Dexion to a site in a new industrial park which satisfied both its main criteria: it was near the market and had an adequate supply of labour. And the state was also able to supply the money through a loan granted by the New York job development organisation.

The Southern states, whatever their local advantages, have to match the financial inducements offered elsewhere, though no state will ever admit that it has outbid another on mere financial terms. One German company, which finally settled in Virginia, said that every other state it had investigated had offered either 90 per cent or 100 per cent financing, in most cases by guaranteeing mortgages or loans from financial institutions like banks or insurance companies. At the time, the going rate for medium- or long-term capital was so high that it would have made the project "prohibitively expensive". So the company arranged a deal with a local group developing a particular area for industry, which covered the land and the complete building on very generous terms—1 per cent under the "prime rate", itself the rate normally charged to the very biggest businesses, for a twenty-year loan. And Dunlop, in moving to Huntsville in Alabama, a town suffering from the decline of the formerly booming space business, was able to take advantage of an Industrial Revenue Bond. So at a time of tight, expensive money, Dunlop got a twenty-four-year, 6¼ per cent loan.

To big companies secure in their international credit ratings, these local financial boosts can be useful, but not as critical as when smaller concerns are choosing a site. For them an American investment is always a major step; and most European companies, apart from the very biggest, are still totally unaware of the very wide variety of financial sources in the US anxious to provide money. But even more important can be an adequate supply of trained labour. A German company in Virginia put very well the feelings of many companies when its spokesman said: "Almost every other state claimed to have more suitable skilled labour available, but we believe that really skilled labour is not available in any location and that a certain amount of training or retraining has to be faced. Yet, due to the nearness of large metal-working industries such as the Newport News shipyards with 23,000 employees, we feel that we have a good base and are not forced to introduce metal-working industry as such in the area we are settling in." A more direct paraphrase would read— look: there are skills and skills; we know we're going to have to teach new employees our ways, but at least the people won't just be peasants but men who've been bashing metal for some time. And we won't, thank God, be pioneers.

Europeans who do not want to burden themselves with too much training can rely on the states to provide technical and vocational schools to match their needs. New investors may be able to organise markets, sites, finance for themselves, but none can provide the labour; the states recognise that, as North Carolina puts it, "if you're going to provide jobs for our people we must provide qualified people for the jobs". For in most cases the right labour force is the key to new industrial development.

Of course sometimes there is one factor so overwhelmingly important that no amount of persuasion will work. When the Intalco consortium, including Pechiney, was engaged on a two-year search for a site for its aluminium smelter, the New York

State authorities went to great lengths to lure them on—efforts which included lending the consortium an aircraft for reconnaissance purposes. But to no avail: in aluminium by far the most important factor is the cost of the vast amounts of electricity consumed. And New York could not compete with the cheap hydro-electric power available on the West Coast.

In most cases, however, the reasons for moving to a particular site are less simple. Before ICI committed $50 million to building a plant to make polyester film at Hopewell in Virginia, it had investigated eighty-five sites all along the coast from Florida to New Jersey. It finally pitched on Hopewell "the chemical capital of the South", because it offered the best average on factors which included low construction, labour and tax costs as well as co-operation from Virginia for training employees through the "Community college system". This mixture of labour cost, deep water and training schemes is a potent one as far as European companies are concerned.

For all the apparent variety of motives which lead companies to invest in the South, ranging from the deep water in Virginia to the climate (as one company put it, "we Germans are always looking for sunshine and Virginia offers a lot of that"), the underlying attraction of the South remains the fundamental capitalist one that labour is not only available, it is cheaper and less unionised than in most alternative areas.

This fact is made extremely clear by the states themselves in their promotional literature—and not just the Southern ones. Illinois puts forward as an advantage "the low time-loss from strikes". But it cannot compete on this score with the Southerners:

> There is an ample supply of labor in Virginia . . . it is important to note that only 15·5 per cent of non-agricultural employees belong to unions. Important too is the fact that the laws in Virginia prohibit a closed or union shop which means that no worker can be forced to join a union. So, basically, Virginia's right-to-work law guarantees the individual's right to exercise his own prerogative. Of the

fifty states, only nineteen have this law and Virginia is the
northernmost state on the Eastern seaboard which has
enacted it.

North Carolina competes with Virginia by saying that "the rate
of unionisation in North Carolina is second lowest in the USA
and virtually all segments of the population support the right-
to-work law now in force ... work stoppages in North Carolina
resulting from strikes are the lowest in the USA. Labour turnover and absenteeism is also low".

The absence of unions and the consequent reduction in the
risk of strikes are very important to German and Swiss companies and one state is sometimes prepared to assure prospective
employers that there isn't "a union within fifty miles" of a
proposed site. Equally crucial is the ability to choose employees
from as many applicants as possible—which can help states
trying to spread their new industries over a large number of
deserving cases.

Even when a new plant is unionised, as Dunlop's is at
Huntsville, the union involved grows with the factory and lacks
the encrusted attitudes found in older factories. But the general
absence of unions could well vitiate much of the good work now
being done in the South. For industrialisation involves a slow
erosion of segregation in economic opportunities, partly because
the characteristic racialism of so many "hard hat" blue-collar
white workers tends to be found in the skilled jobs in older
industries like plumbing and construction work. In South
Carolina the vocational training schools were the first edu-
cational institutions to be integrated in the state. The job
opportunities are in new industries without a racial tradition,
and a high proportion of the unemployed are coloured, so
willy-nilly the newcomers are being pitched into a social,
economic and industrial scene at a time of maximum turmoil
and change.

But unionism will inevitably come to the South, indeed the
American unions are making strenuous efforts there already.
As one state put it bluntly: "A black will organise into a

bargaining unit much faster than a white and employers don't like this." This problem—of attempted unionism and employer resentment at black solidarity—will undoubtedly affect the Europeans, many of whom have come to the South to escape from unions and are less equipped to cope than large American companies (they tend to be as naïvely anti-union as the average Southern firm).

The crunch may not come: instead of one dramatic confrontation there could be a series of local deals. Already one governor, the liberal Republican Linwood Holton of Virginia, is adamantly clear that unionism is inevitable, at least in large factories, and that his officials should not emphasise the absence of unions in their sales pitch to foreign companies. For the overwhelming impression given by the more successful investors is how far it is possible to treat the United States as an infinite number of small localities, one of which can easily become home from home to a European company. This is vividly illustrated by one of the most remarkable single phenomena in the whole invasion, the way in which a medium-sized town, Spartanburg in South Carolina, has become the host for more than a dozen foreign companies whose executives have influenced their surroundings enough to ensure that there is a larger range of delicatessen-type foods available in the supermarkets than in most other towns of around 100,000 inhabitants.

Spartanburg is a natural centre for any industrialist supplying the major part of the American textile industry, which lies within easy reach. The town is in the heart of the Piedmont area, which stretches down the south-eastern slopes of the Appalachian Mountains for several hundred miles and stands at the crucial junction of two major motorways, one along the foothills, the other coming up from the coast.

But for twenty years Spartanburg has also had the benefit of a remarkably far-sighted spokesman, Dick Tukey, at the Chamber of Commerce. A large, red-faced, amiable extrovert in the main-stream tradition of the American booster, Tukey was in fact a far-sighted enough pioneer to realise that foreign companies provided one of the best sources of potential employment for this area. So now he has the flags of half a dozen European countries on his desk and will run the appropriate one up the Chamber of Commerce's flagpole when someone from home visits one of the several hundred Swiss and German businessmen in the town. In return, his European friends give him cigars from Austria, as well as "true Cubanos", the real Havanas the Americans cannot buy because of their boycott of Cuba.

It was the salesman Tukey, not the hail-fellow-well-met cigar-lover, who in 1965 persuaded the German Hoechst company and its then partner in Hystron Fibers, Hercules Powder, to come to Spartanburg. As soon as he heard that they were looking for a site in the area—which already had one major fibre company with a European interest, Fiber Industries at Greenville down the road, with its $37\frac{1}{2}$ per cent ICI shareholding—he set to work. And it took him only twenty-six days to get Hystron signed up in a project which is now worth over $100 million, and is the biggest single overseas investment made by the German company—as well as Spartanburg's largest single employer.

But Hystron was an exception to Tukey's normal target, specialised textile machinery companies. For these he offered no special inducement, except his own enthusiasm. But when a company is interested he bothers about every detail, even arranging the real estate for them, and reckons that his "job isn't done 'til they're making profits". The close-knit world of specialised textile machinery, a world whose home is in Germany, Austria and German-speaking Switzerland, has responded eagerly to Tukey's initiative. New arrivals now come through word-of-mouth recommendations from earlier investors who are enthusiastic with their praises. The companies involved, Sulzer, Menzel and Kusters, Scharer and Reiter, Stibbe and Theiler, are mostly unknown outside their own field. But in it they have world reputations. In fact Tukey has taken a leaf out of the Europeans' book. They specialise in one product or market: Tukey has concentrated on attracting one particular industry which was especially suitable because the Europeans had such a strong position in it. Tukey now makes regular trips once or

twice a year to Europe to see old friends and new. Two years
before the exhibition was due he had booked a stand at the 1971
International Textile Machinery Association's triennial bean-
feast. In fact none of the individual European investors in
Spartanburg (apart from Hoechst) is very large. Many of them,
like Brown Boveri in electrical engineering, are being extremely
cautious in their investment plans. The best known, Sulzer, is in
fact unwilling even to assemble its products in Spartanburg,
preferring to rely entirely on imported machines. Yet merely
servicing and selling the 5,000 weaving machines Sulzer has
sold in the last decade has entailed an investment of $750,000.

Other companies in Spartanburg are gradually moving from
locally owned agencies to assembly shops owned by the European companies. They fabricate bulky, low-cost components
like steel sheet frames; and companies worried about service and
the unfamiliar appearance of European controls are soothed by
the use of American-made instruments. In any case the American product tends to be more reliable and cheaper in this sort of
mass-produced item, while the knitting machinery, the complicated monsters which finish and dye carpets, and so on, are
still made in Europe.

Part of the care that Tukey and his colleagues take with
foreigners, in what they call their "international complex",
includes special classes in English for the wives and children of
executives. These tend to be very enthusiastic about Spartanburg even though a lot of them start by "clinging together over
the weekends". But it is odd to hear a solid Swiss executive
waxing lyrical about the place. One told me at great length of
how the town had the two best brass bands in the state, how the
one from the high school won the "Cherry Blossom" competition
in Washington, and how the town built a special campus to keep
its nursing school because Federal aid was available only for
such schools when they were linked to a university.

Some of the reasons given rather contradict general European
ideas about the US. "Maids," said one Swiss, "are available
very cheaply, and domestic help is no problem." The same man
made the very important point (which would not strike an

Englishman) that one of the principal luxuries of the American way of life to Europeans who were used to the idea of living in relatively small and crowded flats, is that in the United States it is possible for most executives to live in a house.

CHAPTER 9

PEOPLE, MORES, MONEY

The American prefers to work with the limits of
a precise timetable, but within the framework of
this timetable his productivity is at least as good
as that of a Frenchman.
—Spokesman for a French company

EVEN in Spartanburg, where normally stuffy German executives are quite prepared "to roll up their sleeves like Americans"
some people "never quite learn the language" and the culture
shock for newcomers, especially those whose first language
is not English, is considerable. "The first year things are too
different," says Tukey. "They have to shift priorities a little
bit." But, he concludes, after a few years they really like it and
most Europeans wanted to renew their contracts when the time
came, usually after three years.

This pattern, of early problems followed by a later content-
ment, is a recurring one. It even applies to French executives
whose life style at home would perhaps be more different from
the American than that of any other nationality. Pechiney
added that postings to the US were now considered so worth
while that there were more executives than there were jobs
available. This is a general feature which has much to do with
the place occupied by the American subsidiary in a European
group set-up. It tends to be concerned with the most glamorous
products and have the biggest potential: exactly the sort of
framework for a keen young executive, anxious to be noticed

by head office, yet wanting more freedom and a better chance to show his paces than he can get in a staff job at home.

Since American business practice tends to be, to European eyes, more formalised and better structured, Europeans can give responsibility younger and earlier in a man's career than would happen at home. Because of the framework of budgetary and managerial controls in an American company the risks involved in promoting somebody are considered much less than they would be in Europe.

The contrast to the habits of American companies abroad could not be more complete. Many of these subsidiaries were treated as simply convenient backwaters for the less successful. An outpost, however fast-growing, was not the sort of place to which keen young men wanted to be sent. This situation has changed over the past few years as the foreign subsidiaries have grown in size and importance. Even so, they tend to form a world of their own. General Motors has a corps of two or three hundred Americans who occupy most of the top positions in the overseas subsidiaries. But they are a separate group from the management of the company's domestic operations. Only a few exceptional companies like Ford have an open exchange of executives combined with some high-powered, high-flying men in foreign subsidiaries. The international division is still not a natural way to the top in American companies, and the choice of a chief executive in overseas-operating companies is normally a routine one.

For the Europeans, by contrast, the choice of a chief executive is much more difficult. For one thing, it is by far the most important instrument of control available to a parent company, and the relationship with the man chosen is of crucial importance. Because a company in the US is regarded as unique the parent has to exercise a more delicate touch than it would with more ordinary foreign subsidiaries.

The choice of the initial chief executive is often comparatively simple since the head of an existing sales organisation can be promoted. Or, as is the case with Bowater, Canadian management can be transferred across the border. It is the subsequent appointments that are crucial; in the case of Philips, the appointment of a group executive from outside the US company marked a clear change from the previously total independence of the American company. In the case of BAT a top-level appointment soon after the war changed the whole nature of the company for the better; at the same time Unilever made two successive appointments which haunted the company for twenty years. Even Shell had difficulties in the late 1960's. Pechiney's problems with two successive over-dependent chief executives shows up another complication—and one which is vastly increased when, as with Pechiney and Howmet, the subsidiary is quoted and has a substantial local minority shareholding.

At its worst, the independence shown by the head of a US subsidiary can completely negate the point of having a company there at all—witness the history of one company recorded in Lawrence Franko's thorough survey:

"Our American subsidiary's president communicates with us three months after anything important has happened—if he communicates with us at all. He also insists that everything goes through him, personally, if and when we need to transfer marketing or technical information in either direction across the Atlantic. How can we take advantage of the fact that 40 per cent of the world market and 60 per cent of the innovation in our industry occurs first in the US with this kind of set-up?"

Franko discovered just how unsatisfactory were three of the four ways by which European companies tried to tie their US subsidiaries into the total group organisation: The simple "mother-daughter" relationship, and delegating responsibility either on the basis of product groups or geographical areas. The basic problem is how to exert a continuing control by the parent without undue interference; how to ensure an effective feedback of information from the subsidiary; and—because the US subsidiary is so much more important than any other— how to generate a suitable enthusiasm at head office. Franko found that a senior director responsible for the US could often perform the right mixture of duties: "ambassador at court" to explain American peculiarities; transmitter of the latest US developments which could affect the rest of the group (together with the authority to make sure they are not ignored); and knowledgeable, tough but not petty or detailed, guidance of the subsidiary. But he also found that Europeans suffer more than American groups, because they are less ready to adapt their organisational structure to cope with changing corporate circumstances.

Within the subsidiary itself, there are fewer complications. Companies usually face a shortage when trying to appoint executives overseas; in most countries there is very little local managerial talent and a dearth of able people at the head office who want a job away from the centre of power. For the Europeans in the US the situation is completely different; their own executives are keen, and there is ample local talent.

Where its own people are concerned the biggest problem can be not to induce them to go, but to get them to come home when they have completed a normal tour of duty, especially when the local subsidiary is important and fast-growing and the headquarters is in a company town or unattractive backwater. Adding to the competition for the limited number of jobs available for expatriates is the fact that once the company —especially one in a high technology industry—is established in the United States, a sort of "reverse brain-drain effect" is created, in the words of a man from Elliott-Automation. Europeans who, frustrated for lack of opportunity at home, look for jobs with the company, hope to get the best of both worlds—the security of working for a European company with the excitement and high salary available in the United States.

It is relatively easy for Europeans in the United States to settle into a local community, for they are extremely well-placed to take advantage of American social and cultural snobbery. In many conformist middle-class circles there is a cachet attached to the words "imported" or "European" whether they refer to wine, nannies, dinner guests or the next president of the country club.

Local eminence ranges from Commander Edward Whitehead, with his well-photographed Country Club life, to Gian-Luigi Gabetti. When he ran Olivetti-Underwood, he was on the board of the Museum of Modern Art and the Metropolitan Opera in New York. But he may be an exception; his company is now so much a part of the American scene that at least one foreign student at the Harvard Business School has been sent to study Olivetti-Underwood as a typically American concern—even though it is 100 per cent owned by the Italians. Even less acclimatised companies try to integrate managers and their families into their local community. When Mitsubishi took over its former licensee's plant in Texas some form of culture shock could have been expected. But Mitsubishi softened the blow by taking on everybody at the same salary and with the same title. The effort to accommodate themselves to local conditions went further, as *Business Week* recorded:

> The President of Mitsubishi Aircraft International, UCLA educated Hacisaburo Shima, 56, uses just the initial of his first name to spare Texas drawls. And the small colony of ten Japanese does not neglect community relations. Recently, they sponsored a Mitsubishi Golf Tournament at the local Country Club and H. Shima's unorthodox stroke won him second place.

It used to be very difficult for the Europeans to hire or retain executives of any calibre. Many, like Spaght's professors, suspected that local recruits could not achieve any position of any real authority within a foreign-owned company. British insurance companies were not alone in underpaying executives by American standards because otherwise they would have been ludicrously overpaid when compared with Europeans at home.

All this has now changed: I found no one who had any difficulty in hiring good local management. Head hunters, as ICI pointed out, are readily available to choose the right men. The managers themselves are far more used to the idea of job mobility than their European equivalents and are often rather

eager to work for European companies which tend to be growing faster than local concerns.

The Europeans are also more flexible in their idea of individual career opportunities than Americans who often prac-
tise a rather rigid specialisation among their staffs. Barclays
DCO, whose growing business in California is one of the very
few European-owned banks outside New York City (and one of
the few European-owned businesses on the West Coast), finds
that American executives who have previously been restricted
to one banking specialty enjoy, as Barclays puts it, "being
changed into all-round bankers".

In most cases, however, American executives are hired not
for all-round jobs but for specialised ones. They can even bring
a bonus of goodwill with them. Before the war, Shell's success
in the aviation fuel market was greatly boosted by the employment of the late Jimmy Doolittle, then already a heroic figure
in the aviation world. And more recently, when ICI was looking
for a chemical engineer to run their new polyester film plant
in Virginia, they were lucky to find a local man who had not
only had experience of getting chemical plants in the South
working properly, but was a local hero to boot (literally—he
was one of the very few all-American footballers ever produced
by Virginia).

The problem of integrating American executives into a
European-owned set-up seems fairly minimal. New employees
tend to accept a company as they find it. Take-overs create
inevitable tensions, but cases like those of Pechiney and Howmet
are rare; for the companies being taken over tend to be either
(like Libby) noticeably failing; or (like many of the businesses
acquired by Philips since the war and by the European chemical
companies more recently) they are one-man or family companies where the family wants to get out or the man wants to
retire. Wyandotte Chemicals, taken over by BASF in 1969, had
a poor profit record; in addition the controlling shareholders,
the heirs of Captain Ford the founder, were anxious to sell out.
Even so BASF has retained Wyandotte's former managing
director, Robert C. Semple, as at least the nominal head of its

entire US operations. To BASF—echoing many Europeans—
the point of this was clear: "If you are known as people who, if
you buy a company, you sack the management, you cannot buy
companies." This acceptance of the limitation of the bidder's
authority obviously can impede progress, and contrasts with
the necessary, if unfeeling, ruthlessness so often displayed by
Americans in Europe. In several cases recently (of which the
biggest was the take-over by British Petroleum of a great deal
of Sinclair Oil's marketing network in the North-East),
American corporations are selling off only a part of their
activities, and will retain any executive who does not fancy
being employed by foreigners.

These tend to be the exception in any set-up. All the European companies I came across seemed to know exactly how
many Europeans they had working for them, what jobs they
were doing, the reason for their presence and how long a
European would hold a particular job. In other words, Europeans tended to be treated as specialists, consultants, and
advisers rather than straightforward line managers—a guarantee that the transition to Americanisation will be smooth.

This lack of stress extends to the relationship between the
European-owned company and its local suppliers and customers. As Elliott-Automation puts it, "at the top level top
people don't worry who owns what—but who commits for the
company". Americans assume that any company with a
physical base in the country and local executives is by definition an American company unless it is clear that the important
decisions are being made elsewhere.

It is in fact rather easier for the Americans to become
accustomed to dealing with the Europeans than it is for Europeans to get used to American conditions: although there are
exceptions even to this. When I asked a senior man from
Barclays DCO whether he had not found it rather difficult
starting a branch in the alien environment of California, he
said, no, not really, but then the last branch he had opened had
been in Ethiopia. And certainly for companies like Barclays
(and British-American Tobacco) which are used to the control

of subsidiaries in a variety of sensitive countries, American peculiarities must seem fairly negligible.

Yet the Americans have their quirks and quiddities. It is impossible, for instance, for Europeans to grow accustomed to the peculiarly American notion that no business transaction can be even contemplated without the presence of innumerable lawyers who form a sort of palace guard round any important executive. This phalanx, of course, is to deal with the corporate law-suit, that normal instrument of US business life, which is so alien to European eyes. As one British executive told Franko "receiving $100 million law suits (anti-trust, patent infringement, and what have you) in the mail every day took some getting used to."

Another worry is how to convey the information necessary to control a subsidiary: sometimes the sheer peculiarity of the US market cannot be conveyed; or (as we saw in Chapter 5 over the merger of CIBA and Geigy) the problem may be to persuade a non-American company that an American government agency (in this case anti-trust) has any authority over it. A more regular and everyday problem can be how best to transfer the true financial statistics of a business. "Unsystematic transfer of information surely adds to the already inherent difficulties of communicating between European parent and US subsidiary", says Franko and he quotes one cry of despair:

"Every year we send a copy of our one-year budget and five-year plan to our European parent. The format and context of these documents is completely determined by us. We're not really sure if anyone at headquarters even really does anything with these budgets and plans. We almost never receive any comments or questions about them."

One Swiss company draws up two sets of accounts. Every month trading figures presented à l'Americaine are sent back home; but every quarter another set is drawn up on the Swiss model for inclusion in the parent company's actual accounts— though these are never used by the subsidiary at all.

Even more difficult for everyone to accept is the unrelenting hard work imposed on any company in the United States by the competitiveness of the market, and the intolerance towards any slip in delivery date, specification, or pricing. Courtaulds summed up the position very well by saying that the Americans "don't object to others coming but there's competition every minute of the day."

Another businessman told Franko how the competition was "quite happily ruthless" and all the companies Franko interviewed emphasised the sheer speed of response of American businesses. The true fascination of the US for Europeans lies in this combination of knife-edge competition and the sheer opportunity. In the words of Etienne Junod of Roche, "In the US market if you can combine a good philosophy of marketing with a good product it goes whffffft."

In some respects, like the fragmentation of business, American conditions make it much easier for the European newcomer. So does the American willingness to try something new. "Europeans," said one expert, "are horrified at the idea of cold-calling", which the Americans actually enjoy (though Europeans tend to mistake mere friendliness for a desire to order a product). Cold-calling involves doing some research beforehand, and this need shows up the Europeans' biggest weakness, that they don't know their market well enough. John Rhodes of Booz Allen (who himself believes that European business is catching up on American) told the *Wall Street Journal* that the biggest European problem was not enough market research. "A lot of European companies think that because the US market is so big, all they have to do is put their wares out on a counter and wait behind a cash-register". This recurring complaint assumes that the American market is so different and important that European products will, in most cases, have to be adapted or even completely redesigned for it. So the assumption among American companies, that their products can be sold abroad off the shelf, is simply not viable.

Even when the adaptations have been made, and the specialised slot found, a company can suffer badly because it then forms part of an industry and shares that industry's problems. One of the few foreign investments on the West Coast was a British company which was forming aluminum with Boeing as its main customer. And when the aerospace industry plummeted in 1970 it was naturally caught. Howmet also suffered in the same recession, as did Plessey's merger partner, Alloys Unlimited, though Bestobell found a positive advantage in taking over an aircraft subcontractor when the industry was in the doldrums, for "if you wait till the time is right then everyone will be doing very nicely, thank you, and won't want to sell".

But in general, it is much easier for a company selling a consumer product to find a niche which will isolate it from an industry's troubles. The sales of Volkswagens have risen virtually every year since 1949 with the sales patten unaffected by the general fortunes of the American car industry. But if a company strays from a specialised path, or relies too much on a fashion product or follows the industry instead of leading it, then—as the story of the Capitol Records subsidiary of the British EMI group shows—it can end up with 'flu while the industry as a whole merely sneezes.

Capitol was a relatively well-established company as it was set up in 1942. After the war, even though it was 92 per cent owned by EMI, it behaved extremely independently. The EMI management only went to occasional board meetings and refrained from interference largely because of a fear it shared with Unilever, that if it meddled actively the anti-trust people would demand that their rules and regulations be applied to the parent company—which at that time was distributing the products of a number of American record companies outside the United States. Capitol flourished after the war and became the third largest record company in the US, a success based largely on EMI's repertoire of recordings, a sound enough speciality. Then in 1963 came the Beatles and the craze they induced for other British sounds: Capitol's sales jumped in three years from $55 million to $90 million; and profits, in this highly geared industry, more than quadrupled to $6·4 million.

The control from London, such as it was, proved inadequate to cope with the backwash of this success, a crisis deepened by attempted diversification and technical change. Capitol issued its shares on the American market to buy a company called Audio Devices to help with the change from records to taped music sold in cassettes—of which Capitol, like Philips, was a pioneer. The industry was also moving over from mono to stereophonic records. During this change, all the companies had to write off large sums on their stocks of mono records—and one company made a trading loss during the period.

Capitol was also following an industry trend by building up a record club, and, to add to EMI's problems, its American rivals had recently become far more aggressive and therefore unwilling to allow their records to be marketed by EMI in the rest of the world.

In the US itself everything went wrong. The club was more unprofitable than had been foreseen, Audio's management was unable to cope with the development EMI wanted; so in two years profits slumped back to their 1963 level—only now EMI had a smaller share ($72\frac{1}{2}$ per cent) of a larger and apparently less successful company. Capitol was then brought more firmly under EMI's control. New management was introduced, largely from rival record companies; Audio was reorganised; and the record club was merged with one owned, improbably but successfully, by the Longines Watch company. But even since then, the new management has had problems in coping with the very rapid changes in public taste—and the problem of selling records on a sale-or-return basis.

In part, the story of Capitol since 1967 is that of the orthodox reorganisation of a subsidiary whose troubles stem largely from a growth too fast for the management to cope with, at a time when the whole industry was suffering from the costs of a major technical change. But it includes elements which are peculiar to a subsidiary of a foreign company: the relative failure with a line of business—the record club—where the company was neither a pioneer nor a specialist; the way in which the crisis could become more serious than it would have

in an ordinary subsidiary with less competition and more
parental control; and the basic instability because Capitol's
sudden growth was essentially due to one product—the Beatles
—and that a fashionable one, compared with the older assets
—recordings which may have sold less spectacularly but which
at least provided a solid basis of earnings.

Curiously, the single factor that Capitol has not had to cope
with over the past decade is the one most frequently mentioned especially by British companies, as the most crucial in
their calculations, providing a ready excuse for not invading
at all: finance. The British, and indeed the French as well,
can claim that the existence of stringent exchange controls on
the export of capital for direct investment is a major deterrent.
The British rules are also designed to ensure that the outflow
involved will not interfere with exports—and they also cover
any contingent liability. So if a British company wants to issue
shares in order to take over a foreign company it has to make
sure that the foreign shareholders cannot sell the shares in the
British company for five years. For when foreign shareholders
sell to a British investor there is a loss of foreign exchange. The
rules assume that during the five years when the shares are
frozen the company will make enough profit out of the foreign
company to ensure that when the shares are unfrozen the
company is a big enough asset to offset any loss of foreign exchange. Similarly, British companies have problems when
guaranteeing loans to their subsidiaries in foreign currency
which would inevitably lead them to pay out in the event of
the new subsidiary's failure.

In fact, to obtain foreign exchange at the official exchange
rate for investment abroad, the company has to be able to
show the likelihood of so quick a profit that the money will
return within eighteen months. Even to get permission to buy
foreign currency for direct investment in the free market (and
for the dollar this amounts to a premium of up to 25 per cent)
the company has to prove a three-year pay-back period: both
criteria effectively exclude most manufacturing investments,
otherwise the company has to raise the necessary capital
abroad. These regulations are far less formidable than they

sound. In an enquiry conducted by the Industrial Policy Group, a loose association of fairly right-wing businessmen, it was found that no company in the group, which included most of the British companies with the biggest overseas investments, had ever had to abandon a major scheme because of the controls. As an official of the French Treasury told me admiringly in 1969, when Britain's economic prospects were grim and its international debts overwhelming, "your exchange controls are very intelligent, much more so than ours—but perhaps they are too intelligent"; so sophisticated that they let through any sensible plan even though the country could not afford it at the time. The Treasury and the Bank of England are sometimes prepared to allow schemes because they make financial sense even though other Ministries, which are more concerned with Britain's technical and export position, may be worried that future export prospects could be damaged.

The British exchange controls ensure that only schemes which have been solidly thought out and make industrial and financial sense can get through. As one British company put it: "You have to make the basic case for the Bank of England as you would for your own board." Yet any limitation turns out to be due not to the hostility of the exchange authorities, who rarely if ever reject a scheme, but to the unwillingness of British companies to produce proposals. In the US the host government also creates financial difficulties, many of which spring from its efforts to help its balance of payment problems by ensuring that as much capital as possible is imported and as little as possible exported. These are dealt with in Chapter 12 which covers all the dealings of the American government with the European influx.

The Europeans, however, have some powerful allies. Not only are the American states and local consortia anxious to guide and help finance the invaders, but the larger American banks are also very well aware that they have a promising source of business in assisting European companies to expand in the United States. And their detailed knowledge of the American scene gives them a considerable edge over their European competitors. This is a major change from the situation a few years ago when, according to the finance director of BASF Inc., even the biggest European company "had to take the picture of the European plant from the wall; go into the bank; and show them the picture, because they were completely unknown; and try to convince the bank in this way that they were somebody".

These banks have been prolific with ideas for helping foreign companies, the most useful of which as far as the British are concerned is that of "back-to-back" financing. This is a sort of swap arrangement born of the fact that both the British and American governments have been trying to contain the outflow of capital. It involves finding an American company in Britain and a British company in the United States, both of which need money abroad but have surplus funds at home. They are matched and they lend each other the money on their home ground. The trouble is there are too few British companies wanting to invest abroad—a further proof that it is not exchange control but managerial lethargy which inhibits a greater British effort.

Expanding sales generally involve direct investment; in the same way the expansion of direct investment beyond a certain point often requires some form of local issue of equity capital. In the past, there have been few such issues (just as there has been little direct investment). But now they are likely to multiply even though a considerable gulf may remain between different nationalities. To the Swiss, unused to the idea of telling the investing public anything, the requirements of the American government's Securities and Exchange Commission are the equivalent of a striptease, an unthinkable, unnecessary and even immoral requirement. The Swiss are also extremely unhappy about allowing foreign—particularly American—shareholders any substantial interest in any company they own. The Germans' investments are too recent for the attitudes to be clear yet. But to the Dutch and the English, more inured to the idea of exposing the delights of their corporate bodies to the public, the introduction of local shareholders appears a merely tactical decision without any moral overtones, though, even to British eyes, the SEC regulations seem decidedly tough.

Historically, those British and Dutch companies which have been prepared to go public have done rather better than others, mainly British, which have not (partly because they were not profitable enough to do so). The exceptions seem to prove the rule. Until its recent expansion, Brown & Williamson was too small to be worth floating: so far the right opportunity for take-over-by-flotation has not occurred. For Bowater, as we have seen, the problem is a strategic one which has nothing to do with the SEC. Most other British invaders with any desire for expansion have either gone public or are acting on the assumption that they will do so—in one case taking over American companies with shares, at the moment unquoted, with the promise that they will be marketable within a few months.

The major Swiss companies in the United States have not in the past suffered from the problems to which market quotation provides an answer—basically the narrowness of the credit base of any unquoted concern (and, apart from the special case of Roche and Elno Bobst, they have not suffered because executives had no stock options). The Swiss were in specialised chemical products and drugs, fast-growing sectors which need little capital and produce high profits. But this was an historical accident. The newest arrivals, especially the German chemical companies, are likely to find that continued growth in a capital-intensive industry will depend on raising very large sums in the American capital market, far greater than can be obtained without a quotation. At the same time, they are moving away from their previously secretive habits at home; so it is a fair bet that one or more of them will take the plunge of public ownership within a few years, though BASF is likely to copy the Americans by issuing the shares of the parent rather than the local subsidiary.

The desire for expansion still has to fight against a number of reasons why shares should not be issued. There can be a natural emotional feeling that since American companies have not issued the shares of their subsidiaries in Europe, there is no reason for Europeans to behave any better. European companies in the United States, especially those which have been established for some time and are therefore more likely to go public, are not generally thought of as foreign. So they have no reason to curry favour with the local public by issuing shares to them—a motive which can be quite important in the rest of the world. And although stock options are often thought of as an indispensable means of luring and retaining American executives, especially senior ones, the pressure to provide this particular incentive does not seem critical. The Swiss companies acknowledge the problem but overcome it by paying slightly over the going industry rate to compensate. And some companies, like Foseco, were quite definite that lack of a stock option scheme had never caused an executive to leave. Most important, the existence of minority shareholders prevents the parent company from treating the subsidiary merely as a pawn in a world-wide corporate game. It becomes much more difficult to change the management, and to arrange, through royalties, fees and inter-company transfer prices, for the group's profits to occur in the most convenient, low-tax countries. Because the issue means a weakening of central control, most American companies abroad try hard to avoid local shareholders.

The issue of part of the equity can involve a conscientious parent in far-reaching concessions to the subsidiary—as we saw in Chapter 4, Shell leans over backwards to be fair in its dealings over royalties and fees with its Shell Oil subsidiary. But another European oil group, the Belgian Petrofina, goes even further in its dealings with its 58 per cent-owned US subsidiary. It has arranged its tax structure to the simultaneous benefit of both its own shareholders and the locally-owned minority in US Petrofina: a wholly-owned subsidiary of the parent does the expensive work of prospecting for oil in the US (work in which the group has been relatively unsuccessful in recent years). The very generous tax allowances for this exploration go straight to the American Petrofina, so that its US minority shareholders get the tax relief involved without incurring any of the exploration expenditure on which it is based.

This behaviour represents fairly extreme generosity; but equity issues need not only be designed, like Petrofina's tax set-up, to appease local sentiment, or to satisfy local institutional investors who want a percentage of a company before they are prepared to lend it any more money. Recently, the Europeans in the US have discovered the use of an equity issue as an aggressive weapon: Beecham used it to provide funds to launch its new penicillin; EMI to take over a company; and, if and when Bowater, Brown & Williamson and Schweppes-Cadbury go public, they will have the same motive.

The most spectacular case so far has been the merger of British Petroleum's US interests—including its fabulous Alaskan oil discoveries—with Sohio. BP's chairman, Sir Eric Drake, explained the full financial reasoning involved, which encompassed virtually all the factors which could be found in such a situation:

> If we had gone it alone we would have been hard put to it, as a foreign concern, to find all the money over here. Nor could we have hoped to remit it all from the UK because of our balance of payments difficulties. But Sohio is a large concern, well known and highly respected in the States, and difficult though it may be for them, these particular problems don't arise. Secondly, your capital market here is highly sophisticated, and is not enthusiastic about putting loan capital, particularly for a foreign concern, without getting a share of the equity too. If we *had* been going it alone, we could hardly have given the American investor a share in the equity until our outfit over here had become a going concern, and this might not have been for five years or so. The deal with Sohio was, we thought, a neat way of letting the American investor have a share in the equity of BP's interests in the US *here and now*.

The BP-Sohio deal is the biggest, but the most constructive use of the American market so far has been made by Plessey group.

Plessey's founder, the late Sir Allan Clark, was himself an American,* and spent three months of every year in the States looking for new products in the electrical component field for his company in England. It was not until he took over Garrard, a leading specialist maker of record changers, however, that he actually had any business in the United States, and in the course of the 1960's Plessey built up sales there of $5 million. In the meantime Plessey had grown extremely strong technically in a number of electrical component and electronic fields and consequently wanted to expand in the United States. In February 1968, six years after Clark's death, his company, by now run by his son John, found a relatively small family aircraft company business called Airborne Accessories, whose owner, Leon Marantz, was anxious to sell. But he was worried that if he sold it for spot cash he would attract capital gains tax immediately; if, however, he took paper, he would delay and control the payment of the tax. Plessey had no cash in the US and Plessey Inc., its American subsidiary, was far too small to go public. So Airborne's owner took the $8·9 million which Plessey paid for his company in five-year notes. After that time Marantz was to take cash for one half of the stock and 16 per cent of Plessey Inc., which of course had been vastly increased in size by acquiring his company, for the other half—though even this was underwritten for cash in case things had gone wrong. Plessy finance the notes very cheaply by five-year loans to be paid out of the company's retained earnings.

But this takeover was merely a preliminary to a subsequent deal in January 1970, through which Plessey bought, for $188 million, Alloys Unlimited, a major company in electronic components. The problem was to find a type of security which would not involve any actual or potential loss to the British balance of payments, yet was acceptable to the shareholders of

---

* So were the founders of Burroughs Wellcome and Baker Perkins, both British companies with, historically, a large stake in the US.

Alloys Unlimited and to the American market. By then Plessey Inc. had sales of over $18 million and was already quoted, but was just not big enough to absorb Alloys. The parent company was and the Alloys people were sufficiently struck by Plessey to be willing to accept the "unknown paper" represented by the shares of the parent company. They were, in fact, a group of barely middle-aged entrepreneurs who had built up Alloys extremely fast in little more than a decade, helped by the research talents of a German-born scientist of Chinese extraction with the unusual name of Hamburg Tang. The Alloys people were impressed by what they described as the "throb and the hum" they detected in Plessey and as soon as they had seen some of Plessey's factories took the proposed merger very seriously. For some years they had realised the need to invest in Europe in order to follow the customers for their electronic components who had already done so. Plessey and Alloys fitted together very well; the combination was able to provide package deals in solid state electronics, aircraft hydraulics, communications equipment (especially in the growing business of linking computers to computers through telephone lines) and in equipment for mechanically sorting post. Plessey needed an American base in order to try to sell equipment to the post office in New York after an initial success using imported equipment in Columbus, Ohio.

Finding a common currency for a merger posed a number of awkward traps. A simple solution was found avoiding all of them by Eric Frye, Plessey's finance director—and an ex-Ford man. The owners of Alloys were allocated dollar shares in the whole Plessey group which were quite separate from the sterling shares. The dollar shares were suitable for quotation in New York but could not be sold to British shareholders, thereby removing the exchange risk. Because the two, theoretically equal, classes of shares were quoted on quite separate stock exchanges, a major problem was created because of the very sharp fluctuation not only in share values in London and New York, but in the relative attraction of shares quoted in different currencies. Plessey had the encouraging precedent of the Shell group, whose two holding companies, Royal Dutch and Shell Transport, are quoted in different currencies (the Dutch florin, and sterling). Although the shares have quoted at very different values in the past, especially when international investors were avoiding shares quoted in sterling, the company itself has not been affected.

In any case, Plessey's purchase turned almost immediately into a can of worms. Alloys' basic business went into its first downturn in the short history of micro-electronics, and, as a components supplier, suffered even worse than its customers, who obviously refrained from using outside suppliers as long as they could. Even worse, Alloys brought with it a number of unprofitable businesses. Plessey's response was ruthless: of the European invaders only Nestlé with Libby has behaved as toughly. Within 18 months 30 per cent of Alloys had been closed down or sold off—usually for less than it had cost. In the year after Plessey bought it, sales slumped from over $140 million to $65 million. Two of Alloys' three founders have gone.

Plessey is an unusual company: the toughness, speed of response and readiness to admit mistakes of its American founder still make it resemble an American rather than a European group. John Clark (now Sir John) claims that he has no doubt Alloys will go ahead. But Plessey has now set up an assembly plant in Southern California which is quite separate from Alloys. The whole story has been summed up as a "debacle"—and in the words of one board member, "A bit too much 'get in there' in our strategic thinking over Alloys, and a bit too much emphasis on the technical fit". For all the present—quite justified—breast-beating by Plessey about its Alloys venture (and even though it is clearly not going to be the vehicle for all its American interests), Plessey is likely to find—like that other aggressive, impulsive family-dominated group, Olivetti, which landed itself with a massive loss-maker—that the American experience will serve it in good stead when competing with American-owned groups in the future, despite its present lack of profitability.

CHAPTER 10

BRITISH PETROLEUM—PRESERVING THE LAST FRONTIER

> What I think is so good about what you've done
> is that you've done it without any money.
> —New York petrol dealer to BP executive.

To most British readers the European challenge in the US in the last few years is symbolised not by Plessey, or Capitol, or Philips, but by BP, by far the largest and most spectacular of the invaders. Its discovery of oil in Alaska in 1969; the almost simultaneous take-over, with a locally borrowed $400 million of some 8,500 service stations formerly belonging to Sinclair Oil; the merger of BP's enlarged interests in the US with Standard Oil (Ohio); the frustrations which still delay the construction of the vital pipeline across Alaska to an ice-free port: all three acts of this particular drama have been written up at far greater length (certainly in the British press) than the whole of the rest of the European challenge put together.

The attention has been well deserved. For the story of BP in America contains all the elements found in the invasion, the specialised skills, the use of local partners and of the market; and in BP's case the skills and the conditions were such that, by spending $30 million on looking for oil in Alaska, BP gained control over assets worth $2 billion. BP's interests alone will be several times greater than all the French and Italian investment in the US combined. Because it was so big and sudden and public, the story boosted British national pride. Because it involved the first commercial exploitation of Alaska, North America's last frontier, it brought a clash between an old dream —the gold-rush lure of fabulous mineral wealth in the frozen North—and a new awareness of the damage that could be done to the country, and to the people in it, through the exploitation of such wealth.

There was nothing in BP's post-war history to suggest that an invasion of the US on such a scale was either possible or likely. By the time BP had recovered from the shock of the confiscation of its Iranian oil interests in 1951 and their subsequent, but only partial, restoration, it was in no position to tackle the US market other than by selling to local companies its freely available supplies of cheap crude oil. And these sales were largely blocked by the imposition of strict quotas on imports of oil into the US at the end of the 1950's. So BP more or less gave up any hope of entering the American market while they were in force, unless it was fortunate enough to discover oil in the US. Indeed as recently as April 1967 a managing director of BP told the New York Society of Investment Analysts:

> At the risk of being impertinent I am going to dismiss the USA with only a few brisk sentences. In view of our other commitments our chances of finding capital to enter into your market in a significant way are not very great and as we see it at the moment our only opportunity of greater participation here would be if your government were to relax import controls over crude oil.

Virtually the only asset which BP in fact salvaged in the US from the 1950's was a strictly intangible one: Charles Spahr, then president, now chairman, of Sohio had been a potential customer for BP's crude oil and he and "Billie" Fraser (now Lord Strathalmond), a BP managing director, had become friendly. So, when BP, ten years later, was casting around for a suitable American partner, it was the most natural thing in the world for Fraser to make formal contact with Spahr.

While BP was prevented from using its natural assets in the

US (and was, like another giant British company ICI, concentrating its efforts in the 1960's on Europe rather in the US),
it was also learning the hard way some of the difficulties of the
North America market. BP found considerable problems in
developing its Canadian interests without a big splash, but rather
through the purchase of a small local oil-producing company and
the gradual build-up of a retail network. During some of the
crucial years the head of BP's interests in Canada was Alistair
Down, who, as a managing director and deputy chairman of
the parent company, played a large part in the strategy of BP's
subsequent entry into the US. BP's unprofitable years in Canada, spent trying to grow gently in a fiercely competitive
environment dominated by a few large companies, were not in
fact wasted since they provided an indication of what to avoid
in the US. Canadian experience also gave Down the benefit
of working with a local lawyer whom he had trained to think
in a European, rather than American way—to concentrate on a
few key issues rather than on a mass of detail.

At first sight, it was surprising that BP did not move more
gently into the US market. For, as we saw when discussing
Shell's story in the US, the US oil market, unlike similar
markets in the rest of the world, is not dominated by a few
large integrated companies, with cut-price firms operating in
the interstices. In theory any size of firm can make a living.
But because of BP's experiences in Canada, because of its overall
size and because, as the New York investment analysts were
told, its managerial and financial resources were fully stretched,
a gradual, patient, specialised operation would have been
pointless, and could not have taken advantage of BP's greatest
asset, its incomparable ability to find more oil than any other
major oil group.

This background makes it sound as though BP's discovery of
oil in Alaska were merely a lucky throw of the dice. But it was
not: BP had been prospecting nearby on and off for nearly a
decade, and it was only a matter of luck that the first discovery
was made by another company. Yet the New York analysts
were not being deceived. There was no guarantee that it would

be Alaska rather than any other of the dozen new prospects in the world which BP was investigating at the time which came up such a gusher, enough to provide BP with over five billion barrels of reserves, and thus, at one step, to give it over a tenth of all the reserves of crude oil in the country.

The BP story effectively started as recently as July 1968 when a medium-sized American oil company, Atlantic-Richfield (Arco), announced that with its partner Humble Oil it had made a major oil discovery near Prudhoe Bay on the North Slope of Alaska, under one of the most inhospitable landscapes on earth. This mass of tundra, with below it as much as 1000 feet of permanently frozen earth or "permafrost", is unbearably cold and windy during the everlasting gloom of winter, so cold that steel is liable to crack, so windy that men could not hear an aeroplane crash a few hundred yards away. In summer it melts, for a few weeks the gentle slope is a mass of flowers, and then turns into mud in which everything sticks solid.

Yet the discovery had an electrifying effect. "A big new oil strike is something Americans thought they would never experience again," said one BP man; the fact that the discovery was in the very furthest North did not detract from the furore. The excitement was not only industrial, it was political as well: without it the US had reserves of crude oil enough for only nine years' consumption, and discoveries were not keeping up with consumption in what the Alaskans call "the lower 48 states". So the Alaskan strike promised to delay the time when the Americans would have to rely, as does Europe, on Arab and Persian oil, and thus sacrifice the unique political freedom it retains in the Middle East because it is not as dependent as Europeans on the goodwill of Arabs and Persians. From the start, the Alaskan oil flowed so freely, and was of such a sweet, sulphur-free quality, that it would have been an economic proposition whatever market it was destined for. But because government protection ensured that crude oil fetches perhaps a third more in the US than it does in the rest of the world, the benefits of the discovery were multiplied into a bonanza—the restrictions added $1 a barrel to the value of any oil found.

The locals immediately grasped the fact that BP stood to benefit as much as Arco from the discovery and started buying the shares. BP had been plugging away further up the slope, but it had licences (bought for virtually nothing) in an arc all round the Arco discovery, and that winter it started drilling. Progress was slow—metal objects like spanners or the stems of the drills kept breaking in the cold and no one could hurry in such conditions; and although the well (the now famous Put River No 1) was directly between two existing discoveries, it had still not been proved when BP was given an unique opportunity to buy a ready-made network—for oil it was not yet quite sure it had discovered.

Atlantic Richfield, the other Alaskan pioneer, had taken advantage of its discovery to merge with the comparatively dozy but larger Sinclair Oil; to satisfy the anti-trust authorities it had to sell off 8,500 of Sinclair's service stations. At first it thought only 6,500 would have to be sold; these were in the North-East and were a thoroughly run-down chain, living down to Sinclair's unfortunate corporate symbol of a dinosaur. In none of the states did Sinclair have the 7 per cent of the retail petrol market required for a really satisfactory marketing operation. The stations were rarely decently located and the coverage was extremely thin. There is a story of one BP executive touring these stations by air; as they were landing at one sizeable town he noticed a Sinclair sign and pointed it out to the ex-Sinclair man with him who gently explained that he had now seen a full quarter of Sinclair's outlets in the town.

Nevertheless BP had to take on even such an unsatisfactory set-up because of its sheer size: the opportunity to buy such a network and on such favourable terms occurs only rarely. But there were some fairly stiff upper-lipped jokes at BP's London headquarters as the company agreed to commit the necessary $300 million—jokes mainly concentrated on the detached way in which BP's exploration chief, Monty Pennell, would break the truth if Put River turned out to be dry. The general consensus was that he would concentrate on the geological interest of the North Slope.

In fact all went well and, as the locals had suspected all along, BP's concession housed half the oil on the North Slope, giving BP, with one discovery, as much oil in the ground as the previous biggest find in the US, the East Texas field. In April 1969, a few weeks after the Sinclair purchase, Put River's promise was confirmed. And BP had another stroke of luck. The US anti-trust authorities required Arco to sell off a further 2,000 stations in the South-East which were far better than the original 6,500. And it helped, not hindered, BP that in the Atlantic-Sinclair merger the top Sinclair management elected not to stay with their service stations and left behind only the lower echelons. They, to BP's great relief, turned out, in many cases, to be abler than their superiors.

But BP could not rely just on Alaskan oil and the Sinclair stations. It needed more outlets even than Sinclair's 8,500 service stations—and some really good, marketing-oriented top management. By merging its US operations with Sohio later in 1969 it acquired both. As Sir Eric Drake, BP's chairman, told the Georgetown conference, presumably with BP's Canadian experience in mind:

> ... marketing here is not at all the same thing as marketing in BP's traditional marketing areas. If we *had* tried to go it alone over here, I'm sure our marketing people would have had many hard lessons to learn. But Sohio's reputation is on all sides admitted to be of the highest order, and under our deal with them, it is *their* marketers who will be developing the marketing assets we bought on the East Coast and then transferred to them.

BP also needed to link up with a profitable company. For one of the major advantages possessed by oil companies operating in the US is their ability to diminish their tax burden considerably through a variety of tax allowances, largely concentrated on money spent on exploration. But these allowances are of no use without profits against which to set them. Sohio could provide all three advantages, outlets, management and profits.

Sohio is the original Standard Oil Company, the very base of John D. Rockefeller's original monopoly (other Standard Oils are "of" somewhere like New Jersey or Indiana or California). In the past forty years—and especially in the last dozen while the present chairman Charles Spahr, a lean, taut engineer, has been in charge—Sohio has grown into a company unique in the world oil scene. Whereas other companies try to expand geographically to cover as much of the world as possible, and try also to integrate their own oil supplies, Sohio had stuck by its own state and continued to buy three-quarters of the oil it needed. Its fierce concentration—combined with ruthless weeding and if necessary physical pulling down of unproductive stations—gave it 30 per cent of the Ohio market, more than any other single company has in any other US state. Some of these markets are so fragmented that the leading company has not much more than 10 per cent. Only in the last ten years has it sallied out of Ohio, notably in western Pennsylvania—the Pennerie area containing Pittsburgh; such was its marketing skill that within a few years it was competing for first place.

The contrast with the stations BP had bought could not be greater: Sohio was concentrated, with brilliant marketing and none of the jobbers (middlemen) who are used by virtually all other US oil companies to sell in thinly populated areas; Sinclair's thin, sixteen-state sprawl of 8,500 stations was served mostly by jobbers. So it was not surprising that Sohio received over a quarter more revenue for every gallon it sold than did Sinclair-BP.

Yet Sohio needed BP: Spahr fully understood how the discovery of oil in Alaska had considerably speeded changes in the structure of the US oil industry, after which the industry would be far more integrated, and grow increasingly to resemble the rest of the world oil scene. In such a situation, Sohio, with strictly limited supplies of crude oil at home, and very little abroad, was looking for a partner exactly like BP—and would indeed, have approached BP had not Spahr's old friend Fraser at BP got his call in first.

Before BP was allowed to take an initial 25 per cent stake in Sohio, a percentage which would escalate into control if BP could deliver enough crude oil to Sohio by the mid-1970's, it had to run the gauntlet of anti-trust. By interfering, the government was in fact, merely taking back a proportion of what it had already given BP: through its protectionist policy it had transformed BP's Alaskan oil into a uniquely valuable asset; and anti-trust itself had given BP its entrée into the retail market by enabling it to buy the Sinclair stations. At the same time the anti-trust authorities had just stated they would investigate the proposed merger of any of the US's 200 largest corporations—a list on which Sohio figured at No. 131.

At first it seemed that anti-trust wanted to block the merger completely on the grounds that BP was a potential competitor to Sohio in or near its home market and so could have gone it alone; and thus the merger prevented possible competition in the future. This view was absurd, principally because it exaggerated BP's strength: its oil was in the Far West, its outlets in the East, and its resources far too strained to allow BP to get into the Mid-West in the foreseeable future without the Sohio merger.

This opposition jolted Spahr; it outraged BP's head office, which did nothing to discourage the considerable shock in European business circles at the blockage—in fact BP talked to other major European companies anxious to expand in the US, so as to enlist their support, as well as to the British government and press.

So Drake got down to negotiating with John Mitchell the Attorney-General—who very rarely involves himself in anti-trust questions. In fact (though not in theory) Drake had little choice, as he told the Georgetown conference

> There was another course open to us—to go ahead with the merger and let the Department challenge it in the courts. This would have been costly and would have meant years of uncertainty, during which we would not have known where we were. And in any case it would hardly

have been wise for a foreign concern like BP to advertise its entry into the States by immediately challenging the Administration in the courts.

BP's collaboration paid off after a very tense confrontation at which, as Drake described it to Paul Ferris of the *Observer*, "they tried to say 'we'll let the merger go through, but we consider it illegal'. So at any time within the next ten years they could have brought suit against us. Sounding purer than perhaps I am, I said, 'I will not take my company into what is an illegal act'." This stand was based on a slight misunderstanding of the word illegal. "To our minds," Drake said at Georgetown, "this meant that we were actually breaking the law (by going through with the merger) which isn't a thing a respectable concern such as BP likes to be told in the UK. To *your* minds all it meant was that what was *proposed* didn't as it stood conform with the law. This *is* rather different, because once you realise what it means, it is up to you to see that it *does* conform, and this is what we tried to do by going for and getting a consent decree."

Dealing with the anti-trust is a poker game. The department may never have intended to try and ban the merger at all, but merely to ensure that it led to greater competition in Ohio. In the end Sohio and BP were forced to agree to some harsh terms in the consent decree. By these, Sohio had to sell off, within a couple of years, stations selling 400 million gallons of fuel a year, cutting its share of the Ohio market to 20 per cent, to an oil company which has less than 2 per cent stake in Ohio, a condition which considerably diminishes the number of potential purchasers. It may also serve to reduce another effect of the decree; to enable BP-Sohio to compete more effectively elsewhere in the US by exchanging their Ohio stations for others in different states. There are few, if any, companies with stations available for exchange elsewhere which do not have 2 per cent of the Ohio market. Even so, American oil men will say, the settlement with BP was fair—and quicker than two US companies in the same situation would have obtained.

After all, the anti-trust authorities only finally agreed to the merger of Arco and Sinclair, which pre-dated BP and Sohio by a year, nearly a year after withdrawing opposition to BP's proposals.

The shock of anti-trust was short and sharp; the uncertainty over whether BP's oil could be transported out of Alaska lasted longer and could prove even more severe. Immediately the Prudhoe Bay Field had been proved in 1969, BP, Arco and its partner Humble Oil (of the Esso group) had proposed to build a 900-mile pipeline across Alaska to Valdez, an all-weather port, as the most economic way to transport Alaskan oil to market. Subsequent events—the partial success of the voyage of Esso's ice-breaking tanker, the SS *Manhattan* through the fabled North West passage to the East coast of the US in the summer of 1970, and the cost of the proposed alternative pipeline through Canada to the US Mid-West—merely confirmed that the trans-Alaskan pipeline was the best way out for the oil.

The three companies rushed ahead—even bringing pipe into Alaska—before permission to build the pipeline had been given. But they hit a combination of factors. The first concerned Alaska and the damage the pipeline would do to the ecology of the only virgin wilderness the growing number of conservation-minded Americans felt remained to them. The worry, like the oil, was new-found: "two years ago," said one Alaskan, "it was the hostile, frozen North. Now, all of a sudden, it's the goddam delicate tundra."

The problem lay partly with the nature of the permafrost. If the pipeline were buried, it would warm the whole area round it and turn the permafrost into permaslush. If it lay on the ground, the heat would, equally, melt the surface and also disturb the wild life. Migrating caribou, it was learnt, would be unable to follow their favourite streams; though the oil men claim the caribou are happy with the new inhabitants, lemmings, dashing on a suicide path every seven years for the Bering Sea, would, it was feared, turn at the pipeline and scuttle back to the Canadian prairies, eating everything in their path. BP sent Peter Scott, the well-known British natura-list, to Alaska as a token of its concern; but tokens were not enough.

The American conversationists were aroused and filed suit against the Department of the Interior to prevent it from granting the permit for the pipeline, as did some of the local Indians and Eskimos. They were a further complication; it was clear that the advantages to Alaska of the oil money—which included $900 million raised through a further sale of oil leases in September 1969—would, as usual in these circum-stances, flow to the urban middle class engaged in service industries. This suited the majority of local politicians well enough; but it was guaranteed to arouse the opposition of groups—similar to the conservationists—which had seen else-where how the country's original inhabitants had either been left in abject rural poverty, or, if they did secure any money from mineral rights, were unable to adjust to modern American life and drifted into sullen, drunken, urban squalor. These groups, were, basically, anxious that the wealth brought by the oil companies did not ruin the country and its inhabitants, as they felt the rest of the country had been ruined.

They found a staunch, if unexpected, ally in Walter Hickel, Secretary of the Interior (the Department concerned). Hickel, had been a notable non-conservationist, pro-development Governor of Alaska. He was anxious to be a better conser-vationist than his critics and to disprove Washington rumours that he had been appointed to President Nixon's cabinet at the instance of Robert Anderson, Arco's chairman and an impor-tant Republican supporter. Added to Hickel's unexpected stubbornness was the new anxiety about the environment; and, the normally powerful oil lobby was in no hurry to press for a pipeline which would benefit only Arco and BP—both up-starts, and one of them foreign as well—and Esso, the biggest oil group in the world. The Alaskan consortium did not help the case by taking the opposition rather casually. The whole affair was left to engineers without the delicate political touch required to disarm political objections; and they were not backed by any determined effort by their American superiors. BP felt obliged to follow the lead of its American partners and was therefore helpless.

Worse was to come. When Hickel finally left Nixon's cabinet after a well-publicised drift away from the President he was replaced by Rogers Morton—who, as a former chairman of the Republican Party, was presumed to be favourable to the oil companies. Nevertheless, like Hickel, he disappointed them. In January 1971 his Department produced a massive, if lukewarm, report that the trans-Alaskan pipeline was the least undesirable means of getting oil out. Yet even this did not satisfy Morton who put the decision back far enough to ensure that construction would not start until 1972 at the earliest. At the same time the end of the US-Canadian tension over a joint fuel policy for both countries led to a proposal for a pipeline right across Canada to the Mid-West; this could be a red herring but a dangerous one for BP—in order to use its options to give it control of Sohio its Alaskan oil has to be in full flood by 1977 at the latest; and even the shorter trans-Alaskan pipe will now not be ready until 1975 at the earliest.

Nevertheless the atmosphere changed in the spring of 1971. The oil companies finally started to make a fuss; the considerable increases in the price of non-American oil pointed up just how urgently the US needed the Alaskan oil; the Secretary of Commerce came out against his cabinet colleague—and for the pipeline. (Spahr even managed to sell some of the gas found with the Alaskan oil.)

Spahr, now in charge of BP's US assets as well as Sohio's, has more important jobs to do, to replace the gallonage lost by Sohio in its home state through the anti-trust decree; outside the state he has to weld together his and Sinclair's marketing operations. It is a measure of the size of the job and of BP's success that all the energies of Spahr, one of the best marketing men in the US oil industry, are needed and available to do the job.

But it is still unclear whether BP will ever control more of his activities than it does now with its 25 per cent, non-dividend paying stake in Sohio. To exercise its right to sub-scribe to enough of Sohio's capital to give it control it has to be delivering oil in massive quantities by 1977 at the latest. The incredible number of legal obstacles now laid across the pipeline's path—some by extreme preservationists who swear they will never allow it to be built—make this timetable (which appeared lavish in 1969) look decidedly tight. BP executives now appear resigned to the possibility that they will be left, at the end of the decade, with their 25 per cent stake in Sohio—and a lot of oil. Whatever happens, this is increasing in value enough to look like a good investment, even if it cannot be translated into full control of Sohio.

The story of BP is a well-publicised business-ecological political drama, a symbol of a renascent European business community charging into the US; but it does differ in many ways from other invaders. The comparison can easily be made because another European oil company, Belgium's Petrofina, has also invaded the US market since the war with a success which turned its American subsidiary, 58 per cent-owned by the parent, into one of the fastest-growing companies in terms of both sales and profits in the US in the 1960's. Petrofina, like so many Europeans, started modestly. In the mid-1950's it bought a small Texas oil company. Unlike most other Europeans it concentrated in the Mid-West; but, like so many, it special-ised. It bought Cosden, a small petrochemical producer, in 1963; and increased sales of Cosden's products by upgrading them, and bringing in new developments from the group's central research, so that the volume of Cosden's sales went up by less than a quarter in the six years 1963-69 while their dollar value rose two and a half times to $50 million. Over half American Petrofina's profits, in fact, now come from petro-chemicals, and a substantial part from just one product, poly-styrene, a basic plastic, demand for which is growing at around 15 per cent a year and of which Cosden is one of the top ten producers in the US. To get, as Cosden has done, an increasing share of a fast-growing speciality, is the aim of most foreign challengers in any market.

US Petrofina has been so successful that it probably contributes a third of the parent's total world-wide profits from only a quarter of the sales volume. Yet, in common with so many European challengers, Petrofina has kept its European connections out of sight—so much so that it was recently used by *Business Week* as a typical example of an independent American oil company. In October 1970 the Compagnie Française des Pétroles started its invasion of the US behaving just like most European invaders, small and regional. Its Canadian affiliate completed the take-over of a small mid-Western refiner and operator of 600 service stations. And in April 1971, after another small take-over, CFP's "Total" signs appeared on a few hundred petrol pumps.

Everything about BP's entry into the US was different from CFP's, Petrofina's and thus also of the majority of the European challengers. As we have seen, it was big from the start. Within ten years of its arrival, in fact, BP ought to be controlling an empire in the US equal to that of Shell Oil ten years ago—after Shell had been in the US forty years; even now BP and Sohio's interests have net assets of $1 billion and sales of $1·4 billion. Secondly, BP's entry was not preceded, as most other invasions have been, by direct export sales.

Third, the invasion was public—not the usual quiet arrival—and brought about a number of problems with the US government, notably over anti-trust and the trans-Alaskan pipeline, so that every step in BP's progress has been conditioned (either for good or ill) by Federal regulations—whereas other invaders have only come across the Federal government's presence after their arrival. Fourth, because the invasion was so large and sudden, BP created a significant managerial problem for itself, whereas other companies, by growing more slowly, have been able to generate their own management internally.

Fifthly, BP, unlike other European companies, could not choose the most favourable market conditions for the time of its entry into the US. It had to take its Alaskan discoveries as a once-in-a-lifetime chance. Yet the break came right at the end of a decade during which the US oil business, insulated by import quotas from the rest of the world, had enjoyed ten healthily profitable years; and BP, alone of the big seven in the world oil industry, had reaped no benefit from this boom to counteract the exceedingly sticky time they were all enduring in the rest of the world, especially in Europe, during the 1960's. And margins in the US started to crumble with the economy even as BP thundered in. Finally, the invasion was directly induced, as few other recent ones have been, by US restrictionist and protectionist policies.

In oil, as in no other industry, the US government giveth and taketh away. With its quota system it had taken away from BP the chance to enter the US market by importing oil from its rich reserves elsewhere. But with the same apparatus, it gave BP far more powerful weapons when it did in fact discover oil. For, had all the major oil companies been allowed to import oil into the US freely over the previous ten years, BP would merely have been one among a number of companies with a surplus of crude oil elsewhere in the world—and many of the others (especially Gulf and Standard of New Jersey) would have had large US marketing networks already in existence. BP's Canadian experience, as well as its last ten years in Europe (a free market where it was a recent entrant in a key market like Italy), shows how difficult would have been its independent entry into a free US oil market. In a free market Sohio would merely have been an exigent contract buyer—it certainly would not have needed to merge with BP.

But because of the US government's multiple involvement in the industry, the mere possession of large reserves of oil in the US gave BP some unique advantages. Elsewhere in the world it was confronted by a competitive open market for any additional discoveries of crude oil, a market that was comparatively unprofitable for much of the 1960's. In the US it had a guaranteed market; an equally sure profit; the oil in the ground represented a solid credit base on which to build a marketing empire; and the possession of the crude oil gave it enough allure to attract Sohio. All these advantages the Federal government gave through its protectionist policy. But then this, like its policies in most economic fields was never designed to keep out direct European investment—whatever BP may have thought when grappling with Attorney-General Mitchell or Mr Secretary Hickel.

BASF—THE ENVIRONMENT
HITS BACK

THE delay Hickel inflicted on BP was serious enough. A worse blow to a European company came at the end of March 1970 when he administered an effective *coup de grâce* to one of the most ambitious developments put forward by any European company, the proposal of BASF to spend $200 million on a petro-chemical complex in South Carolina. In this case, too, Hickel was acting to discipline a project on the grounds that it would pollute the environment. And the story of BASF, like that of BP in Alaska, concerns the struggle against a foreign company, trying to open up previously undeveloped country, and hitting against the Americans' new-found concern with their country. But whereas in the pipeline story the conservationists were real, the BASF story is more tangled. It harks back to the days in the 1920's when Shell was fighting California nationalists, and, as in that battle, involved a bewildered and unhappy foreign company in the intricacies of American local political life.

The proposed plant was not an addition to an existing industrial complex, but, it was hoped, a spark which would give new life to a very depressed area—in the same way that oil is supposed to bring new life to Alaska. It was to be on the side of one of the two peninsulas jutting into the Atlantic which form Beaufort (pronounced Bewfort) County, beyond Charleston in the far south of South Carolina. The County's 55,000 inhabitants desperately needed a boost: in 1969 it was singled out by a

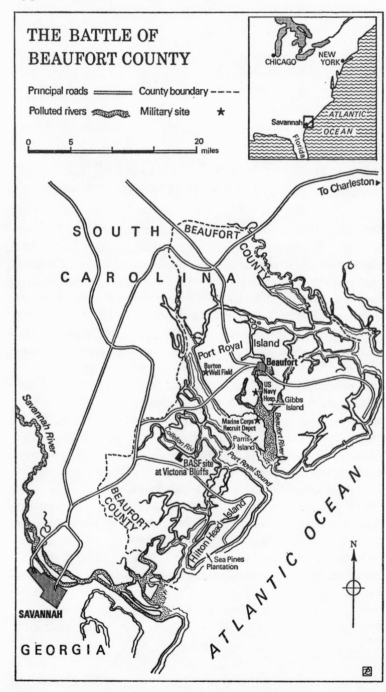

THE BATTLE OF
BEAUFORT COUNTY

Principal roads ═══════ County boundary ─ ─ ─

Polluted rivers ∿∿∿∿ Military site   ★

0   5   20
└──┴──┴──┴──┴──┴──────────────┘ miles

CHICAGO   NEW
           YORK

                        ATLANTIC
Savannah   OCEAN

Florida

To Charleston ▶

S O U T H   BEAUFORT
                            COUNTY
C A R O L I N A

                    Port Royal   Island
                                          Beaufort
                    Burton
                    ★ Well Field
                                 US
                                 Navy
                                 Hosp. ★   Gibbs
                                           Island
Savannah River
                         Marine Corps ★
                         Recruit Depot
                         Parris
                   Colleton Riv. Island
                                                   Beaufort River
                    ■ BASF site   Port Royal Sound
                    at Victoria Bluffs

              BEAUFORT
              COUNTY
                                 Hilton Head Island
                                                     A T L A N T I C   O C E A N

                                      Sea Pines
                                      Plantation
                                                                    N

SAVANNAH

GEORGIA   A T L A N T I C   O C E A N

Senate Committee (which, ironically, included Senator Hollings from South Carolina) as one of the most glaring examples in the United States of undernourishment, illiteracy and general depression. Television crews descended on the area and, much to the annoyance of the locals, photographed the most wretched hovels, the most sickly-looking children.

They were not difficult to find: for none of the County's four sources of employment provides any opportunity for skilled workers, and even unskilled employment, especially for the Negroes who make up two thirds of the population, is difficult. The cotton fields have been taken out of production; the County's large-scale market gardens, growing mainly tomatoes, have been virtually ruined by competition from California which has more sunshine. Agricultural work for these sorts of crops is, in any case, very seasonal. And fishing for clams and oysters, another major source of livelihood, provides few jobs; even this is disagreeable and seasonal—opening and cleaning clams in a steaming, smelly, corrugated-iron shack is no one's idea of a solid, desirable, economic base.

War—or rather military installations—has replaced agriculture as the principal economic basis of the area (70 per cent of Beaufort's income comes, directly or indirectly, from military spending). The reason for this is simple: until he died early in 1971 the local congressman was Mendel Rivers, the Chairman of the House of Representatives Armed Services Committee. And, thanks to the Pentagon's efforts to please him, the Charleston-Beaufort area has far more than its fair share of military bases. In Beaufort itself, the dreaded Marine Recruit Training Base at Parris Island and a Marine air station together provide 500 jobs. And this is only the direct result of military expenditure. Commercial spin-offs include a whole line of motels on the outskirts of Beaufort itself, filled every mid-week by proud parents who have come down to see their boys pass out as real Marines. By the time BASF arrived, even Rivers was saying it was undesirable to count any more on help from the military—the number of jobs available for civilians on the bases fluctuates as wars come and go, and like opening clams, or picking tomatoes, they pay little and offer no hope of economic advancement or spin-off. No wonder so many Beaufort people had wandered north in search of jobs—or even better welfare payments.

Parris Island is at the end of one peninsula: Hilton Head Island is at the end of the other—the one on which the BASF plant would have been sited. Hilton Head itself is 20,000 flat acres of scrub and pine—a sort of sub-tropical Surrey—surrounded by endless sandy beaches, fringed with unhealthy oak trees draped with Spanish moss (which makes them look as though they have grey stalactites or witches' beards hanging from every branch).

The island provided the main opposition to the scheme, while the Beaufort peninsula itself housed the businessmen and people's organisations which were boosting BASF. For, twenty years ago, despite the anguished cries of conservationists anxious to preserve the island, the biggest off the American coast for some hundreds of miles, in a state of virgin wilderness, nearly a third of the land on Hilton Head was bought by a group of enterprising lumbermen from Georgia. These included two brothers, Fred and Orion Hack, and a Lieutenant-General, Rufus Fraser (the rank was only in the National Guard, the American Territorial Army, but he was always accorded full military honours). Since then, thanks largely to Fraser's son Charlie, the island has become a green retreat for organisation men, with ranch-type hotels and houses artfully scattered in the woods. There are seven golf courses (not only because these executives tend to be keen players, but because land on the edge of a fairway is worth more than if it is in the middle of a wood). The inhabitants of Hilton Head are often military men who had come to know the area because of the bases; but they include officers as senior as Vice-Admiral Rufus Taylor, a former deputy head of the Central Intelligence Agency. However, the retired officers were not the only Hilton Headers with the experience and contacts to make a fuss about a scheme they did not like. There were also a number of senior executives from large oil and chemical companies, fleeing an industrial scene their employers

had done so much to pollute. One Hilton Header, it was
rumoured, had been sacked by BASF when his firm was taken
over, and for him the episode was a grudge fight. Other
inhabitants without a personal motive, but with useful knowledge and contacts, included a former research vice-president
from Esso and William F. Kenney, who retired in 1969 as a
vice-president and chief lawyer for Shell Oil after twenty-nine
years advocating its rights in legal battles—a real poacher-
turned-gamekeeper who boasted that he had "never lost a case"
against conservation. Ironically the single Beaufortian with the
most obvious pull, a plantation owner called Du Pont, stayed
scrupulously neutral throughout. Even more ironically, the
coloured inhabitants of the island—the people most affected by
the scheme—remained inactive during the battle. Even though
they owned around two-thirds of the land they felt powerless in
a battle which divided the rich whites they had been taught to
think of as their superiors into opposing camps.

Because there were so many well-heeled people on Hilton
Head, Beaufort County's average income was by no means low,
but the average contained a few rich and many very poor people.
And the rich did not contribute much to the County's economy.
The employees they needed were for unskilled, dead-end jobs
like caddying and for help around the hotels: they even tended
to do their shopping in Savannah just across another river,
rather than in Beaufort itself.

Despite the potential power of the opposition, the scheme
seemed a foregone conclusion when it was announced early in
October 1969. It was strongly backed by South Carolina's state
government; the Governor, Robert C. McNair, had even been
to BASF headquarters in Germany. The site itself is round the
coast from Hilton Head and quite invisible, an apparently
harmless place. It is long and narrow, of 1,800 acres, three miles
long, stretching from the main road down to the Colleton River,
which had conveniently been dredged by army engineers some
years before and provided one of the few unused potential
harbours on the East Coast of the USA. For ten years the state
authorities had tried to find a developer for the site and a number

of companies had turned it down, even though the state was prepared to sell the site very cheaply and provide a great deal of help. A number of BASF officials had gone there with state officials during the two years the deal took to negotiate. Despite this background the Hilton Headers expressed shocked surprise at the suddenness of the decision.

The scheme was designed not only to generate jobs directly, but also to provide the base of a whole industrial complex to banish poverty from the whole area. The first announcement merely said that BASF would build a $75 million complex to make dyestuffs and styrene, and to employ a few hundred people though a couple of thousand would be involved in its construction. But it was enough to ensure that the state would spend $2½ million on a Technical Training School in Beaufort itself. This sort of school is often the best way to break the vicious circle created in any depressed area: skilled men leave because of the lack of job opportunities, potential employers are scared off because of the lack of skilled labour. In this case the lack of skilled labour was used by opponents of the BASF scheme as an argument against it. But South Carolina is a poor state, often forty-seventh in the statistics indicating general welfare ("Thank God for Mississippi"—for preventing South Carolina from being the bottom of the league—state officials are apt to say). So it could not afford to build a new school in advance of a scheme like BASF's.

The six months between the announcement of the scheme on October 2 and the suspension of construction on April 8, 1970 saw one of the bitterest and most unfairly reported dogfights in the recent history of pollution. Most of the time it appeared that this was a peculiarly American battle and that BASF was an innocent bystander getting hurt in a quarrel between two other forces. The opposition started immediately by claiming that the plant would be totally incompatible with Hilton Head's way of life—which, to BASF's supporters, merely indicated that the Hilton Headers were afraid that they would have to pay their caddies a bit more. The opposition turned to the pollution question only at the end of October when a symposium in

Washington singled out BASF as a chemical company with a specially bad pollution record at home. And it really got under way with two major disclosures in late November and early December. The first was that the dyestuffs plant was merely the first stage of the scheme: the second was to be a naphtha cracker. This would be fed by naphtha imported in tankers coming up the Colleton River. It was assumed, probably rightly, that the state's political influence in Washington would ensure that the necessary import permit would be granted for the naphtha. The revelation of the plans for the cracker added a whole new dimension to the argument. To the conservationists it meant a guarantee of irreparable harm to the landscape. For although the site itself was well wooded and a normal chemical plant could have been lost within its vastness, a naphtha cracker is inevitably several hundred feet tall and would thus pollute the landscape very considerably (the area is very flat so that a water tower on Parris Island, much lower than any naphtha cracker, is visible for miles around). Furthermore, there was danger that the tankers bringing in the naphtha would spill and thus actually pollute the water. But the existence of the cracker also gave much greater credibility to the idea that this plant would lend new life to Beaufort. For the second stage would produce plastics from the naphtha and, although the chemical complex itself would not employ more than a thousand people, the plastics could attract exactly the sort of light industry which the area needed. Even before the scheme was abandoned, two plastics companies had in fact agreed to invest in factories on the site; and to confirm hopes that the plant would result in a complete New Deal for the area, over two hundred former inhabitants, many suitably qualified as engineers, who had been forced to look for work away from home, wrote in asking for jobs.

The opposition was already well under way when the second bombshell was dropped. In mid-December came the unfortunate discovery that a dyestuffs plant, owned by the American Tenneco Company, was pouring virtually untreated acid into a river a few miles up the coast, even though it had been open only a couple of years and had conformed to the state's anti-pollution laws. This sort of disclosure, which could probably have been made in any American state, was naturally grist to the opposition's mill and in the first three months of 1970 was loudly publicised.

By then the scheme had brought together an unlikely combination in the name of pollution. The Hilton Headers were joined by a Wall Street broker who owned the island directly opposite the site and who was a big contributor to Republican funds. A symposium organised by Orion Hack attracted some of the lesser luminaries in the world of anti-pollution. They were followed by some radical activists who mixed uneasily with the Hilton Headers. Some of the more respected and ardent conservationists were decidedly cool to the cause of the Hilton Headers. One local academic pointed out to me that "I do not put industry at the top of the pollution list"; he went on to agree with the pro-BASF lobby on the "marginal productivity in job-terms" of the tourism from which Hilton Headers (suddenly converted to the idea of economic progress) hoped for so much and dismissed the word "unique" which was being used to describe the landscape involved as a word "trotted out without much justification" in this sort of case. Despite the idea that pollution (not land values or caddies' wages) was the key issue in the dispute, by far the most balanced article of the many written on the subject was in the journal of the American Museum of Natural History.

The conservationist view of the area was best expressed in a particularly purple passage in an article in *Harper's Magazine* by a journalist who lived nearby. "The coastline involved," he said, "is an uncertain and capricious play between land and water, still arrested at that moment in the history of the earth when the sea was just beginning, reluctantly and tentatively, indecisively, to relinquish the land, a slight release and hesitation and change of mind still enacted every day. Grassy marshes yawn off level and limitless, past solitary marooned islands of palm and pine, into cold red sunsets—one of those plots on the planet where man is still incidental to nature."

Indeed it is this solitary and primaeval quality and not any specific feature which is unique about the landscape. But this quality is inevitably ruined by any major evidence of man's presence. The Hilton Head pioneers had effectively destroyed the unique quality of the area they had bought by pulling down many of the trees and training the landscape into an exurban blandness. It was, intellectually, ridiculous of them to complain that somebody else was going to spoil it in another way, one which would be more economically productive than the developments on Hilton Head.

Yet, for all the dubious credentials of the conservationists, there was about the battle a feeling, made more piquant by the fact that the industrial invader was not an American, that what was at stake was the rape of a virgin landscape and the ruin of an innocent world by sophisticated outsiders. Underneath the click of the golf clubs lay the Alaskan feeling all over again. In the words of Representative Sanders, a maverick local politician: "Make no mistake about it, as compared to the highly industrialised society of Western Germany—the fatherland of BASF—the coast of South Carolina with its poverty and vast expanse of virgin land is viewed by many as nothing more than another emerging nation, whose people are for exploitation and—more important—for sale."

Dr Hans Lautenschlager, who was then in charge of BASF in the US struck the same note; "We always felt that the US as compared to Germany is somewhat underdeveloped—excuse me that expression—in the use of plastics. Because you wouldn't believe it, but from, I would say, Philadelphia to Miami, there is nothing. Really—no plastics plant."

BASF's men were obviously bewildered by the whole affair. They had been lavishly welcomed by the Governor and all the state authorities: they had been sold the land cheaply, had been promised a four-lane highway and a railway spur to the site. Now, suddenly, they were the villains of the piece. They were not particularly well integrated into the American way of life: as one of their supporters complained, "they sent an engineer down here who really didn't understand the language". They failed to appreciate that the Governor was not all-powerful. South Carolina's influential senior Senator, Strom Thurmond, a Republican close to Nixon, was ostentatiously open-minded about the affair—which the BASF supporters found quite extraordinary and inexplicable. How, they said, could a politician dare to oppose a scheme which would be of such economic benefit to the state?

BASF itself, unlike a major American corporation in a similar situation, had no friends or lobbyists in Washington. It could only protest that it would meet any pollution requirements imposed by the state—an offer brushed aside by its opponents because of the scandal over the Tenneco plant and the fact that South Carolina's pollution control office was admittedly too understaffed to be effective. These control authorities were fairly helpless in a situation where fourteen state agencies and six Federal agencies had interests or responsibilities, often conflicting ones, in the marshes and woods, an overlap which made proper planning impossible. But certainly the BASF case was not enhanced by the rather simple assumption of many people in South Carolina that industrial activity inevitably brought pollution, an assumption natural in a state long dominated by high-pollutant textile and paper interests.

BASF's opponents had a field day. The American national press was full of favourable articles. Some, locals will tell you, were influenced by the free hospitality being offered on Hilton Head. But most were a reasonably honest reflection of the anti-industrial pollution feeling then growing so strongly in middle-class America. BASF, again unlike most large American corporations, knew none of the major editors or publishers involved and was not a major advertiser, so had no leverage through less reputable (but often useful) pressures. Nor was Governor McNair a particular hero of the Eastern liberal press after a college shooting incident in the summer of 1968 which had made him appear just another segregationalist southern Governor. Indeed the coalition supporting BASF, which included a local Beaufort man who had been Senator Goldwater's campaign manager in 1964 and the local radical fighters for Negro rights, was just as makeshift as the opposition.

So the newspapers soft-pedalled some of the more obvious discrepancies in the opposition's case: the way in which the Hilton Head interests, oblivious to the true qualities of the site, proposed to bring in a sort of tourist entertainment centre as an alternative source of employment; the fact that the worst pollution in the area was caused, not by Tenneco, but by the lack of adequate sewage treatment plants either on the island or in the military installations in Beaufort itself. And the pious worries about what the water-hungry BASF plant would do to the water table of the area came oddly from people whose golf-courses were kept green by lavish applications of the same liquid. Complaints about the financial help being given to BASF by the state came incongruously from the Hilton Headers, whose arrival had been greatly helped by the construction of a $14 million toll-free bridge and highway.

The "conservationists" did not rely only on the press and their symposium. They went in for a very thorough public relations campaign which included wholesale distribution of the details of their case through postal shots and some wildly misleading advertisements, for example the classic smear "BASF, and its parent company, IG Farben, have a long record of working closely with governments and it is to their benefit to do so". This was a clear attempt to arouse the presumed hostility of the people of South Carolina towards the former German chemical cartel. Farben, of course, had been broken up at the end of the war twenty-five years before. It could not remotely be described as BASF's "parent company", and the name probably meant nothing to anyone in the area—except the people who paid for the advertisement.

Announcements about improving pollution control in South Carolina, lawsuits from fishermen (including a well-publicised one by a Negro fishermen's co-operative), and general declamatory noises from all sides, filled the air during the first three months of 1970. By then the scheme had obviously lost momentum and at the end of March Hickel got into the act with an unprecedented letter to BASF. His excuse for interference was that public money would be involved if the army's corps of engineers deepened the channel up to the site and that Congress had made him responsible for the country's estuaries. So Hickel asked for a blanket agreement from BASF that they would adhere to any environmental safeguards proposed by anyone then or in the future. BASF was unused to the way in which American politics are largely composed of loud public noises and soft private deals. In these terms the letter was clearly only the opening shot in a war which would inevitably end in some form of face-saving compromise. But BASF took Hickel's sweeping requirements as a formal government order and protested that it had "always understood that water and air standards had to be met". It then decided to suspend construction at the site, giving as an excuse the uncertainty surrounding the requirements that would have to be met.

In this, BASF was being disingenuous. While Lautenschlager and his men had been battling to get the South Carolina project under way, the parent company had spent $95 million buying the American Wyandotte Chemicals company. And at least one of Wyandotte's sites, at Geismar on the Mississippi in Louisiana, was more suitable for a new plant than the Beaufort one. It was "in the middle of fifty miles of petro-chemicals" and was already developed for the sort of plant BASF needed. Locally, the suspension of work following Hickel's letter was seen as an indication of a permanent withdrawal because of the Wyandotte acquisition: "If they want to move," said one BASF supporter in disgust, "they'll use this letter as a crutch to hobble out on." And hobble they did. Even while the state authorities were assuring everyone that the work would still go ahead, one of BASF's main board directors was telling journalists at Ludwigshafen, back in Germany, "I have just come back from killing the South Carolina project". But the formal withdrawal did not materialise until the middle of January 1971, when Lautenschlager's successor and Governor McNair issued a statement that BASF would withdraw and sell the land back to the state. To darken the outlook still further, Mendel Rivers died early in 1971, so the people of Beaufort County do not even have the hope of more Marine bases to work at.

Yet the story is not entirely a futile one: there has been a noticeable new vigour in the anti-pollution effort by the state since the publicity—the Tenneco plant and one owned by a powerful textile company were even closed for a few weeks because they did not meet the state pollution requirements. There was also a political repercussion. Governor McNair was not up for re-election, but his associate governor, John C. West, beat the Republican candidate more easily than he might have done if the Republicans had shown the same zeal in favour of BASF as had the Democrats.

Economically, too, there could be a happy ending to the story. The Hilton Headers have now accepted that some kind of economic development is necessary. They commissioned a study from a well-known firm of architects, proposing farming and fishing cooperatives. But the South Carolina development authorities are still adamant that they need proper industrial development. Whether they get it depends on whether other possible investors are put off by BASF's experience, or whether the temptation of the cheap land, access routes and labour, combined with that rarity, an unused site for a deep water port, will prove sufficient attraction. But whatever happens, the attitudes inspired by BASF's adventure ensured that Beaufort will never again be neglected as it was in the past.

The BASF saga serves to darken the rosy picture given by state authorities, and offset their assurances that they can provide exactly what the newcomers want—indeed development officials from another state summed up the story simply: "South Carolina let 'em down." It shows also the latent hostility against a foreign firm which can be unleashed if it happens to offend any powerful body of opinion. And it shows how helpless such a company is in the face of such hostility and how clumsy and unhelpful its efforts to protest its innocence and good intentions can be. In this case, because of the Wyandotte acquisition, BASF's impetus was not severely eroded—it anyway had enough financial problems in 1970-71 to welcome the relief from the enormous capital expenditure involved. And the story, showing how an over-visible posture can hurt a foreign company, makes one realise just how sensible most invaders have been in the past to adopt a meek and low profile all round.

CHAPTER 12

ARE THE FEDS FRIENDLY?

The US is completely open to a firm wishing to invest here as opposed to Europe where the foreign investor has to first pass through a maze of red tape and regulations before he can establish. However, in the US, once established, a company has to comply with numerous Federal state and local regulations, whereas in Europe any established company is relatively free from government regulation. Further, SEC rules, the necessity to consider the other stockholders and disclose much information to them, and strict tax laws, were all new.

—European Company

SINCE the early 1960's the American Federal government has been doing all it can to encourage foreign direct investment. The Federal government's "Invest in the USA" programme is backed, as we saw in Chapter 8, by a considerable effort at state level. The Federal programme has two motives. One is to benefit the US balance of payments. The other is to help provide an insurance policy against possible action against Americans abroad. "Countries with substantial investment interest in the US, for example," a US government official admitted at a recent conference, "will be highly circumspect about actions inimical to US investment within their own borders"—unluckily for the US, the countries where unfriendly actions are most likely are the developing countries, those with few, if any, investments in the US. But there is no doubt that the welcome is genuine, for a decade or more, though until the dollar crisis of August 1971 it tended to be a rather low-key affair. But within a week of the Nixon measures, one Cabinet member had said he would not be happy until European investment in the US was as big as the American challenge in Europe. The need for massive capital inflow and the realisation of the vulnerability of US investment in Europe are transforming official attitudes to genuine, high-level, enthusiasm.

By any of the criteria generally applied for deciding whether a country's investment climate is favourable to foreigners, the US stands high. The currency is (relatively) stable, and completely convertible. There are no restrictions on the payment of dividends or the repatriation of capital. Foreign ownership of most types of businesses is permitted, and, by and large, foreign-owned concerns get the same help from Washington as do local firms. There is no need to fit any particular scheme into the framework of an overall economic plan. Local capital is freely available, the natives are friendly.

Yet it is surprising how many obstacles the Europeans have found which emanate from government laws and regulations. These, of course, are not all Federal. Foreigners are invariably surprised to find how much legal power resides at state level—and how the states' requirements vary.

The variety of obstacles, often quite minor, are not insuperable, but they do provide an excellent excuse for inactivity. They seem bewildering and illogical to Europeans but can easily be understood if seen as products of US history. They spring principally from four motives: early fears of domination by foreigners of what was then a thinly populated, underdeveloped continent; later attempts to tax effectively any company operating in the US and to control any company which became too powerful; still more recent obsessions with security matters; and—a development of the last decade—a desire to maximise the inflow of foreign capital and reduce the outflow of native funds. It is the early fears of wicked financiers from Europe (and New York) which led to the various prohibitions, by the states and by the Federal government, on foreigners owning certain types of business in the US: ownership of deposit banks is, as we saw in Chapter 8, banned in most states, of insurance companies in some, of alcoholic drink companies in a few; fear of land grabs has led a few states to restrict alien ownership of land. In some cases the law can easily be by-passed: aliens are not allowed to develop hydro-electric power stations or "acquire or exploit mineral lands", but there is nothing to stop foreign-controlled US corporations from doing so.*

Fear of alien control over industries of national importance, combined with industrial lobbying, has ensured that the subsidies available to US international shipping do not flow to foreign corporations, which are also allowed only a quarter of the equity in coastal shipping, radio stations and internal air transport. These, and other protectionist restrictions are relatively unimportant though some of the industries involved could benefit from competition. As Drake of BP pointed out, "Under the Jones Act, shipping plying between US ports must be US-built and US-manned. This multiplies the cost by a factor of something like three when compared with costs elsewhere". More seriously, the Americans abroad could suffer from backlash because their government's subsidies are available only to native concerns in these industries. Common Market officials have already expressed concern at the degree to which American-owned companies have taken advantage of government inducements to invest, and the way in which such help allegedly adds up to half the money paid out within the Six. BP suffered also from another form of protectionism—the very strict immigration laws enacted by the US in the 1920's—and was not alone in complaining about the difficulty of getting work permits for even the relatively few foreigners such companies wish to bring in. This sort of bureaucratic irritant is frequently mentioned as an obstacle—underlaid by a feeling, one would guess, that a country which was truly as anxious to

* This is no mere gesture; boron, one of the more profitable natural products of which the US has a monopoly, is found almost exclusively at a mine in California owned by US Borax, long British-controlled and now a subsidiary of Rio-Tinto Zinc.

help foreigners as the Americans claim to be could do something to remedy the situation.

The visa problem is a minor one. The biggest single way in which the US government helps its own companies, through defence contracts, is, usually, simply taken as a fact of life. Yet it is vitally important because defence procurement dominates the relationship between government and industry in the US to an extent undreamt of elsewhere. In other countries, too, there is a perfectly legitimate concern that national security should not be imperilled by the involvement of too many foreign-controlled firms. But this does not prevent a good deal of government help through regional aid, investment grants, and the like, which is lacking in the US, apart from the relatively minor programmes of the Economic Development Administration and the assistance available to small businesses. So the American government can truthfully claim that its help is available to all companies, whoever owns them, while the peculiar political, security-conscious, nature of defence supply ensures that, in practice, such help is overwhelmingly slanted towards native concerns. Because of its generosity, the European lag in electronics and aerospace is likely to remain.

"Security" is also an excellent excuse for disguising straight protectionism. Historically, it was used to justify the expensive protection of shipping; and recently in the ball-bearing industry where, one manufacturer complained "half of our product line has been taken away by the Japanese", a congressman immediately complained that "there is a real danger that the US will lose its capability in precision bearings. National security is directly involved".

Because of their lack of basic political pull the European companies inevitably stand at a considerable disadvantage in bidding for defence orders even when they are relatively low-security items (what matters in these cases is not the nature of the item itself but the use to which it is going to be put; the more secret the use, the greater the security clearance required by the supplier). Even apart from straight political pull (and cynics will say that this leaves little of importance), the buyer has to consider the degree of "foreign ownership, control and influence" on a bid. Clearly it is easier for companies which have only a very loose relationship with their parents to get the highest clearance and thus be in the running for research and development contracts on really advanced projects. Three which appear to be considered secure are North American Philips, the Swedish-controlled SKF ball-bearing firm, and Shell Oil. Philips is enormously helped by its trust deed and, though not a major supplier, enjoys a cosy relationship with the Pentagon: one Dutch-born director was in fact president of a suppliers' organisation, the Armed Forces Electrical Association, for three years running. SKF is virtually independent of the Swedish parent for anti-trust reasons. And Shell Oil is too big and well established to be considered foreign.

Yet other companies seem less worried about their ability to compete for everything except the highest security contracts. As a routine matter they provide a special all-American board with security clearance—as Elliott-Automation and Alloys Unlimited have done; and there do not seem to be too many problems for a European company taking over an important supplier—as Plessey wished to do with Collins Radio, one of the US Navy's favourite companies. In fact, American policy with regard to foreign suppliers and products oscillates. For some years in the mid-1960's the Americans were anxious to buy as much as possible from the British so as to offset the cost of the F111 fighters the British were then buying. But they found few companies prepared to go to the elaborate expense of submitting a specification in the detail required by the Pentagon. Then came a shift. "As an interim measure designed to alleviate the impact of defence expenditure on the nation's balance of international payments", the defence procurement agencies have, since 1968, been obliged to add 50 per cent to the price, before duty (or 6 to 12 per cent to the price after duty),* of any foreign supplier, thus, in theory, effectively ruling out any foreign supplies at all. It was in 1969, for instance, that the

* The higher level of protection is applied if the product is made in an economically depressed area.

Pentagon cajoled one key German supplier of optical glass to spend $1 million on a factory in Pennsylvania to supply the specialised glass it needed.

Yet another factor sprang into prominence during 1970, that offsets this encouragement to direct investment (which turned out to be more theoretical than real); the desire for economy and cost cutting. Under these circumstances it is obviously cheaper to order from a foreign supplier's own home production line, rather than duplicate it expensively in the US. The classic case is the Harrier, the first operational vertical take-off and landing fighter in production, made by the British Hawker Siddeley Company. This was desperately wanted by the powerful US Marine Corps whose influence pushed the necessary order through Congress. Washington, however, was anxious to ensure that only the first dozen aircraft (out of a possible total order of a hundred) were made entirely in Britain. So Hawker arranged a joint venture with the American McDonnell Douglas aircraft company to assemble the majority of the aircraft even though most of the parts were so specialised they had inevitably to come from Britain. Then, in late 1970, came an order for another batch to be built, economically but un-Americanly, completely in Britain. And this order survived even the problems associated with the collapse of Rolls-Royce, a disaster which can be used in the future, quite legitimately, by American defence contractors as an additional reason for not relying on foreign-owned suppliers, wherever they are situated.

What matters in fact, when selling to the Pentagon, is the uniqueness of the product and the keenness of the buying department. Hawker was lucky; the Harrier is unique and the Marines were extremely keen. Under these circumstances it is a toss-up whether political pull will ensure that the product is made in the US, or the cost element that it is built abroad. But uniqueness implies that a great deal of research and development had already been done on a product; and this will rarely if ever be funded by the Pentagon. So, even though US-owned companies are now complaining bitterly about the lack of orders and research help from the Pentagon, Europeans will remain effectively excluded from the benefits derived from what is still a reasonably well-endowed foundation, whether they invest in the US or not.

The Pentagon is a genuine force discriminating against the Europeans. The American tax system should not, in theory, be one, but Europeans often see it as such. This is partly because it is unavoidable. Most European companies in the US after all are not in defence-oriented businesses, and if they do come across the Pentagon it is probably for routine supply purposes where there are really no complications. A company can choose its area of business, it can keep out of industries and areas where it will be at a disadvantage as an outsider. Indeed, as we have seen, this ability to pick and choose is a major part of the European challenge. But wherever it goes the European company has to take the whole American tax system as it finds it.

The system itself is very different to that found in continental Europe, principally because it relies mainly at the Federal level on Income Tax levied on people or companies, rather than on the indirect taxes like the Value-added Tax or Social Service charges which form so high a proportion of the tax paid to European governments. The importance of Federal Income Tax creates a number of worries. At the most personal level, executives are concerned that their own government will ask for and get far more details of what they earn in the US than it could if they were completely home-based. (In fact there is an increasing volume of exchange of such information, either to collect taxes more effectively or, as with the Swiss-American agreement of 1970, to chase down fraudulent operators.)

At a corporate level, the system's reliance on income tax works both ways. Whereas in Europe aid is often available in the form of cash grants, American government help to corporations is mostly in the form of allowances, credits and depreciation provisions, which are only useful when a company has some US profits whose tax bill it can reduce with the help of such grants. And the newcomer has none. Indeed, as we saw in Chapter 10, one of the reasons for the merger of BP's American interests and Sohio was the particularly generous provisions available to the oil industry. But the newcomer, especially if, like so many Europeans, he is bringing in some specialised know-how or product, also has an element of choice as to how he can divide his profits, a choice which can help him to reduce his tax bill.

He will normally have a subsidiary company in the United States, but dividends from that subsidiary to the parent company are effectively subject to an American withholding tax. Depending upon the tax treaty his country has with the US, this can range from nothing to a full 30 per cent. But the foreign company can reduce the liability because payments of interest or royalties paid on patents, technical knowledge, know-how, copyrights, trade marks or the like, are tax-exempt. So the foreign company can reduce its tax burden by arranging for as much income as possible to be taken by the parent as non-dividend income. However, the tax problems of a foreign company are not confined to the Federal corporate level. At a recent conference, Walter Damm of the Banking Commission of the European Common Market gave a long list of other tax barriers: "Such State and local taxes as sales tax, franchise tax, and property tax are quite important and confusing, at least in the beginning; they differ from state to state and are not covered by double taxation agreements. If a subsidiary receives supplies from a parent company, the latter may find itself subject to US Federal and State taxes for the profits effectively connected with the conduct of trade or business conducted with the US. Temporary residents in the US are taxed there, not only on their US earnings, but on their world-wide earnings and capital gains. If the subsidiary obtains double taxation relief it may lose such relief because the parent is a non-US company."

This list is by no means complete. But it does show up two of the inevitable complications in establishing businesses in the US. First, the recurring point that state and local governments play a far more important part than in Europe; and although state sales and income taxes are never very high (and some states

only have one of them) they are still a nuisance and a complication. But Damm's list also shows how much more zealous
and protective of its rights the US government has been than
many others, and the legal and administrative complexity to
which this state of affairs gives rise. As Professor Kindleburger
puts it, "the power to tax is the power to destroy; it is also the
crucial power to exact deference to the sovereign". And the
US government, with a watchful xenophobic Congress behind
it, has always been eager to ensure that foreigners—and indeed
its own citizens trying to escape US jurisdiction by going
abroad—have paid up what was due so that its sovereignty
remained intact.

Even when the Americans fall in line with international
custom this anxiety can undo good work. Before 1966 foreign
companies in the US had to cope with what is called the "force
of attraction" in tax matters. If they had a branch or subsidiary
in the US, all the income they derived in the US from whatever
source, whether it was interest on money loaned out by the
parent, royalties, or sales made by any company in the group,
was all lumped together with the income from the subsidiary.
So instead of being taxed at the rate appropriate to the type of
revenue they represented, they were all taxed, in theory anyway, at the full rate of corporation tax. Since this was sometimes more than double the rate applicable on capital gains or
interest, the rule amounted to some fairly effective discrimination against foreign business.

In 1966 the Foreign Investor's Tax Act ensured that different
types of income, from business and from investment, from
passive or active involvement, would be separated for tax
purposes. Even this attempt to put foreign-owned businesses on
the same basis as US-owned ones aroused Congressional
suspicion. According to one expert, "many things that the
Administration proposed in the interests of equality seemed like
they might be a give-away to members of the Congress". And
the good work was partly negatived by subsequent attempts to
tax the non-US income of American citizens and corporations.
The American Internal Revenue Service has bent over back-

wards with elaborate rules to stop this applying to the non-US income of American companies controlled by foreigners. So the rules involved can be circumvented but, as another tax expert put it, the complications "cut back a lot of the psychological kind of benefit in stimulating investment, that was hoped for by the 1966 Act". Even now foreign companies have to ensure that the stock they own in US corporations is not used as collateral for a loan; and there is still some strength left in the old "force of attraction" rule.

Tax rules also play a part in deterring foreign corporations from exploiting a patent actively in the United States rather than a one-off sale to an unrelated American corporation where no entanglement, leading to tax problems, can arise. If the foreigner licenses his patent he has to make extremely sure that he is basing the operation in a country with a suitable tax treaty with the US; and if he sells the rights to his own subsidiary in the US he gets all snarled up with Federal income and dividend-withholding taxes. This sort of complication comes as an unwelcome addition to the problems of actually producing and marketing the product on which he has a patent. If a foreign company takes over an American one it may have to go in for some fancy legal gyrations to satisfy the sellers of the company, who may for their own tax purposes want to sell stock in the company rather than assets and be paid in equity or loan stock rather than in cash.

All these problems, however complex, are at least concerned with a fairly rational if convoluted tax law. But some of the worst recent problems encountered by foreign companies, not only in tax but when trying to finance their American companies locally, stem from the way in which the Americans have used their tax system to influence their balance of payments. These troubles are often accidental, which makes them difficult to pinpoint or forecast, and the regulations were often not drafted with foreign-controlled companies in mind at all. In the words of Walter Slowinski, a distinguished American tax lawyer, "each time something had to be done about the balance of payments, they ran to the internal revenue code, except in the last gesture it was to the foreign direct investment regulations and the code was getting pretty tired of being picked on, you know, for public policy objectives".

The biggest nightmare for foreign corporations arises from the workings of the Interest Equalisation Tax. This was enacted in 1963 to prevent capital raised in the US for more than one year by any institution or company from a developed country being exported, thus virtually insulating the American capital market from the rest of the world. A foreign company is inevitably unsure if the Inland Revenue Service will rule that money borrowed by the American subsidiary for more than one year from a bank or other financial institution, like a pension fund or an insurance company, counts as an issue by the parent company and is thus liable to the tax. The IRS has told American corporations abroad to make sure that their local subsidiaries are not "thinly capitalised". If they do try and borrow more than five times their equity capital then, says the IRS, the parent in effect becomes the borrower even though there may be a chain of companies, international financial subsidiaries and the like, between the borrower and the parent. So foreign companies must try and obtain exemption from the tax when raising loans for a subsidiary in the United States. They have to prove that the loan is supported by the asset value of the US subsidiary, that all the funds will be used in the US and not shipped out, and that funds raised in the US are not a substitute for money that would otherwise be brought in.

But even if the company does get clearance from the IRS this is a strictly one-off business and every subsequent loan needs separate clearance. No wonder there is a group at work in the American Investment Banking Association to amend the IET to exempt issues by US subsidiaries of foreign companies from the tax, even if they have a guarantee from the parent company. The grounds the investment bankers are using are that the United States benefits from the extra business generated by the issue of such loans; they could add that the loans are going to result in increased manufacture of items, many of which were previously imported.

The IET also rears its ugly head in any attempt to try to take over American companies using shares in foreign concerns. Plessey's take-over of Alloys Unlimited was delayed for some time because Plessey needed a ruling that the dollar shares it was issuing in the parent company would not count as foreign securities and therefore attract IET. But at least this tax is administered by the IRS, a highly competent and professional body, which is also applying definite rules and is not deliberately unhelpful.* Even so, the complications and uncertainties created by the IET have led some foreign companies to finance their American activities through the Euro-dollar market (which creates further problems in timing and interest payments and guarantee). And some of course are simply too small, too timid, or too confused, to raise the money necessary for entry at all.

Yet there is an even murkier area of difficulty; the danger that funds raised in the United States may be considered as in some way a substitute for funds imported from abroad. This factor brings in two more institutions, the Federal Reserve Bank and the Office of Foreign Direct Investments within the Department of Commerce in Washington. The banks have to operate their voluntary credit restraint programme so as to prevent this substitution effect even on money borrowed by foreign companies to cover their requirements of working capital, let alone more permanent investments. The banks (as well as institutional investors) are scared that the Fed, which has in fact effectively ignored this aspect of the restraint programme, will apply it, so that they could be landed with the consequences. This may be an unreal prospect but the banks are more concerned to placate the Fed than please a foreign customer, so the fear, however unreal, has a very real effect.

Even worse is the problem of trying to satisfy the OFDI, partly because it is a recently established department with a shifting population of administrators. And its existence adds yet

* It has, for instance, speeded up the very necessary clearance of takeovers by foreign companies so that the majority get an assurance that neither side will attract any tax liability within a couple of months.

another hurdle for the overseas customer trying to show that locally raised funds are not a substitute for imported capital. When, for instance, a foreign company borrows from an American one on a "back-to-back" basis, everyone concerned must certify that the US dollars are not substitutes for imported ones. In many cases it is quite impossible to prove that the foreign company could not raise the money elsewhere in the world and bring it into the US. It may simply be more convenient, or cheaper, to raise it in the US (it is probably the company's policy to raise as much as possible locally anyway); and such is the nature of the international capital market and of companies' own financial situations that a company may be awash with cash or unused credit facilities only a few months after claiming, quite rightly, that it was stretched to the limit of its resources. In other words, to get over these hurdles the foreign company has to certify something—that it couldn't raise the money elsewhere—which is in practice often uncertifiable. Since the European companies rely on the usually excellent capital facilities in the US to a greater extent than American companies abroad, these worries form a real deterrent and make the Europeans feel harried, rather than helped, by the government department with which they have most contact —the taxmen.

The sheer unpredictability of the tax complications and their apparent lack of contact with real life makes them unique. But the Europeans have also to cope with regulatory agencies which are largely unknown at home. So, unlike American corporations, they, and their executives, have not grown up with these agencies and kept their rules and requirements in the back of their minds throughout their lives. In fact they are coming as complete innocents upon a scene where the agencies have been going for a very long time and have now acquired considerable sophistication and strength in dealing with companies to guard against the most sophisticated dodges dreamed up by generations of dubious entrepreneurs to bamboozle, poison or deceive the American public. The Europeans are unlucky in that the three agencies with which they mostly come into contact, the

Securities and Exchange Commission, the Food and Drugs
Administration and the Anti-trust division of the Justice Department, are among the most highly developed of all the Federal
government's watch-dogs—in some other cases they are either
toothless, like the Federal Communications Commission, or
historical monuments unable to cope with the realities of
modern life, like the Interstate Communications Commission
which deals with road and rail questions.

The SEC is frequently mentioned as a very considerable
hindrance because of its detailed provisions for ensuring that
any company whose stock is quoted on an American exchange
provides adequate information. Until recently the amount of
information the SEC required, especially when new stock was
issued, was far greater than that demanded by any European
exchange. So the contrast was a terrible shock. But in the past
few years Europeans have been catching up rapidly and in
some cases their requirements are rather more severe than
American ones: German accounting principles on stock valua-
tion and the disclosure required by the London Stock Exchange
during take-over bids are two cases in point. And American
companies have to provide a far less detailed split of where their
profits come from, geographically as well as by trading activities,
than do British ones—had the American conglomerates, for
instance, been forced into the English pattern, the nifty and
dubious footwork exhibited in their accounts during the last
few years of the 1960's would have been impossible.

For British, German and Dutch companies the problem with
the SEC is often a largely formal one, in that it requires accounts
to be presented in a certain way so that a group has to re-
formulate the same information to a different pattern. And even
some Swiss and French groups, like Rhône-Poulenc, Pechiney
and Alusuisse, have gone ahead with consolidated accounts
which could be easily adapted to SEC regulations, not to
satisfy the Americans, but the international investment community.

In fact the major crisis involving the SEC is now past history.
It started in 1964 when the SEC extended its requirements to

any foreign company which happened to have American share-holders. There was a fearful row but a very reasonable set of regulations were devised. Foreign companies were given two years' complete exemption; the rules then applied only if they had 300 shareholders resident in the US; exemptions were given from regulations about share trading by directors and other "insiders" and the naming of proxies; and, unless the shares were to be quoted on an American stock exchange, the informa-tion required was largely tailored to that given by the company to its own home stock exchange. This sort of workable com-promise is only possible when you have one institution in charge of a particular field and it has reasonable discretionary powers and a competent staff; and none of these conditions applies in the tax area.

But even the existence of one strong agency is no guarantee that the Europeans will not suffer badly from US regulations. A classic case in point is the Food and Drugs Administration which is responsible for licensing new products in a field where the Europeans are particularly strong and have large numbers of products which they want to bring in from abroad. Although the FDA will accept some clinical evidence from abroad, its rules generally involve a foreign company in expensive clinical and field tests in the United States. And the thalidomide tragedy, where a drug subsequently proved to have appalling side-effects was allowed into many sophisticated markets, including Germany and the United Kingdom, but banned from the US, did nothing to increase the FDA's willingness to accept results of foreign tests.

This situation creates two problems for European companies. When they introduce a product abroad the fact that the FDA will delay its introduction in the US for up to five years gives their American competitors time to catch up; and they may have very considerable problems in trying to get the particular company in their group which discovered the product to do tests which the FDA will accept. CIBA pointed out, for instance, that if its Portuguese company finds a drug it can scarcely be expected to conduct the FDA's tests on its own slim resources.

The existence of the FDA, and the absence of any internationally accepted testing code, means that there is an inevitable temptation for non-American companies to do the majority of their research in areas like drugs, pesticides, herbicides and veterinary products, in the United States. This means that once the FDA has passed them they can immediately be introduced in the biggest market of all before competitors have time to catch up, and, because the FDA's tests are so strict, other countries are more ready to accept its findings than it is to accept theirs.

But even the FDA only covers a minority of European companies and none of them thought of it as worse than a finicky but fundamentally sensible organisation doing a genuine job of protecting Americans and, only incidentally, protecting American companies as well. The same cannot be said of European attitudes towards the anti-trust division of the Justice Department. They think it unfairly biased against Europeans; they are sure that it is capricious and likely to turn against them even if they have been established for some time in the US; and, generally, they are all afraid of it as people living in a totalitarian society are afraid of the secret police. The mere fact that you are innocent, that you have had the best legal advice as to what you are doing, the fact that you have been untroubled for a very long time is of no consequence. The threat still remains. The European companies are wrong to think in this way but there is no doubt that anti-trust, even more than the tax authorities, is a legitimate bogeyman in two rather separate ways: first what it is likely to do to European companies' activities; and second, and rather different, what they are afraid it can do even to their operations outside the US.

CHAPTER 13

THE OGRE OF ANTI-TRUST

IT is a sign of the increased interest being paid in Europe to investment in the US that the anti-trust regulations have suddenly loomed up as a major obstacle; for they are by no means a new one. As far as European companies in the US were concerned, the fear of anti-trust hung over the inability of Unilever and EMI to control their American subsidiaries as tightly as they would have liked, and as the Americans can in Europe; and in cases as diverse as the mergers of CIBA and Geigy and BP and Sohio, Beecham's problems with its drug patents, Bayer's partnership with Monsanto and Lever's acquisition of "all" detergent, we have already seen how anti-trust has affected the Europeans in a wide variety of ways even after they have been established in the country for some time. European companies without direct investments were also affected: in a number of cases in the twenty years after the war the American courts made several attempts to extend their jurisdiction to foreign companies. These cases arose from the work of the anti-trust division of the Justice Department in policing the most basic of all the American anti-trust prohibitions, section 1 of the Sherman Act of 1890, which declares simply that "every contract, combination in the form of trust or otherwise, or conspiracy, in restraint of trade or commerce among the several states or with foreign nations, is hereby declared to be illegal".

The zeal of the American courts is based on the way in which the law can, in American eyes anyway, be applied to foreign companies. As an international lawyer, J. J. A. Ellis, puts it: "The extraterritorial application of US anti-trust law is governed by the 'effects' theory (i.e. the effects of acts performed abroad upon US domestic or foreign trade interests) and does not depend on the nationality of the enterprise involved." The Americans quite simply believed that their laws were beneficial and so were anxious to apply them as widely as possible. In effect, by ensuring that their laws covered any activities which might affect them in any way, they were half-consciously guarding against a danger of which the rest of the world has only just become aware: the way international companies can effectively reduce the sovereignty of a country. As Professor Kindleburger says, "US law assumes that both US companies abroad and foreign companies in the US direct the operations of their subsidiaries in ways that conform to US purposes".

The zeal of the American authorities, when breaking up international cartels and agreements to pool patents and carve out spheres of commercial influence, was reinforced because they felt frustrated in their inability to get at the Europeans involved. As A. B. Neale's standard work on anti-trust puts it:

> Sometimes it may be suspected that an American company has an understanding with foreign companies that they will not invade the North American market and it will not export to their markets, but no express agreement relating to the American side of the bargain can be found or proved. Yet the foreign companies concerned may be quite open and explicit about their arrangements and obligations. It may seem very frustrating not to be able to bring before the court those who have agreed not to supply the American market, a course of action which rather clearly restrains competition in the United States.
>
> It must also be tantalizing, in some cases, to the enforcement agencies to feel that the files of the non-American participants in a suspected cartel agreement are probably bursting with exhibits which would not only lay bare the workings of the restrictive scheme but would even record

an uninhibited satisfaction at the suppression of competition envisaged and intended by the parties; whereas the
files of the American company concerned, meticulously
guided and reviewed by lawyers who have anti-trust risks
constantly in their thoughts, may yield but meagre or
arcane indications of the true situation.

In their efforts to stop conspiracies in restraint of trade, to get
evidence from foreign companies and some redress against the
foreign companies, the Americans have in the past gone so far as
to serve writs on foreign businessmen in the US on business or
personal visits; and when companies had assets within the US,
writs have been issued threatening to seize them in order to
force the parent company to appear in court.

In the past, less extreme attempts to apply American anti-
trust law to the activities (especially the non-American ones) of
non-American companies have naturally aroused considerable
nationalist opposition in the foreign countries concerned even
when the cartel being broken up was a very real one. When the
American courts were finally destroying the cartel agreements
between Du Pont and ICI in the early 1950's, the British courts
were used to ensure that British Nylon Spinners retained its
rights to the Du Pont nylon patents which ICI had transferred
during the US court case, probably in order to take them out of
reach of the US courts. During the same period the British and
other European governments intervened to protect their own
oil companies from being dragged into an investigation of price
fixing arrangements. The successive attempts by another
American government agency, the Federal Maritime Commission, to acquire documentary evidence from British companies
of rate fixing on transatlantic shipping agreements, provoked a
series of public rows during the 1960's, and the Canadians have
blocked attempts to allow their companies' documents to be used
by the American authorities. The Swiss and American governments became deeply embroiled because of the widespread
ramifications of the cartel arrangements under which the
Swiss watchmakers operated. Because this agreement did not

have the specific authority of the Swiss government, the Americans felt free to pursue its consequences as far as an investigation of the Swiss companies' arrangements in the rest of Europe, activities which affected the Americans because the non-Swiss companies involved keep out of the US.

But these cases, however large and public, did not affect the vast majority of European companies which are not part of international cartels. What worries them is the application of another Act altogether, clause 7 of the Clayton Act of 1914, which stops take-overs "where the effect of such acquisitions may be to substantially lessen competition between the Corporation whose stock is so acquired and the Corporation making the acquisition, or to restrain such commerce in any section or community, or tend to create a monopoly in any line of commerce". The prohibition was virtually ineffective for thirty-six years after it was first enacted because the courts ruled that the section was designed to cover only secret share purchases and (in a separate judgment) that the Act did not allow mergers to be undone anyway. Ordinary acquisitions were virtually unaffected. The Act did not really bite until the Celler-Kefauver Act of 1950 closed the gap. The political climate of President Eisenhower's 1950's was not conducive to vigorous anti-trust activity. So it was not until 1962 that it became clear just how widely this provision could be applied to cover take-overs where the combined company did not even have a quarter of the market concerned. Then a merger between two shoe companies was blocked, even though together they produced under 5 per cent of the nation's shoes, and as retailers sold less than 10 per cent. The early 1960's also saw a series of decisions on "potential competitors". These effectively ensured that companies strong enough to enter a market—geographical or industrial—but which had not done so, would not be allowed to use the take-over of an existing company to do precisely that. Nor, as Bayer and Monsanto found, were partnerships allowed when either side could be judged able to compete in the new market by itself. A joint venture can also create a long-term problem. As Ellis points out, "the more successful a joint venture the greater the risk that at some future date it will draw the attention of the Department of Justice"—Mobay was an extreme case because the joint venture got 50 per cent of its market. The only exceptions allowed were if the victim was so obviously failing that it was not providing competition or if the bidder needed a new product line to remain an effective competitor itself. Because, it was ruled, Procter & Gamble could have entered the bleach market by itself, it was forced to sell off Clorox, the biggest maker of household bleach in the US, ten years after P & G had bought it. By contrast, as we saw in Chapter 4, Unilever was allowed to buy the rights to "all" detergent from Monsanto in order to retain effective competition against P & G.

This concentration on attacking mergers has also affected the European companies because the very vigorous anti-trust division of the Justice Department administers the Sherman Act and section 7 of the Clayton Act—the two sections with which they generally come into contact. Many other anti-trust provisions are policed by a much less vigorous body, and one now under attack because of its alleged softness towards the industries with which it is dealing, the Federal Trade Commission.

A more crucial result for the Europeans has been the establishment of a virtual double scale of values. Their American competitors had built up their positions in the relatively free days before 1950. As newcomers the Europeans are having to obey rules which, had they been in existence earlier, would never have allowed the construction of the massive existing American corporate entities with which they are competing. To take an extreme example, Will Durant and Alfred P. Sloan would not have been permitted to build up General Motors as they did by a series of take-overs under the present criteria. Conversely, because there were no anti-trust rules in Europe, American companies have been able to buy up competitors and companies in complementary businesses in Europe freely, although under their domestic regulations the bids would have been disallowed because the companies concerned could have got into the market by themselves. Yet it is only recently, after a large number of potential or actual European competitors had been swallowed up, that the American authorities have tried to establish that an American company could not take over a European one because it was an actual or potential competitor in the US market. The anti-trust authorities know of only one case where they would have acted to stop an acquisition on these grounds, and before they could do so the foreign government had forbidden the take-over anyway on straight nationalist grounds. The only public attempt there has been to protect the independence of a potential European competitor—and then an unsuccessful one—was when Gillette took over the German Braun company, a move which would, anti-trust feared, prevent Braun entering the American market with its own electric razors to compete with Gillette. In another case Litton Industries was allowed to take over the German Adler typewriter company, although it already owned an American manufacturer, because otherwise it would not have been able to compete with IBM, which dominated the electric typewriter market.

In the late 1960's under Richard McLaren, anti-trust turned in other directions, all of which affected the Europeans. After the fuss created by the BP-Sohio merger McLaren went out of his way in an important speech in March 1970 to say that a foreign company "can hardly expect better treatment than domestic firms, anti-trust promises that he will receive no worse". But he went on to make a parallel between anti-trust proceedings and ecology which combines very aptly two of the ways in which Europeans are having to suffer from present-day American preoccupations which affect them peculiarly badly because their products, companies and facilities are newcomers to the scene. "The ecologists," he said, "stress that we should take into account the long-term consequences of the introduction of a product into the environment before the product is in fact introduced. I think this principle of ecology is a pretty good one for anti-trust too." This desire to think about future consequences of present actions has led the Justice Department under McLaren to apply with renewed vigour the "incipiency clause" in existing legislation under which he can prevent a merger (like that between Gillette and Braun) which might have an anti-competitive impact on the US market in the future, though it would not do so immediately.

Foreign companies are also affected by a renewed attack by the Department on licensing agreements. To quote McLaren's March 1970 speech again: "We should be especially wary of artificial barriers to the entry of foreign firms or their products into our domestic markets." These barriers included "unduly restrictive patent, know-how, and technology licences as well as outright cartel-type arrangements". The mere fact that a licence was granted for a very long time, itself always a suspicious fact, is now under detailed assault. McLaren was especially concerned to ensure that cross-licensing of patents between the technical leaders in an industry did not permanently eliminate competition (American corporate lawyers have often told their clients that this sort of agreement could not be expected to last indefinitely anyway). Later in 1970 McLaren was as good as his word and acted against a very long-standing agreement between American Westinghouse and the Japanese Mitsubishi companies under which Mitsubishi exploited a large number of Westinghouse's patents. If McLaren is successful Mitsubishi could, if it wanted, use the know-how it acquired under licence from Westinghouse to compete with Westinghouse in the American market. Whether it *would* compete is another matter: the American authorities can only try and remove the legal restrictions on competition; they cannot force the companies concerned to compete.

This break-up of international licensing agreements could benefit European companies by making it possible for them to attack the American market, using American know-how. The general openness of the US market, the relative absence of the cosy market-sharing arrangements and price rings which still persist in Europe, all features which favour the Europeans, are often due to anti-trust's past activities. So it is rather hypocritical of the Europeans to expect the best of both worlds—the market opportunities opened up by anti-trust, yet complete liberty to exploit them. Yet the benefits in this case are long-term theoretical ones, and appear less substantial than the short-term disadvantages of the general attack on licences. Beecham has probably been the single company most affected by one aspect of the Justice Department's attack. For several years the Department's primary objective in the drug field has been to establish through anti-trust court cases the legal principle that patent licences cannot be limited to marketing drugs in the form of finished products ready to be taken by a patient. It has been trying to force the drug companies to sell the bulk material to all-comers (this attack comes belatedly after twenty-five years in which a number of American drug companies made scandalously large profits out of their monopoly of new drugs). The attack has hit Beecham badly because it had the patents on the most important drug involved.

Zenith, another drug company, imported Ampicillin, Beecham's semi-synthetic penicillin, in bulk from Italy where patents on existing drugs are not applied. Beecham sued because its patent rights had been infringed, Zenith sued Beecham on anti-trust grounds. The anti-trust authorities, which often tend to throw the book at companies they are attacking, have even assailed the validity of Beecham's patent. In theory, if anti-trust succeeds in this case, it will destroy the whole drug patent system by allowing in new drugs in bulk from countries like Italy without patent protection.

Beecham is an extreme case of the way in which foreign companies, because so many of them are new to the scene, are in the very front line against attempts by the anti-trust department to assert its powers more fully. But many more companies have been affected (or assumed they would be) when they think of buying an American company. Recently, anti-trust has ensured that virtually any take-over by a major company in its own or a related industry will at least be examined: if a company is big enough any bid, however small, is likely to be forbidden because it could enter virtually any industry by itself—it is said that General Motors would not even be allowed to take over a petrol station. European companies are not likely to be judged that harshly; but because they try, in general, to extend their activities in the US to correspond with those elsewhere, some examination is inevitable. However, recent cases do show that the anti-trust authorities are not implacable: once the Dutch KZO company had shown that it knew nothing about salt production in mines rather than salt pans (and thus, lacking the relevant technology, was not a potential competitor), and had no intention of getting into the US market on its own account, it was allowed to take over International Salt. Alternatively, the merger partners can plead that either the bidder or the victim is weak, though the idea of a "failing" company, open to take-over, is very narrowly defined. According to its published guidelines the anti-trust division regards as failing only those firms with no reasonable prospect of remaining viable; it does not regard a company as failing merely because it has been unprofitable for a period of time, has lost market position or failed to maintain its competitive position in some other respect, has poor management, or has not fully explored the possibility of overcoming its difficulties through self-help. Yet Nestlé succeeded in this plea when taking over Libby, and BASF avoided problems for the same reasons with its bid for Wyandotte.

Then again the bidding company itself can plead the weakness of its own competitive position. Lever did so in the case of "all" detergent; and BP could have said that its financial and managerial resources were far too stretched for it to be competitive on its own in the Ohio market in the foreseeable future. But no company really likes to be exposed to an examination in which it biggest argument will be its own weakness. Like BP, it is much more likely to settle for an out-of-court settlement which will at least allow it most of the benefits of the merger reasonably quickly. But, judging by recent cases, the Justice Department assumes that any strong European company can enter the relevant American market by itself unless proved otherwise, so the weakness case has to be spelled out on each occasion. When British Insulated Callender's Cables, the largest British cable makers, proposed a share swap with General Cables, the second biggest in the US, the Justice Department at first objected, saying that a link between two such strong companies would not increase competition. Better, said the Justice Department, for BICC to tie up with one of the smaller American cable makers. And it needed a good deal of convincing that BICC would not have entered the US market alone or without a link with a company as powerful as General Cable before it would let the deal through. Even then it imposed several restrictions, including a weakening of the proposed links between the two, and forced BICC to let other American companies have licences on its valuable patents.*

Anti-trust is not likely to intervene, even if the European company could enter a market anyway, has every intention of doing so and the victim is a viable concern, provided the foreign company is making its first investment. This idea, that Europeans should be allowed a "foothold", can allow some sizeable investments—BP's foothold in the American petrol market after all consisted of the 10,000 petrol stations and two oil refineries it bought from Sinclair Oil. But this "foothold" concept, which is McLaren's way of encouraging the Europeans, imposes a very crucial decision on the European company concerned when it first enters the American market. It cannot afford a mistake: it has only one bite at the cherry—even if the first acquisition is too small or inadequate it will still face a much more rigorous attitude from anti-trust when it tries to strengthen its position with another purchase.

So anti-trust would be a formidable barrier to Europeans even if it consisted of a fixed body of law administered in an unchanging way. But of course it is not. As we have seen, the 1960's were particularly fruitful in new applications of anti-trust, particularly in the field of eliminating competition through licensing and encouraging it by ensuring that potential competitors did not enter a market the easy way by taking over existing companies. (In theory this attitude should encourage

---

* As usual there were a number of sub-plots: in this case neither company was vertically integrated by being connected with a copper or aluminium producer, so the two could use a link to assert themselves against the large and cartelised copper producers.

European companies to come in by themselves, whereas in the absence of anti-trust they would either have invested in a joint venture with an American company or taken one over. But in real life timid companies which are not allowed to enter through a take-over or a joint venture are much more likely to stay out completely than come in by themselves as anti-trust intends they should).

The Europeans are also affected by the sheer uncertainty as to the applications of the anti-trust laws. Because it is so enormous a field the Justice Department can only concentrate on a few aspects of it at any one time. The emphasis depends partly on court decisions and new laws and partly also on the mood of particular Department heads. As Sir Eric Drake says, "the officials with whom we were dealing were only doing their best to interpret the law of the land, the interpretation of which inevitably varies from Administration to Administration". This unpredictability makes anti-trust especially daunting to European companies, bringing with it the fear that what they are doing now may be smiled on unofficially by the present Administration but could become a central object of assault for a subsequent one. Points of attack can seem inconsistently chosen even within a single case. BP had no existing stake in the Ohio market for petrol and Sohio had only 30 per cent of it. Yet anti-trust concentrated on this possible limitation to competition, while it ignored the fact that between them BP and Sohio controlled 90 per cent of world production of acrylonitrile, a vital raw material for making acrylic fibres like Orlon. There are only two known processes for making this, BP has the exclusive rights to one, Sohio to the other.

In view of this sort of paradox, it is not surprising that there have been calls for a multinational anti-trust authority as well as many requests for the anti-trust division to give positive, permanent, binding permission when foreign companies try and get into the US market. Neither of these ideas seems practical. The problem of policing an international anti-trust agreement would be insuperable even in the unlikely event that the Americans, concerned only with competition, could agree the terms of such a law with the Europeans and the Japanese, who are still concerned with strengthening their own industries through anti-competitive mergers in order to face the Americans. And the jealous shadow of Congress is long and deep enough to prevent any discrimination in favour of European companies. McLaren himself ruled out, for instance, a suggestion of mine that just as some parts of a country are given exceptional help because of their economic problems, so European companies and other new entrants in a particular field of activity should be granted the status of "disadvantaged corporations" and allowed more leeway in anti-trust matters than normal companies.

If Europeans tried, as they legitimately could, to copy what the US is already doing to limit acquisition of companies by potential competitors and to force the split-up of existing groups (many of which would, inevitably, be American-controlled), they would probably find that Congress would immediately put the pressure on the American administration to strengthen its rules to the disadvantage of the Europeans. Because of the power of present American rules and the weakness, irrelevance or inconsistency of European ones, Europeans would always find themselves trailing in any race to split up multinational concerns. So the Europeans may well continue to panic at the apparent haphazardness, unpredictability and waywardness of anti-trust. They can have no idea when, whether or on what grounds, any of their activities in or out of the US may be attacked. If the merger of CIBA and Geigy was delayed because of the need for clearance, will anti-trust claim similar jurisdiction on the proposed merger of other foreign groups which have interests in the US—or are strong enough to have such interests? Can BP-Sohio be sure that some future action may not be brought against its world monopoly in acrylonitrile? Can ICI, BASF and Rhône-Poulenc guarantee that their joint ventures in the US are safe?

Yet they will learn to live with these uncertainties and the ogre may appear less serious in the next few years as the companies entering the US get progressively smaller. For the smaller the company the less likely it is to be able to compete by itself in any particular sphere, and therefore the more likely to be cleared as a potential partner or bidder for an American company. Even bigger companies can often expect some countervailing diplomatic pressure by their own government against the Americans—help which benefited both BP and BICC. But they cannot rely on the provision of such help—let alone that it will have any effect on the US attitude.

The fear of anti-trust could also become less dark as European companies become more used to it, as they start to behave like Americans and consult the appropriate lawyers before major moves. They may even come to appreciate its positive qualities —the fact that it is a body of law, however uneven its applica- tion, and not (like the British Monopolies Commission) almost totally unpredictable, and the way it opens up markets for them. But the mere growth of their interests in the US could leave them open to attack on two grounds: anti-trust may want to break up existing joint ventures because the European partner is now strong enough to go it alone; and the anti-trust authorities may return to the Sherman Act and find new access for attacks on foreign companies for their part in cartel arrangements. Until very recently, after all, European companies as big as ICI or BP were represented in the United States only by tiny offices in Washington or New York, so that the Justice Depart- ment found it difficult to get to grips with them. But now that they have a major stake in the US they have given hostages to fortune, and as Ellis pointed out, "the European company will have to realise that the US anti-trust laws might at some time in the future be applied extraterritorially to its activities outside the United States". It is this fear which has led SKF, Unilever and EMI to steer clear of proper control of their American activities in the past. Although McLaren has gone out of his way specifically to deny intention of becoming a global anti-trust policeman, one of his successors might feel very differently. So, as on most other anti-trust matters, the Europeans will have to accept that, as newcomers, they will be in the front line as far as the restrictions and attacks of anti-trust are concerned.

CHAPTER 14

THE AMERICAN EXPERIENCE

> It is, of course, always galling (apart from political
> considerations) in any country to see an enterprise
> doing well without local people being interested.
> It is contrary to human nature, however well a
> concern like that may be directed, or however
> much it may have the interest of the people at
> heart, not to feel there will be a kind of jealous
> feeling against such a company.
> —Sir Henry Deterding of Royal Dutch Shell
>   in the 1920's

The Europeans would be superhuman if they did not grumble,
as do so many Americans, against the frequent barriers created
by the vagaries of the Pentagon, the tax authorities and the US
government's many regulatory agencies, and did not try and
invoke help from home when attacked. But such requests put
them (and their home governments) in a weak position to
complain when American companies call upon the power of
their own parent government to protect them when they are
threatened. They should accept, and expect the American
companies to accept, the Calvo doctrine. This asserts that
foreign investors have no recourse to their own government for
protection and must seek remedy for any injury done to them
exclusively in the local courts. This idea is obviously anathema
to American companies; but if European companies are con-
tinually expected to keep quiet about American judicial

proceedings, American companies really cannot fuss about decisions elsewhere. For the Calvo doctrine is essentially the only way in which equality between big strong countries and smaller, weaker ones can be established in the face of multinational companies.

For all the Americans are doing is using their laws to protect their society against "over-mighty subjects". Because they have so much experience of the unchecked power of large corporations they have evolved a far more effective mechanism than other countries for dealing with them. The fact that the various provisions involved seem to strike hard on foreigners can also be seen as the very natural way the Americans protect themselves against the double threat posed by large companies which are controlled from outside the country. For, as Adriano Olivetti, one of the most philosophical of the invaders, pointed out in a Harvard Business School case study of his company: "You cannot be a business 'visitor' over a certain size. It isn't fair to just take all that money out of the economy—any economy, even as strong and as rich an economy as the United States. You also have to make a contribution to the economy. Moreover, quite beyond such ethical considerations, if you ignore the responsibility of contributing to an economy, something will happen to stop you. National economies have various ways of protecting this fairness."

The Europeans should realise, like Olivetti, that the Americans are merely ensuring that their own society is not overaffected by the invaders, and that it is this assurance that helps to make Americans personally so relaxed about the European invaders—even if they fight hard, and sometimes chauvinistically, against their products.

Countries without such a framework are now coming to realise how much power they lose if much of their industrial life is controlled by international corporations. They lose tax revenue: centralised control of the cash-flow of the companies makes it much more difficult to exercise control over monetary policy; similar central direction reduces the freedom countries have in deciding how best to encourage industrial investment;

above all the tendency among really centralised groups, like IBM, to fragment its research and production effort into specialised units in different countries, means that one of the major supposed advantages to foreign direct investment, the development of new industries, is not achieved.

In the US all is different. A watchful host government is confronted by companies whose American subsidiaries are treated not as the robot operating arms of an all-powerful central corporate brain, but as independent concerns. So a reasonably satisfactory three-sided working relationship seems to have evolved between the host country, the parent company and the local subsidiary. The host is strong and confident because it is getting the benefits of direct investment with none of the disadvantages; the parent company is anxious to adapt itself to local surroundings; the subsidiary is independent enough of the parent for the host country not to feel that it is losing any great degree of sovereignty. All that is missing in the relationship is American recognition that the Europeans are bringing any particular qualities into their country. The most obvious benefit introduced by any newcomer to a market is simply that he is new and is not therefore bound by the unspoken framework within which local companies are operating. The Europeans have certainly brought this fresh approach to old markets, from Lever's Lux Flakes to Wilkinson's stainless steel razor blades. But they have brought more than a fresh eye. Their willingness to conduct long-term basic research even within companies which are not large by American standards, their emphasis on the somewhat neglected values of specialisation, the way in which they try and shield employees of all ranks against sudden or unfair dismissal, as well as their desire to learn from their surroundings, are all features of European corporate life in the US which the Americans would do well to emulate. European countries are now beginning to grapple with the problem of ensuring that the activities of multinational organisations do not produce any further loss of sovereignty. They have in front of them the awful example of the Canadians, desperately looking for ways to buy back their own country from the Americans, or at least to prevent any further slide into economic colonialism.

All the alternatives to the balance of enlightened self-interest which appears to have been worked out in the US have very serious disadvantages. The first, international control of multinational companies, is now being actively mooted. It would provide for the creation of some form of truly international policing over their activities, through a supra-national anti-trust organisation, and some form of agreed tax code which would discipline these companies and force them to pay taxes equitably in the countries where they operate. This idea seems, frankly, remote, and a counsel of despair, since it ignores the very disparate national policies involved. An apparently more realistic idea is that of regional control by organisations like the European Common Market Commission. Even this could lead to a most unpleasant economic war between the US and Europe. The EEC is slowly drawing up a European company law, and trying to organise greater technical co-operation between members so that they are not defenceless against the Americans; negatively it is studying ways to discriminate in favour of European companies in the oil industry. If this negative approach gathers momentum it could lead to the most fearful protectionist war in which the barriers would be erected, not against imports of goods, but of capital. The same applies to the positive steps slowly being taken by the EEC to evolve a proper European anti-trust policy; the first target, the American-owned Continental Can group, was successfully attacked; but a really effective anti-trust policy à l'Americaine, which would involve a good deal of disinvestment by American companies and a natural halt to new acquisitions by major ones (because they could enter the market by themselves) is a long way off. And, because the Americans have such a jealous nationalistic Congress, any such move would produce some form of reprisal in the US.

Alternatively, the Europeans could try and draw up some form of code of conduct for foreign-controlled companies to cover their minimum obligations towards the countries in which they are operating. This code could deal with the ways in which, as we have seen, the European companies in the US differ so markedly from American companies abroad: the relative independence, leading to so much research and development, and so many local initiatives; the personnel policy which ensures that foreign staff will be kept to a minimum in numbers and will be deployed in the most tactful way; the adaptation of policies to fit in with the local social and economic environment; and, implicitly, the abandonment of the attitude of superior paternalism which characterises so many American companies abroad. But the crunch comes with the issue of shares to the local public as a token of real integration. This can even, as in the case of Shell or Petrofina, ensure that the subsidiary sometimes benefits at the cost of the parent. For until every major foreign-owned company operating in any country is obliged to issue a substantial proportion of its shares to local investors, then it will, as Sir Henry Deterding said, be a visitor, and a privileged one at that—and the welcome for a favoured guest can never be permanent. So, any code of good citizenship would inevitably include a provision for such an issue. A combination of national pride, irritation at corporate imperialism and sheer greed at the thought of the value of the shares to be issued could ensure that a code of this nature was carried out fairly generally within a few years. A similar idea is that propounded by Christopher Tugendhat in a recent book: he proposes an annual review of foreign-owned companies in which a suitably qualified government body would ensure that its activities were of benefit to the country.

This idea of responsibility to the host community—and indeed any attempt to discipline international companies within a national or regional framework—has one major disadvantage; Companies are spread more widely than the political authorities. As Professor Raymond Vernon puts it in his book, the multi-national corporation "is not accountable to any public authority that matches it in geographical spread" —and represents all the countries in which it operates.

Whatever other countries do, the swing in the balance of

power between Europe and America should ensure a further heavy investment in the US. For there are still thousands of European companies with the size, specialised products, or technical expertise sufficient for them to enter the American market through direct investment. Yet they are still mumbling the ritual excuses to themselves: that the market is so big, that all the firms are so gigantic, that labour is impossibly expensive, the natives hostile, finance impossible. These excuses grow thinner through the years and, increasingly, any sizeable company which is not involved sounds defensive. Although European investment dried up after the Nixon measures in August 1971, the real possibilities these measures raise—of unpredictable import duties, of trade wars, threats virtually unknown since 1945—are bound to increase the tendency to invest rather than export. After all, the desire to overcome tariff barriers is largely absent from the European invasion, yet is a prime motive in most direct investment elsewhere.

The corollary to a certain increase of the European investments in America is a continuing reappraisal of American attitudes towards investment in Europe. Undoubtedly American companies will cherish and encourage their successful investments overseas which, as they were in the late 1950's, are now often more profitable and operating in economies which are growing faster than in their home base.

But there is already evidence of a double shift in American attitudes. Squeezed at home by the Nixon recession, companies are setting a limit to the time they will carry losses from foreign subsidiaries: this may lead them to pull out of a market where their products are just too alien. Early in 1971, for instance, Kraft stopped trying to sell its processed cheese in France, home of a hundred delicious natural cheeses. This new-found toughness among the American companies is likely to afford European companies some relief from uneconomic American-backed competition in their own back-yard, especially as the spate of new entrants is no longer as fast as it was in the mid 1960's.

Within the companies themselves, control from the centre will become more, not less, rigid, as they grow in importance and as trans-Atlantic telephone and computer links improve. Under these circumstances, a countervailing force is needed to assert the rights of European host countries to exercise control over what goes on inside their borders, whoever owns the institution involved. American companies are fond of proving that any steps they take to adapt themselves to local conditions (above all the issue of equity capital) are likely to prove profoundly inimical to their own strength, and thus, by their extrapolation, to the economic strength of the non-Communist world. Probably only a really xenophobic anti-Americanism among Europeans will convince them otherwise; but once such an idea has real political force behind it, any countervailing efforts by the Americans to mitigate the nationalist backlash are likely to be ineffectual. Yet it is still not too late to try and persuade the Americans that the interests of their companies are not synonymous with those of the countries or the regions in which they are operating; and that consequently the nations involved will seek to super-impose their views on those of the company's. For unless they come to terms with local interests, they are going to find that Europe will follow Latin America and Africa in asserting national control over foreign-controlled enterprises in the crudest possible way, by nationalisation or even confiscation.

Vernon states the position pessimistically: he ends up believing that "the constructive economic role of the multi-national enterprise will be accompanied by destructive political tension". Again the Nixon measures—and the degree to which American corporations hastened the underlying crisis through their heavy investments overseas—have perceptibly increased the underlying tensions.

Anti-Americanism in Europe is now no longer confined to the left (and the French). It is a growing political force which could lead to some fairly ruthless European action against the Americans in their midst.

The Europeans have an excellent case for some sort of action against the Americans simply because, unlike the Peruvians or the Zambians, they can point to a ready-made alternative mode of behaviour by their own companies in the United States. And if the Americans refuse to follow the good example they have been set they can scarcely claim any generosity of treatment from the host governments, or expect sympathy because of any action that may be taken against them. This is not a theoretical warning note. One Canadian political party contains a strong faction which would nationalise American companies without compensation. In Latin America even military regimes are steadily expropriating American concerns and concessions, or are sharing them with European and Japanese companies which are more responsive to local wishes (and less insistent on 100 per cent ownership) than the Americans. At the same time, Pechiney and Olivetti, Shell and Petrofina have not suffered unduly because their pattern of behaviour in the US has been so different from that of the Americans abroad. And in the long run the style of the European infiltrators could ensure that they will be infinitely more secure in the US than the Americans can ever be in the rest of the world.

NOTES AND SOURCES

MOST of this book is based on conversations with, and documents supplied by, government and state officials, and executives of companies and banks involved—primary but inevitably confidential and prejudiced sources. It has been supplemented by the remarkably few written sources I could find. The most valuable of these are the annual series of statistics on the foreign investment position of the United States published by the US Department of Commerce in their Survey of Current Business in either September or October each year together with an acute commentary on the situation. Unless otherwise mentioned in the notes, all statistics in the book come from this series and the facts on current business events from the *Financial Times*, *Business Week*, and the *Wall Street Journal* of the appropriate dates.

Page xiii. The conference at which Mr Ball was speaking was organised by the Institute for International and Foreign Trade Law of Georgetown University, Washington D.C.

Chapter 2 The Figures

Passim. Jean-Jacques Servan-Schreiber: *The American Challenge*, Atheneum 1968.

Pages 17 & 20. J. H. Dunning: *British Investment in US Industry*. Moorgate and Wall Street, Autumn 1961.

Page 21. Stephen Hymer and Robert Rowthorn: "International Oligopoly" in *The International Corporation*. A symposium, edited by Charles P. Kindleburger, MIT Press 1970.

Page 23. J. H. Dunning: *The Role of American Investment in the British Economy*, PEP 1969.

Chapter 3—The New Balance of Power

Page 29. Robert Aliber's theory is to be found in *The International Corporation*, op. cit.

Page 30. Kindleburger's theory is in *American Business Abroad*, Yale 1969.
Page 31. Pavitt was giving a paper to a conference on the Multinational Enterprise at the University of Reading in May 1970. This summed up very well the considerable work done by OECD on the "technology gap".
Page 31. Dunning: "Technological Transfer" in *The International Corporation*, op. cit.
Page 34. Dunning at the University of Reading conference, op. cit.
Page 36. Kindleburger in *American Business Abroad*, op. cit.
Page 36. Dunning in *British Investment in US Industry*, op. cit.
Page 37. Lawrence Franko in *European Business*, Autumn 1971.
Page 37. Raymond Vernon, *Sovereignty at Bay*, Longmans 1971.
Page 37. Michael Brooke and H. Lee Remmers, *The Strategy of Multinational Enterprise*, Longmans 1970.
Page 37. Hymer and Rowthorn in *The International Corporation*, op. cit.

Chapter 4—The Giants

Many of the historical facts about Shell are taken from *Enterprise in Oil— A History of Shell in the United States*, by Kendall Beaton, Appleton-Century-Crofts 1957, a pedestrian but detailed volume. The early days of Lever Bros. are told in Charles Wilson's excellent *History of Unilever*, Vols. 1, 2 and 3 (Praeger 1968). The soap wars of the 1950's are very well described in two articles in the June 1959 and June 1963 editions of *Fortune*.
Page 56. Robock was reported in *Dun's Review*, March 1970.

Chapter 5—The Veterans

Page 68. *The Economist* insurance survey was in the issue of July 29, 1967.
Page 70. Gwen Nuttall was writing in the *Sunday Times* Business News for September 27, 1970.
Page 71. Forbes' article on Nestlé is in the issue for October 1, 1970. James Poole also wrote on Nestlé in the *Sunday Times* Business News, October 11, 1970. See also *Entreprise* for June 10, 1971.
Page 78. For Hoffman La Roche see *Fortune*, August 1971. The interview with Dr Mattia was in *Life*, March 7, 1969. I have also used an excellent article on the marketing strategies of five European companies in the US (Roche, ICI, Olivetti, Volkswagen, Pechiney) in *European Business*, Autumn 1970.

Chapter 6—The Pioneers

Olivetti is by far the best documented of all the Pioneers. There is an article in the July 1967 edition of *Fortune*, the Harvard Business School did a case study the same year, and there was an interview with Gian-Luigi Gabetti in the *Columbia Journal of World Business* in September/October 1967. The rationale behind Olivetti's presence was brilliantly expressed in an address given by Sergio Pizzoni-Ardemani before the National Association

of Manufacturers on October 11, 1965. Pechiney and Olivetti both feature
in the article in *European Business*, op. cit.

Chapter 7—Partnerships and Specialities

Page 104 on Schulte & Dieckhoff—See *Frankfurter Allgemeinen Zeitung*, 12
June, 1970.
Page 106 on Dunlop—See *The Times* Business News, October 12, 1970.
Page 107 on British Banks—see *Financial Times*, March 17, 1971.
Page 108. *The Property Boom* by Oliver Marriott, Fernhill 1967.

Chapter 9—People, Mores, Money

Page 141. *Business Week*, June 6, 1970.
Page 145. *Wall Street Journal*, February 10, 1970.
Page 148. Industrial Policy Group. The Case for Direct Investment.
February 1970.
Page 149. The BASF Director was speaking at the Georgetown conference.
Page 153. So was Sir Eric Drake in a speech which cogently sums up BP's
experience. I have therefore drawn extensively on it for Chapter 10.
Pages 155 & 156. Plessey's problems were well described by David Palmer
in the *Financial Times*, December 1, 1971.

Chapter 10—British Petroleum—Preserving the Last Frontier

Apart from Drake's speech and the very extensive coverage in the business
press, I have also used Lewis Lapham's article "Alaska: Politicians and
Natives, Money and Oil", in the May 1970 issues of *Harper's Magazine*.

Chapter 11—BASF—The Environment Hits Back

The Hilton Head battle was almost as well publicised as BP's arrival. The
article referred to on page 108 as the best on the subject is by Alan Ternes,
in the April 1970 issue of *National History*. The article in *Harper's Magazine*
was by Marshall Frady in the May 1970 issue. See also the *Washington Post/
Potomac*, April 26, 1970; *Washington Post*, December 14, 1969, *Newsweek*,
April 13, 1970.

Chapter 12—Are the Feds Friendly?

Page 187. Georgetown conference, op. cit.
Much of the information in this chapter was derived from the proceedings
of the Georgetown conference, and the chapters by Walter Damm and
J. J. A. Ellis in *The Multinational Corporation in the World Economy*, Praeger
1970. The quote from Kindleburger on page 195 is from his *Power and Money*,
Macmillan 1970. Robert Hill of the Morgan Guaranty Trust helped me
greatly on the impact of US attempts to control their balance of payments.

Chapter 13—The Ogre of Anti-trust

A. D. Neale's book *The Anti-trust Laws of the USA* was published by Cambridge University Press in 1970. Mr Neale also kindly read this chapter and I have adopted many of his suggestions. For Damm, Ellis and Drake see Chapter 12 *supra*. McLaren's speech (page 208) "Anti-trust Today" was given on March 5, 1970 before the National Industrial Conference Board. He also contributed to *The Multinational Corporation in the World Economy*.

Chapter 14—The American Experience

Christopher Tugendhat's book, *The Multinationals*, was published by Eyre & Spottiswoode in 1971. For Vernon, see Chapter 3.

THE BRITISH INFILTRATORS

THIS appendix contains a list of the British-owned, or British-controlled, manufacturing and petroleum companies in the US, control being defined as a shareholding of more than 10 per cent. It does not include the subsidiaries of financial, banking, or insurance companies; nor does it include companies which are solely engaged in sales or servicing. The list is based on one issued in December 1970 by the United States Department of Commerce. This included a number of subsidiaries which had been sold off, and one case where the American subsidiary is now the parent. As well as removing these mistakes, I have added a few subsidiaries acquired or set up after the list was compiled. I have also classified the US subsidiaries under the British holding company's name. In some cases they had been categorised under the relevant British operating company. In this way I have given a better idea of the total US interests of large British groups, which, like Courtaulds, say, may trade under several different names in the US.

COUNTRY OF ORIGIN:

ENGLAND

Parent Company	American Subsidiary	Location	Product
APV Holdings Ltd.	APV Co.	New York	Head exchangers
Allied Colloids Mfg. Ltd.	Allied Colloids Mfg. Ltd.	New York	Chemical auxiliaries
Armstrong Equipment Ltd.	Armstrong Hydraulics	New Jersey	Hydraulic activators
Associated Motor Cycles Ltd.	The Indian Co.	Massachusetts	Motorcycles and engines
BBA Group Ltd.	Scandura	N. Carolina	Belting and brake lining
Baker Perkins Holdings	Baker Perkins	Michigan	Bakery equipment
Barrow, Hepburn & Gale Ltd.	Barrow Hepburn & Gale	New Jersey	Speciality chemicals
	Colloids		
	Cellate		
	Colloids of California	California	
	Colloids of Carolina	N. Carolina	
Beecham Group Ltd.	Beecham Inc.	New Jersey	Cosmetics, toiletries, drugs
	Horlicks Corpn.	Wisconsin	Malted milk products
	S. E. Massengill	Tennessee	Drugs, disinfectants
Bestobell Ltd.	General Conductors	California	Aircraft pneumatics
Bowater Corp. Ltd.	Bowater United States Corp.	Tennessee	Sulphate, pulp
	Bowater Paper Co.		Paper
	Bowaters Carolina Corp.	S. Carolina	Paperboard
	Bowaters Southern Paper Corp.	Tennessee	
	Catawba Newsprint Co. (J.V. with Newhouse Newspaper Group)	S. Carolina	Paper for 21 daily newspapers
Bowthorpe Holdings	Tyton Corp. (49%)	New Jersey	Wire and cable harnessing

Company	Subsidiary	Location	Products
British-American Tobacco Co. Ltd.	Brown & Williamson	Kentucky	Tobacco products
	Vita Food Products Inc.	New York City	Food products
	Aleutian King Crab Inc.	Alaska	Processing crab meat
	Yardley of London Inc.	New Jersey	Perfumes, soaps
	Lentheric Inc.	New York	Toiletries
British Petroleum Co.	BP Exploration Co. (Alaska) Inc.	California	Petroleum exploration and production
	BP Pipe Line Corp.		
	Standard Oil (Ohio)—25%	Ohio	
	British Petroleum Holdings Inc.	New York City	
British Ropes Ltd.	British Ropes Corp.	Massachusetts	Engineering products
	Donnelly Mfg. Co.		
Brooke-Bond & Co. Ltd.	Brooke-Bond Foods	New York	Food products
British Oxygen	Edwards High Vacuum Inc.	New York	High vacuum pumps
	Getters Electronics Inc.		Vacuum measuring instruments and control levers.
Burmah Oil Co. Ltd.	Southdown Burmah Oil—60% (J.V. with Southdown Inc.)	Louisiana	Petroleum
Cape Asbestos Co. Ltd.	North American Asbestos Corp.	Illinois	Asbestos fibres
Carrier Engineering Co. Ltd.	Schweitzer Equipment Co. Inc.	Ohio	Ventilation equipment
Caravans International Ltd.	Caravans International Corp.	Indiana	Trailers
	Covered Wagon Trailer Mfg. Inc.		
Carrington-Vyella	Bradford Dying Assn. (USA)	Rhode Island	Textile processor
	Solly Allen Ltd.	New York	Textile products
Charterhouse Group	Smith & Wesson	Massachusetts	Line throwing equipment
	Pyrotechnics (J. V. with Smith & Wesson)		

Parent Company	American Subsidiary	Location	Product
Coats Paton Ltd.	Coats & Clark Inc.	New York	Yarn and fasteners
	Gries Reproducer Corp.	S. Carolina	
Cooper Roller Bearings Co. Ltd.	Cooper Split Roller Bearings Corp.	Pennsylvania	Roller bearings
Courtaulds Ltd.	Courtaulds North America Inc.	Alabama	Synthetic acrylic fibres
	Red Hand Compositions Inc.	New Jersey	Marine paint
	Penn Elastic Co.	New York City	Knitted elastic fabric
	Delta Pine & Land Co. of Miss.	Mississippi	Seed breeders
	International Paints Co.	New York City	Surface coatings
Croda-Premier Ltd.	Croda Inc.	New York	Lanoline
Thos. De LaRue International Ltd.	De LaRue Inc.	New York City	Printing
	Federated Bank Note Co.	Pennsylvania	Printed forms
Dexion Ltd.	Dexion Inc.	New York	Steel pallet racks and shelving material
	Dexion Mfg. Co. Inc.	Illinois	
	Dexion of California Inc.	California	
	Dexion of Michigan Inc.	Michigan	
Distillers Co. Ltd.	Gordon's Dry Gin Co. Ltd. (Delaware USA)	Illinois	Gin, vodka
Dunlop Rubber Co. Ltd.	Dunlop Tire & Rubber Corp.	S. Carolina	Tyres, tubes and sports equipment
	Angus Inc.	New York	
	Slazenger Inc.		
E.G.L. Industries Ltd.	Mechanical Products Ltd.	Michigan	Circuit breakers
EMI Ltd. (Electrical & Musical Industries)	Capitol Industries Inc.	California	Records: electronics
	Audio Devices Inc.	Connecticut	Recording tapes and discs
English China Clays Group	Anglo-American Clays Corp.	Georgia	Kaolin
English Calico	American Thread Co.	Connecticut	Yarn and thread
	Atcot Corp.	New York City	
J. H. Fenner	Fenner America	Connecticut	Belting

Parent	Subsidiary	Location	Product
Ferranti	Ferranti Electric Inc.	New York	Electronic equipment
Fisons	Fisons Corp.	New York	Organic chemicals, fertilisers, seeds, gardening materials
	Patco Inc.		
	Lee Patton Seed Co.		
	Albatross Fertilisers, Inc.—50%		
	National Polychemicals Inc.	Massachusetts	
	Doggett-Fison—80%		
Foseco Ltd.	Foseco Inc.	Ohio	Metal treating equipment
General Electric	AEI Liaison Services Ltd.	New Jersey	Mica electronic components
	Eugene Munsell & Co.		Refrigerators
	Morphy Richards Inc.		Lighting
	Royal Ascot Lamp Co. Inc.	New York City	Electrical products
	English Electric Corp.	New Jersey	Electrical equipment and components
	Kaar Communications		Electronics
	Hallikainen Instruments Inc.	California	
	Kaar Electrical Corp.		
Gestetner Ltd.	Gestetner Corp.	New York	Duplicating machines
Guest Keen and Nettlefold Ltd.	Bound Brook Bearing Corp.	New Jersey	Bearings
Hawker Siddeley Group Ltd.	Lister Blackstone Inc.	New York	Diesel engines
	Brook Motor Corp.	Illinois	Electric motors
Grolier Society Ltd.	Grolier Inc.	New York	Publishing
	W. M. Jackson Inc.		
Imperial Chemical Industries	ICI America, Inc.	GA-N.C.-R.I.	Chemicals, pharmaceuticals, and synthetic fibres
	Chemical Mfg. Co.	Virginia	
	Fiber Industries Inc.—37%	S. Carolina	
		N. Carolina	

Parent Company	American Subsidiary	Location	Product
Imperial Chemical Industries —cont.	Nylon Industries Inc.	S. Carolina	Catalysts and dyes
	Katalco (J.V. with Nalco Chemical Co.)	Illinois	
	Rubicon Chemicals (J.V. with US Rubber Corp.)	Louisiana	
	Atlas Chemicals	Wilmington	Drugs, etc.
J. & J. Cash Ltd.	J. & J. Cash Inc.	Connecticut	Woven labels
Johnson Matthey & Co. Ltd.	Johnson Matthey & Co. Inc.	Pennsylvania	Refiners of metals
	Matthey Bishop Inc.		
Jute Industries Ltd.	Stanley Belting Corp.	Illinois	Woven belting and jute products
George Kent Ltd.	Cordova Spinners Inc.	New York	Precision scientific instruments
	Cambridge Instrument Co. Inc.	New York	
	Kent Meters	Puerto Rico	Water meters
Lansing Bagnall Ltd.	Lansing Towmotor Inc. (J.V. with Towmotor Corp. a subsidiary of Caterpillar)	Illinois	Materials handling equipment
Lindustries Ltd.	Survival Equipment Corp.	Pennsylvania	Tools
Macmillan (Holdings) Ltd.	St. Martin's Press Inc.	New York	Publisher
Megator Pumps & Compressors Ltd.	Megator Corp.	Pennsylvania	Pumps
Moorwood-Vulcan Ltd.	Vulcan-Hart Corp. (Assoc.)	Kentucky	Commercial cooking equipment
Morgan Crucible Co. Ltd.	Morganite Inc.	New York City	Electrical and refractory products
	Whittaker-Morgan—40% (J.V. with Whittaker Corp)	Pennsylvania	Carbon fibre materials

Muirhead & Co. Ltd.	Muirhead Instruments Inc.	New Jersey	Electronic parts
	Addison Electric Co. Inc.		Instrumentation for cable makers
James Neill Holdings	James Neill & Co.	New York	Hacksaw blades, tools
Renick & Ford Ltd.	Bacon Products Corp.	Georgia	Processing bacon rinds
Penguin Publishing	Penguin Books Inc.	Maryland	Publisher
Permali	Permali Inc.	Pennsylvania	Industrial laminates
Photo-Me International	Auto-Photo Co.	California	Coin-op photographic machines
Sir Isaac Pitman & Sons	Pitman Publishing Corp.	New York	Publishing
Plessey	Plessey Inc.—81%	New Jersey	Aircraft parts
	Alloys Unlimited Inc.	New York	Alloy components for electronic semi-conductors
Ransomes, Hoffman & Pollard	R. & J. Dick Co. Inc.	Pennsylvania	Belt power transmissions
	Pollard Bearings.		Roller bearings
Racal Electronics	Racal Communications Inc.	Maryland	Electronic equipment
Ranks Hovis McDougall	M. Sheffer & Co.	Illinois	Cider and vinegar
Reckitt & Colman Holdings	L. F. Forman & Sons Inc.	New York	Food products
	R. T. French Co.		Food products
	Widmer's Wine Cellers Inc.		Wine
Redland Ltd.	Universal Highways Inc.	Pennsylvania	Highway signs and markings
	Pismo Safety Corp.		
	Wald Industries Inc.		
Reed Paper Group Ltd.	J. H. Thorp & Co. Inc.	New York	Pulp
	Anglo-Southern Paper Corp.—96%		
	Birge Co. Inc.—65%	New York	Wallpaper and other paper products
	W. H. S. Lloyd Co. Inc.		
	Montmorency Paper Co. Inc.—96%		

Parent Company	American Subsidiary	Location	Product
Reid Paper Group Ltd.—*cont.*	Cahners Publishing Co. Inc.—40%	Massachusetts	Publishing of business journals
	Conover Mast Publications	New York	
Reyrolle Parsons	Rockwell Parsons Corp. (J.V. with North American Rockwell Corp.)	Pennsylvania	Turbines and generators
Rio Tinto-Zinc Corp.	Pyrites Co. Inc.	Delaware	Cobalt and copper
	US Borax and Chemical Corp.—97%	New Mexico	Boron products
	US Potash—30%		Potassium
	Yttrium Corp. of America (J.V. with Molybdenum Corp. of America)	California	Yttrium oxide
	Alloys and Chemicals Corp.	Ohio	Aluminum smelting
	I. Schumann Co.		Aluminum and zinc alloys
	Ireco Chemicals Inc.—50%	Utah	Explosivess
Robinson Ltd.	Ascot Chemicals & Adhesives Co.	New York	Adhesive
Sears Holdings Ltd.	Sears Industries Inc.—52%	New York City	Laundry service
	Consolidated Laundries Corp.	Massachusetts	
	Tiffany Textiles Inc.		Knitwear
Shell Transport & Trading Co. Ltd.	Shell Oil Co.—27.8%	New York	Petroleum
	International Lubricant Corp.	Louisiana	
	Shell Pipe Line Corp.		
	Shell Chemicals Co.		
Staveley Industries	Lapointe Machine Tool Co.	Massachusetts	Chemicals
	Associated Machine Tool Corp.		Machine tools
	Staveley Machine Tools Inc.		
Tennants Consolidated Ltd.	Kay-Fries Chemicals Inc.	New York	Chemicals
Thermal Syndicate Ltd.	Thermal American Fused Quartz	New Jersey	Fused quartz silica

Trafalgar House	Cementation Co. of America Inc.	Tennessee	Water sealing
Tube Investments Ltd.	Cyril Bath Co.	Ohio	Machine tools
Turner & Newall Ltd.	Certain-Teed Products Corp.—15%	Pennsylvania	Millwork and pipes
Unilever	Lever Brothers	New York	Soaps and oils
	T. J. Lipton Co.	New Jersey	Food products
	Morton House Kitchen Inc.	Nebraska	Canner of meat and fish
	Good Humour Ice Cream Co.	California	Frozen dairy products
	Dairy-Delite Inc.		Ice cream
	Usen Products Co.	Massachusetts	Animal food
	Pennsylvania Dutch Megs	Pennsylvania	Macaroni
	Wishbone products	New Jersey	Salad dressings
Vavasseur & Co. Ltd.	Wood and Selick Coconut Co. Inc.	New York	Food products
Venesta Ltd.	Arkwright-Interlaken Inc.	Rhode Island	Bookcloth and tracing
Vickers Ltd.	Racine & Vickers-Armstrong Inc. —50%	Wisconsin	Pumps, valves, controls
	Vickers Instruments Inc.	Massachusetts	Printing machinery
	Crabtree-Vickers Inc.	New York	
Vickers McKay Ltd.	McKay Machine Co.	Ohio	Sheet and strip mill equipment
Wellcome Foundation Ltd.	Burroughs Wellcome & Co. (U.S.A.) Inc.	New York	Pharmaceuticals and chemicals
	Cooper & Nephews Inc.	Illinois	Agricultural chemicals
Winsor & Newton Ltd.	Winsor & Newton Inc.	New York	Artists' colours
Wates Ltd.	Rouse-Wates Inc.—49% (J.V. with Rouse Co.)	Maryland	Prefab building system

INDEX

All references to subsidiaries, whether in the US or in Europe, are indexed under the name of the parent group. For all references to the US government, its departments or its regulatory agencies, see under Government, US.